THE REAL STORY
OF THE JACKSON
THE ONE THEY DIDN'T
WANT PUBLISHED.
YOU'LL SOON SEE WHY.

—Joseph Jackson's brutal physical abuse of his children, and his open infidelities that humiliated his wife

—Life on the road with the Jackson Five, a rocket ride through hell

—How La Toya and other of her famous siblings seriously considered suicide

—The truth about Michael Jackson's "eccentricities" and his women

—The appearance in *Playboy* that ended La Toya's girlhood forever

—The "marriage-in-name-only" that La Toya plunged into to become her own woman

—The shocking kidnap attempt that made La Toya realize her parents would stop at nothing to get her back

The truth. Sometimes it hurts, always it fascinates, ultimately it triumphs.

LA TOYA

LA TOYA

Growing Up in the Jackson Family

La Toya Jackson
with Patricia Romanowski

A SIGNET BOOK

SIGNET
Published by the Penguin Group
Penguin Books USA Inc., 375 Hudson Street,
New York, New York 10014, U.S.A.
Penguin Books Ltd, 27 Wrights Lane, London W8 5TZ, England
Penguin Books Australia Ltd, Ringwood, Victoria, Australia
Penguin Books Canada Ltd, 10 Alcorn Avenue, Toronto, Ontario,
Canada M4V 3B2
Penguin Books (N.Z.) Ltd, 182-190 Wairau Road,
Auckland 10, New Zealand

Penguin Books Ltd, Registered Offices:
Harmondsworth, Middlesex, England

Published by Signet, an imprint of New American Library,
a division of Penguin Books USA Inc.
Previously published in a Dutton Edition.

First Signet Printing, September, 1992
10 9 8 7 6 5 4 3 2 1

Child abuse: brutality, suffering, humiliation, pain, fear, cruelty, physical and mental abuse. Scars that cannot be seen but are left on a child for a lifetime. I dedicate this book to all the children of the world and to people who have suffered any form of abuse, in the hope that one day everyone will see the light and the abuse will end.

ACKNOWLEDGMENTS

I would like to thank the following people for their help and support while I was writing this book.

To Suzanne Gluck, my agent: Thank you for overseeing this project from the beginning. You've been wonderful.

To Jack Gordon, my manager: Thank you for arranging my schedule and setting aside time so that I could do this. And thank you for standing by my side against all odds.

To Philip Bashe: Thank you for getting involved and being there throughout.

To Patty Romanowski: I want to thank you so very much for your hard work and devotion to this project. Even though you were going through many personal traumas, your dedication was always there. Again, I thank you.

To my publisher, NAL/Dutton, and my original editor, Gary Luke: Thank you for understanding and sharing my vision. And to my current editor, Kevin Mulroy: Your perceptive comments and guidance were invaluable.

FOREWORD

Nearly three years after it was publicly announced, here is my book, the one my family doesn't want you to read.

When I started my autobiography, I could not envision that it would be the book you now hold in your hands. In fact, many events recounted here occurred only after I began, forcing me to accept truths about my family that I simply could not see before. To say that my six brothers, two sisters, and I lived sheltered lives barely expresses what growing up in the Jackson family was really like. People assume that because of my family's fame and wealth naturally we'd be more or less cut off from the everyday world.

But in fact, neither I nor my siblings ever led a normal existence, not even as small children, years before celebrity transformed our lives. We were a not-so-typical but classic dysfunctional family. Yes, there was love and happiness, but it was poisoned by emotional and physical abuse, duplicity, and denial.

When I finally left home in my late twenties, I was the proverbial bird freed from her cage. Like a figure stepping out of a family portrait, I could see it clearly for the first time. Now I realize that while we all know the truth about our family, I appear to be the only one willing to admit it.

For most of our lives, none of my brothers and sisters questioned what went on in our home. How could we? A child's ideas about love, trust, relationships, and right and wrong are formed by her parents' actions and words. The proscriptions of my Jehovah's Witness faith, my mother's seeming love and devotion, and my father's inability to express any emotion but anger kept us all entangled in a web of guilt disguised as love, brutality that was called "discipline," and blind obedience that felt like loyalty. Psychologically, we were powerless: so great was my parents' power that eight children could silently witness another enduring merciless beatings or denigrating insults without feeling compelled or entitled to protest.

We couldn't identify it, but we all sensed something was wrong in our house. Most of my siblings "rebelled" by essentially running away from home to teenage marriages. This was acceptable, because my parents could pretend it wasn't our home life that drove them away, but love.

My mother and father recognized that someday all their children would leave, with one exception. Me. I was Mother's best friend, and the quietest, shyest, most obedient child of all. By moving out on my own, I surprised everyone. I also broke the cardinal rule of a dysfunctional family: I stopped living the lie and playing the destructive game.

My family's responses were swift and mixed. Early tear-filled pleas that I return to the Jackson home, Hayvenhurst, turned into veiled threats of violence against my manager and former close family friend, Jack Gordon. My 1989 appearance in *Playboy* magazine provoked a storm of intrafamily controversy that still rages on. Several of my siblings privately offered me their love and support, but others viciously attacked me in the media, one even claiming that I was on drugs or something equally terrible and untrue—both shameless lies. I couldn't imagine how people who loved one another deeply could be so hurtful. Today I understand that this rallying behind my parents' position, whether right or wrong, is characteristic of children raised as we were.

Later, when subsequent threats and aspersions failed to stop this book and force me back to the nest, my mother and father plotted to take me against my will. In the distressing aftermath of their two failed kidnapping attempts, I had to carefully reconsider what this book's publication would mean to me and to them. Yes, I could have appeased my parents, and there's nothing they would have liked better than for me to abandon this. But the longer I experienced the real world, the more I realized that it isn't normal for a father to terrorize his kids, or for a mother to shackle them to her with guilt and deceit. There's no way to negotiate in a family where parental love is apportioned on such flatly ridiculous criteria as your number of hit records or willingness to remain a child forever.

Since leaving home over three years ago, I have repeatedly reached out to my brothers and sisters. It's ironic that we are so closely associated with children's causes, helping others who've suffered, yet we seem incapable of acknowledging our own pain. I've learned that as an abused child, I'm not just one of nine but one of millions. Overcoming the far-reaching effects of child abuse is a painful, lifelong endeavor. But it has to begin with the first step: the truth.

Rather than dissuade me from this book, my family's vehement reactions only steeled my determination to see it through. My brother Michael always told me that wishes come true, but only if you make it so.

To my siblings: I love you all dearly. I wrote this book because it had to be written, so that our children and our children's children won't have to endure what we did. If I have achieved this goal, then it all will have been worthwhile. After this, maybe we can do what we've always discussed but never seemed able to do, which is to be a family. All we have to do is do it.

—La Toya
London, 1990

I

ON JACKSON STREET

"Guys, let's get up. *Now*."

Opening my eyes in the dark, I heard my father's footsteps striding toward the room my five brothers shared. My older sister Rebbie lay sound asleep beside me on the sofa bed, oblivious, but his voice always startled me awake. It didn't matter that it was way past midnight; my father wanted his sons Jackie, Tito, Jermaine, Marlon, and Michael up, dressed, and ready to perform.

"Come on, let's go. I've got some people here to see you."

Through the wall I could make out the rustle of bedclothes and the soft thuds of Michael's and Marlon's feet hitting the floor as they climbed down from their upper bunks. Soon the discordant sounds of Tito and Jermaine tuning their guitars and the crackling hum of amplifiers reverberated through the house. Then they began to play and sing, four voices wrapped in seamless harmony around either Jermaine's or Michael's lead.

Without opening my eyes, I envisioned the scene:

my brothers' flawlessly executed dance steps, the claps of approval from the living-room couch, and the polite bows before the guys sleepily made their way back to bed. Maybe one of them would softly mutter, "Why does he do this to us?" But probably not. The front door closed, car motors rumbled, and the small house on Jackson Street was dark and silent again.

People often ask me, What was it like growing up in the Jackson family? It probably sounds crazy, but in many ways our household appeared like most others, with a loving mother, a hardworking father, and their kids. For much of my life, that's how I thought of us.

To this day my mother remains the heart and soul of the Jacksons, her small stature and quiet manner belying a deep inner strength. She was born Katherine Scruse in Russell County, Alabama, to Martha Upshaw and Prince Scruse, known to us as Daddy. Our own father we called by his first name—never an affectionate Dad, Pop, or Papa, but Joseph. I remember how dignified and handsome my grandfather, a railroad Pullman porter, looked in his crisply pressed uniform. When I was a little girl, I loved gazing at the beautiful gold pocket watch that hung from a long gold chain looped between his vest and pants pockets. Of course, then I didn't really understand what a porter did, but I sensed it was very important, because Daddy always seemed so proud.

Mother was very young when she moved from Alabama with her parents and younger sister, Hattie, to East Chicago, Indiana. Kate, as everyone called her, contracted polio in infancy, and my grandfather carried her to and from the hospital nearly every day for treatment. There was no cure or vaccine for polio in the 1930s, so she was very lucky to have survived. Prince and Martha soon separated, each later remarrying, but Mother remained close to both. In my maternal grandparents I saw the source of her best qualities: love and courage.

With exotic almond-shaped brown eyes, high cheekbones, and soft, feminine features, Mother was strikingly pretty. As a girl, she wore a brace or got around on crutches, and because people feared catching the polio virus, children sometimes taunted her cruelly. Those that got caught had to answer to her sister Hattie, as much a tomboy as my mother was ladylike. I'm sure those experiences hurt Mother's feelings deeply, because she hardly ever talked about it.

Mother's polio made her self-conscious and shy with boys, so she was secretly thrilled to have her very first romance with Joseph Jackson, the handsomest young man in school. Not long after, in 1949 they married and settled a few miles east in Gary, Indiana, on Lake Michigan's southern shore.

It's funny, but my parents rarely told us anything about how they met and fell in love. While I know most children hear this kind of family history repeated time and again, that wasn't the case in our house. In fact, when Michael was writing his autobiography, *Moonwalk,* he and I often asked Mother to tell us. "I need this information for my book," he pleaded, but Mother always evaded our questions. Thus, I'm not the only Jackson to whom Joseph remains largely a mystery.

I do know that he migrated to East Chicago in the late 1940s from rural Arkansas, where he was born to Samuel and Chrystalee Jackson. My paternal grandfather graduated from Mississippi's Alcorn State University, a notable accomplishment for a southern black man back then, and went on to teach high school. The divinely beautiful, irresistible Chrystalee King was one of his students. Her mother, perhaps hoping that hot-blooded Chrystalee would settle down, married off her daughter to Samuel, old enough to be her father.

Joseph was the eldest of their three boys and one girl. His sexy smile, distinctive, sharply arched eyebrows, light reddish hair, and emerald eyes made him a "catch," as they say. But although girls threw themselves at him constantly, he wasn't interested. I remember my grandmother saying of him, "He was a loner. He had no friends, and he didn't want any."

Samuel and Chrystalee split up, married other partners, remarried each other, split up *again,* remarried again . . . Joseph's mother loved going out on the town, and so her eldest son sacrificed his childhood to raise the younger siblings. My uncle once told me that seeing Chrystalee with different men embittered my father, and neighborhood gossip about his mother embarrassed him terribly. Needless to say, this was hardly an ideal, loving environment for a boy.

After leaving school, Joseph boxed professionally for a time, earning a local reputation as a fearless fighter. Broad-shouldered, standing almost six feet tall, he is remarkably strong. One of my few fond childhood memories of my father is of him down on all fours and us kids climbing on top of his back. As we clutched at one another and giggled, he'd boast, "See? I can carry my whole family!" It's a small thing, but I think it says a lot about how he viewed us. Joseph needed to feel that we were his and that he could support and protect us.

By day my father operated a crane at the Inland Steel mill, but he dreamed of being a full-time musician. His taste in music ran from jazz to black rhythm and blues, the natural outgrowth of living just outside Chicago, the cradle of electric blues. In the early 1950s he and his brothers started an r&b group called the Falcons (not the more famous Falcons of "You're So Fine" fame), playing weekends at area colleges and nightclubs. What their professional prospects might have been, who knows. But with us kids coming at a rate of about one per year in the fifties, Joseph eventually had to quit the band.

He never stopped loving music. Even today my father is a fine singer and an excellent blues guitarist, though he hasn't picked up the instrument in probably twenty years. My siblings and I have often playfully debated about where we got our musical talent. While we all agree the singing came from Mother, no one can account for the dancing ability. It sure didn't come from Joseph, whom she always chided, "You can't even keep a beat." It's true. He snaps his fingers or claps his hands to music, but *off* the beat.

When Mother brought me home from the hospital, there were four little Jacksons to greet me: Maureen Reilette, or Rebbie (pronounced "R*ee*bie"); Sigmund Esco, or Jackie; Toriano Adaryll, or Tito; and Jermaine Lajuan. Mother's fondness for unusual names stopped with me, La Toya (which Mother insists she coined) Yvonne Jackson. The four kids to come received more typical names: Marlon David, Michael Joseph (whom we usually called Mike), Steven Randall (Randy), and Janet Damita Jo. A tenth child, Marlon's twin Brandon, died shortly after birth. My mother made her children her life, but my father was indifferent at best, never even coming to the hospital to hold any of his newborns.

Home in Gary was a small, plainly furnished one-story house. It had just two bedrooms, one for the boys and one for our parents; a living room with an alcove, where Rebbie and I slept; a bathroom; a dining room; a kitchen; and a small yard. It was simple and nondescript, but we were comfortable there and never felt that we were poor or in any way deprived.

Contrary to the Jackson Family Legend later contrived by Motown Records, our neighborhood was no ghetto. Gary is a northern steel-industry town, and booming postwar prosperity drew many blacks from the South. The city boasted clean, comfortable residential neighborhoods like the one we lived in. Our schoolmates' parents were lawyers, teachers, and blue-collar workers.

Even so, Joseph decreed that we were not to socialize with other kids. He and my mother believed that our futures depended on education, hard work, and strict discipline. Most parents do the best they can with their kids at home, then send them out into a world full of negative influences and pray for the best. My father took no chances. He banished the outside world from our home until our home *became* our world. It's easy to understand a parent's desire to protect his youngsters, but Joseph took this to an extreme.

No Jackson child could ever be spoiled. Weekday mornings began at around five, when our father rose for work and stomped through the house, waking everyone. We climbed from bed, half-asleep, then set to our chores. "If I have to work," he reasoned, "they have to work too." Even in nasty weather, he forced my brothers to rake leaves outside, shovel snow, or perform pointless tasks like stacking and unstacking piles of bricks before school.

Being the eldest, Rebbie assumed the role of second mother, helping with the littler kids, while the rest of us took turns washing dishes, ironing, and cleaning. One of my jobs was to help Mother cook, because according to Joseph, "You're a girl, and you belong in the kitchen, so you'd better learn how to make cornbread." I oiled the pans for the muffins and cornsticks. It's an irony of adulthood that you manage to forget much of what you were forced to learn as a child. Today I couldn't cook a pan of cornbread if my life depended on it!

After eating breakfast, dressing, and brushing our teeth, we obediently lined up in size order like little stairsteps. Mother checked everyone's teeth, while Joseph followed her down the line like a general inspecting his troops, dispensing spoonfuls of cod-liver and castor oils. Then Mother passed out apples, to kill the vile taste. I don't know why, but I just couldn't stomach the oils. I'd go, *"Ptui!"* and spit them out. So my father forced my mouth open and spooned them in again, laughing all the while. It was in moments like these that I sensed in him an almost sadistic pleasure in his children's suffering. He seemed incapable of sympathy.

Following school we had to come directly home. No dawdling to talk to our classmates and no visiting their homes. It may surprise you that until very recently I could look back and honestly say I didn't regret not having friends. Perhaps if I'd been an only child it would have been different. But with so many siblings, I was never lonely, because there was always something going on. Since we weren't permitted out, my brothers, my sisters, and I passed our free time playing games Mother invented and singing the songs she taught us: "You Are My Sunshine," "Cotton Fields," "Danny Boy," and anything by Harry Belafonte; there must have been hundreds of others. Mother has an exquisite voice and once wanted to be in show business herself, but I think self-consciousness about her limp held her back. Because her father liked country-and-western music, she grew up listening to *The Grand Ole Opry* on the radio. To this day my mother's favorite singer is country star Floyd Cramer.

Even at that young age we all harmonized beautifully. It just came naturally to us. So many times our father straggled in from the mill, and Mother told him excitedly, "You won't believe the boys, Joseph. They make perfect harmony. It's amazing!" Where most other fathers might have at least feigned enthusiasm or offered to listen, Joseph reacted with complete disinterest. My father is basically a quiet man. Except for when he reprimanded or teased us, he acted like we didn't exist.

For as long as I can remember, Mother always made me feel special. Though money was tight, she delighted in dressing me up in dainty dresses and very feminine things, like lace-trimmed anklets and shiny patent-leather shoes. One day I came home from school very upset because some kids kept calling me Gorgeous. Having never heard the word before, I was certain they were making fun of me. I sure felt a lot better after I looked it up in the dictionary. Whenever anyone teased me, my mother consoled me by saying, "Never mind them. I was the same way when I was growing up." We were remarkably alike in many ways, both very sensitive, fastidious (though nine babies changed her standards somewhat), and straight-A students. Like Mother when she was a girl, I dreamed of becoming a nurse. Even my grandfather would comment, "La Toya, you're just like Kate." I was flattered, because I adored Mother. In my eyes she could do no wrong.

When it came to my brothers, I considered myself the luckiest girl in the world. I was everyone's buddy, the family confidante. Rebbie was much older than me, and Janet younger, so as far as the guys were concerned, I might as well have been the only girl in the family. They were—and are—perfect gentlemen, kind and considerate, and they treated me like a princess.

Jackie, the oldest, was quiet and serious. An exceptional athlete, during his teens the Chicago White Sox scouted him at the baseball diamond behind our house. Given the chance, he undoubtedly would have turned pro, but by the time my brother graduated high school music overshadowed everything else, and there was no question of Jackie abandoning the family act to pursue a different career.

Tito, who inherited our father's peaked eyebrows and stocky build, was also quiet, keenly intelligent, and fascinated by machinery. At a very early age he learned to work Mother's sewing machine, and later helped her sew the Jackson 5's early stage costumes. I remember how he always surprised me with little handmade gifts. "Here, La Toya, this is for you," he'd say, holding up a new outfit for my Barbie doll. Tito quickly graduated from building model airplanes and cars to dismantling the television, the radio, or the washing machine, just to see how it worked. Of course, each was reassembled before Joseph came home.

Jermaine, though fourth in line, was more the family leader. He also liked to tease a lot. At the dinner table, if he wanted my dessert, he'd breathe on it, knowing I'd scream in disgust and push the plate toward him. Or he'd chew a mouthful of food, yell "La Toya!," and open wide for my benefit. He always seemed to be starting something, just for fun. Compared to other kids, we were all reserved and polite, but Jermaine was more outspoken and opinionated. He was also stubborn. Once, to avoid school, he hid in a closet all day.

All born within about three and a half years, Jermaine, Tito, and Jackie were closest then, sneaking out their bedroom window to play basketball and peeking in the closet at Joseph's guitar. This we were under strict orders never to touch, let alone strum. But Mother felt so sorry for us being cooped up all the time she occasionally let them take it out, warning, "Now, you know you have to be careful with that guitar." Of the three, Tito was especially adept at picking out songs he'd heard on records or the radio.

One day the inevitable happened: he broke a string. "Oh-oh!" we all cried, panicked. "Wait till Joseph sees this!" Somebody was going to catch a beating. And in our house, punishment never stopped with a single slap or a spanking. My father was deplorably violent, whipping, smacking, and punching his children. For the rest of that afternoon, all of us kids anxiously watched the clock, waiting.

When Joseph got home, Mother took him aside and said timidly, "One of the boys accidentally broke a string on your guitar . . ."

He marched angrily to the closet. Holding his beloved guitar by its neck and fingering the broken string, he bellowed, "How did this happen?"

Mother, at his side, pleaded, "Joe, the boys have talent. And Tito can play guitar—"

"I don't want to hear it!" his voice thundered as we cowered across the room.

"Joe, they really *do* have talent."

My father reconsidered and thrust the instrument into Tito's hands. "Okay," he commanded, "show me what you can do."

Tito, tears streaming down his cheeks, tentatively finger-picked a melody, and Joseph's hard expression softened. His wife was right: Tito *was* talented. As he quickly discovered, they all were. Especially Michael. When he was just a toddler, Mother once caught him in front of a mirror, mimicking Jermaine's singing and gestures. And at age five he received his first standing ovation, for warbling "Climb Every Mountain" in a kindergarten production of *The Sound of Music*.

Soon he, Marlon, Jackie, Jermaine, and Tito were performing locally. To my father's credit, he saw how serious they were and outfitted them with brand-new instruments: a guitar for Tito; a bass guitar for Jermaine, also the lead singer; maracas for Jackie; and amplifiers and microphones. Marlon and Michael sang and danced.

What began as a hobby quickly turned into work. Each day after school the guys rehearsed rigorously, first under Mother's direction, then, after dinner, with Joseph. My father demanded absolute perfection, rarely praising, constantly criticizing, and often hitting. Long before the guys became a national sensation as the Jackson 5, their calling card was precise choreography inspired by their idols, Jackie Wilson and James Brown. I can still see my father standing in the living room, whip in hand. If someone missed a dance step, *crack!* Sometimes after Joseph had attacked one of the guys, leaving him gasping for breath and doubled over in pain, Mother cried, "It's not worth it, Joe! Just forget it. The boys don't have to be singers."

But Joseph never answered. Even with school the next morning, he rehearsed the quintet to exhaustion. For up to eight hours straight, the same notes, the same words, the same moves, repeated until everyone memorized them. Step, dip, and spin. Step, dip, and spin. Step, dip, and spin . . .

Because eight-year-old Marlon had a hard time learning the choreography, he suffered many beatings. Joseph hadn't wanted him in the group at first, but Mother insisted, even though she would concede privately, "He doesn't know his left foot from his right." Marlon refused to quit, though, and practiced constantly. Today, of course, he's a brilliant dancer.

For no reason I could understand, our father singled out his first-born son for the most punishment. I used to ask Mother why Joseph treated Jackie so badly. All she'd say was, "I don't know . . . he just never liked him." As if that made it all right. One of the most talented Jacksons, my brother won many dance competitions as a child. As a young man, he had a warm smile and intelligent brown eyes that made women sigh. I truly believe that Jackie had the same potential as Michael to become a star in his own right. But endless psychological and physical battering wore him down.

As if my brothers didn't suffer enough at their father's hands, he forced them to don boxing gloves and fight one another while he watched. "Okay, Jackie," he'd sneer, "let's see what you and Tito can do." The two selected halfheartedly punched each other right there in the living room, just to get it over with, while Joseph egged them on.

Another of his pastimes was frightening us. For as long as I can remember, he got the biggest kick out of lurking around our windows at night and tapping on the glass, or pretending to break in. When one of us tiptoed to the window to investigate, my father, wearing a gruesome latex mask, leaped up and growled like a beast. We screamed in terror, and Joseph laughed. It wasn't done playfully or as part of a game. Why a grown man would deliberately scare his children out of their wits is beyond me.

Even worse was being startled awake by a hideous monster hovering just inches above our faces. While we shrieked, Joseph ripped off his mask and fell out laughing, as if this was the funniest thing he'd ever seen. It got to where every night I pulled the covers tightly over my head and gently rocked myself until drifting off. Even now, that is the only way I can get to sleep.

In those days, our father was clearly the boss. Mother almost never intervened, but shook her head and lamented, "That Joseph, he's so crazy." You could see in her eyes that she pitied us for fearing our father so. But it would be years before I understood how unusual her attitude was. What makes Mother's resigned acceptance of Joseph's brutality more confusing is that she grew up in a loving home. Certainly she knew her husband was wrong.

For whatever reason, she never stopped him and rarely voiced any strong disagreement. Instead, she tried to make up for his meanness by bending the household rules in his absence. With Joseph at work, she sometimes let us out to play—provided we got back before he returned home and no one breathed a word about the infraction. I usually stayed inside with her and Rebbie, playing with my doctor's kit or Barbie doll, or being a little helper. Just before Joseph was due, Mother dispatched me to find my brothers. I'd run down the street, calling, "Tito! Jermaine! Jackie! Mike! Marlon! Come home!" I couldn't stand the thought of any of them getting the switch.

Each day, waiting for our father's Buick to pull up out front was like bracing for a storm. Either he would be in a good mood or he would explode. We never knew, but we always feared. That persistent fear clouded every moment. At a time when most children are carefree, we were anxious. That we couldn't trust our own father made it hard for us to trust anyone but one another and, of course, Mother.

We had no choice but to obey Joseph's demand of respect. Still, it was very hard for any of us to truly love him. Now I see what a tragedy that was for all of us, but there was no way then we could know that other kids' lives were different. To us, fathers were cold and mean; mothers, warm and loving. That's just how it was. The few times we did get to visit friends, we left as soon as their dads came home, Michael shooting me a nervous glance and blurting, "We've gotta go!" They must have thought we were so strange. It took us a long time to grow comfortable around other fathers. I remember how Michael and I were absolutely stunned the first time we saw a man display affection to his children. All the way home we couldn't stop exclaiming, "Did you see that? The way he kissed and hugged his kids!"

"Yeah. How weird!"

Out of this unpredictable, alternately loving and cruel home life grew an unusually deep love and understanding among my siblings and I. Even for a so-called close family, we were unusual. There's no denying that one force drawing us together was Joseph, our common foe. When you see someone you love being insulted, hit, and otherwise demeaned, your heart breaks for them. I guess we all followed

Mother's example, trying with a kind word or gesture to somehow soothe the pain Joseph had inflicted. In response to his volatile nature, all the Jackson kids grew up basically soft-spoken and extremely gentle. We worried about hurting one another's feelings, and if you know anything about kids, this is hardly typical. Until quite recently, we rarely even raised our voices, and aside from the forced boxing matches, there was no fighting of any kind, not even in play.

All children need to feel worthy and loved, but our father shattered our self-confidence and self-esteem by the time we were old enough for school. Not surprisingly, none of us ever mustered the courage (the foolhardiness?) to defend ourselves against him. Except Michael.

Mother used to say that from the time he was born, Michael was "different": quick to walk and talk, and unusually well coordinated for his age. She's made it a point never to boast about any of us, but of Michael my mother would allow, "I don't want to say he's gifted, but I know there's something special about him."

Bright-eyed, with an impish smile, Michael was a scamp, an inexhaustible ball of energy. Though never bossy, he was a natural leader. Every morning before school, the neighborhood kids congregated around our tiny front porch, waiting for Michael to emerge and declare which game they would all play that day. Everything was "Michael this" and "Michael that.'' In his own little world, he was already famous.

Even then, Michael had clear ideas about the brothers' act and its presentation. If they were shooting promotional photos, the six-year-old posed everyone, instructing in his peep of a voice, ''Okay, Jackie, you stand here, this way. Jermaine, you'll be next to Jackie, but like this.'' No detail escaped his eye. Mother used to hold up for them the stage outfits she'd sewn—a purple two-piece suit; black pants with white shirts—and the youngest of the five pointed and declared, *''These.''* And he was always right.

Spirited and supremely confident as a child, Michael was the only one of us who ever hit Joseph back. Whenever my father raised a hand in anger, everyone else stood still and braced for the blow. Michael raced off. ''When I get you . . .'' Joseph growled, but he couldn't catch him. Michael was so fast, he could pause to fling a shoe at Joseph, and still elude him.

Michael talked back and always had to get in the last lick, even if it meant another beating. Cringing, the rest of us wondered, *Why doesn't Mike quit while he's ahead? He's only making it worse for himself.* Secretly, my brothers, my sisters, and I admired his fearlessness.

I was six when I got the beating of my life. A straight-A student, I always looked forward to report-card day, since it was one of the few times Joseph might praise me. Late one afternoon I happily carried home my first-grade card, and because Mother was at work, presented it to my father. Tearing open the envelope, he glanced at the grades and the teacher's remarks. I didn't know she'd written, "La Toya's work is excellent, but she rarely speaks up in class, and so I feel it might be best to hold her back a grade."

Joseph put down the report card and suddenly smacked my face with his open palm. "Don't you ever shame me again!" he shouted. Then he took off his belt and reached for the switch employed so often around our house. As the metal buckle and the whiplike branch seared my skin, I cried, "No! Stop! Please!" But my father was beyond hearing me.

If I close my eyes I can still see his face, which changed whenever Joseph went into one of his rages. His eyes literally flared, turning cat's-eye yellow, and his forehead seemed to stretch back to the middle of his head. It was as if he'd been transformed into a monster, with no rubber mask this time.

"You will never shame me like this again! Never!" he yelled, punctuating his words with hard slaps. "This will teach you to study!" His boxer's fists pummeled my face and body, and I cried until my eyes were swollen nearly shut. *But I do study,* I thought. *Why are you beating me?* Of course, I said nothing.

Just as abruptly as he'd exploded, Joseph stopped. Yanking me by the arm, he dragged me down the hall to the bathroom, roughly threw me to the hard floor, and walked away. I felt the shock of cold tile against my hot, wet cheek; then a heavy book fell on my bleeding leg.

"You stay in there! And read this!" The door slammed shut.

I lay on that bathroom floor moaning in pain and quietly sobbing for hours. As suppertime neared, each of the guys came in to wash up, carefully stepping around me, never saying a word for fear that Joseph would either beat me again, beat him, or beat us all. Our father controlled us with the constant, implicit threat of further violence. It paralyzed us and indirectly made us accomplices. Curled up there that evening, I felt invisible and worthless. After I'd cried myself to sleep, Mother came in and silently cleaned my cuts and bruises before tucking me in next to Rebbie.

My siblings and I, accustomed to this terror, assumed that Joseph had valid "reasons" for his outbursts. So I believed I must have done something very bad to provoke him. Just what, I didn't know, because neither he nor my mother ever discussed it or any other random punishment with us. A child learns about the world first through her parents' behavior. When they are out of control, as our father was, or meek and defenseless, as our mother seemed, she can't help but think this is not only how things are but how they should be.

Lying on the bathroom floor, I vowed I would never give Joseph cause to beat me again. Perhaps I couldn't control him, but I could appease him by controlling myself. This is the self-destructive "deal" many abused children learn. I promised myself I'd never again do anything to make him angry. I did start speaking up in class more, but at home I silently observed everything from my little corner behind the kitchen water heater. Desperate to please, I would never make *anyone* angry, no matter what. Mother always used to say, "La Toya is the perfect child," as if it were an accomplishment, when actually, I felt there was no choice.

To a very limited extent, my plan worked. Though I remained powerless to stop the relentless psychological abuse, Joseph never raised a hand to me again. Because of that, my brothers still call me "the spoiled one." But verbal abuse is every bit as painful as a beating—perhaps more so—because a beating eventually stops. Cruel, demeaning words repeat themselves in your head long after they are spoken.

I think Mother's parents sensed there were problems at home, because grandmother Martha—Mama, we called her—always did special things for us, like buying our school clothes, or getting Rebbie a fancy party dress. Whenever Joseph announced, "You're going to your grandparents' for the weekend," we whooped with joy. They still lived in East Chicago, yet to us it was like escaping to another world. Mama baked us cakes, pies, and shortbreads, and Papa, her second husband, brought us treats like cookies and potato chips from the store he owned.

Mama's immaculate house was a magical place filled with love. She and Papa were strict, but without the insults and brutality we knew at home. One coffee table held my grandmother's treasured collection of figurines, statuettes, and porcelain dolls from all over the world. They were so beautiful. I cautiously kept my hands behind my back while looking at them, but Michael couldn't resist picking up a piece, flipping it in the air, and trying to catch it. Sometimes he dropped it, for which he received a spanking. Mama also owned a real crystal ball that Michael and I gazed into every time we visited, wishing that one day we'd travel the world.

After Mother became a Jehovah's Witness, we no longer celebrated Christmas at home. So my grandparents, feeling sorry for us, took us to Christmas parties and gave us gifts and money. Although this went against my mother's religious beliefs, she permitted it, seeing how happy it made us.

Otherwise, except for Joseph, as children we all followed the Jehovah's Witnesses teachings and attended meetings at the Kingdom Hall several times a week. There we learned that the Bible was the word of Jehovah, the only true God, and the sole authority. Even compared to other evangelical Protestant movements, Adventism, as it is called, is unusually rigid. Witnesses must go door to door "publishing," trying to reach people with the word of God. They believe Satan rules the world now but that it will eventually be destroyed in an apocalyptic battle between good and evil. Only then will the true believers, an elect 144,000 Jehovah's Witnesses called the Remnant, join Jesus Christ in the Kingdom of God.

Witnesses do not smoke cigarettes, celebrate birthdays or holidays (except the annual Lord's Meal, which occurs approximately around the time of the Jewish Passover celebration), salute the flag, vote, serve in the military, or hold public office. Homosexuality, abortion, gambling, and profanity are considered sins. You may drink, but not to the point of intoxication; see movies, but none rated R or X; dance, but not touch your partner; date, but only if you plan to marry. Furthermore, you can associate only with other Jehovah's Witnesses. This isolationist aspect of the faith conformed neatly with Joseph's determination to sequester us from the world.

Mother encouraged but did not force any of us to become Witnesses, believing we should decide for ourselves. Several of us, including Michael and I, were later baptized in the faith and remained deeply committed most of our lives. Even those Jacksons who eventually abandoned it were influenced by its moralistic teachings.

With eight of us, it was getting harder to make ends meet, so Mother worked part-time as a cashier at Sears & Roebuck. The whole family was dedicated to developing the brothers' talents, and no one minded doing without little luxuries so that Jackie, Tito, Jermaine, Marlon, and Michael could get an essential piece of equipment. At first the neighborhood kids teased them for staying inside to practice music every day, but soon those same kids were perched on our front lawn, listening to them sing and play.

My father continued to drill the guys with the single-mindedness of a football coach, refining their vocals, choreography, and presentation until they were perfect. For inspiration, he played them records by such r&b greats as Otis Redding, Jackie Wilson, the Temptations, Smokey Robinson and the Miracles, and James Brown, whose moves Michael picked up effortlessly.

Around 1965, calling themselves the Jackson 5, my brothers took first place in a talent contest at Roosevelt High School, just around the corner from our house. I distinctly remember them swaying and harmonizing sweetly on the Tempts' recent smash "My Girl." Our whole family was happily surprised they won, since their competition consisted mostly of older kids.

For Joseph, this was the turning point. He immediately arranged weekend dates for them at local store openings and small clubs. From his years as a working musician, he knew how to find bookings, how to handle nightclub owners, and, most important, how to get paid. As Michael has written, some of the places the guys played were like strip joints. For their version of Joe Tex's "Skinny Legs and All," precocious Michael worked the room, scurrying up to women in the audience, crawling under the cocktail tables, and lifting their dresses! The next day, out of Mother's hearing, he'd shock me with his breathless descriptions of what he'd seen.

Appreciative crowds threw money, which my brothers stuffed into their pockets, then turned over to Joseph. From the evening's take, he doled out allowances. Jackie, Tito, Jermaine, and Marlon either quickly spent or saved their money. But Michael always bought a quantity of candy to sell to the neighborhood kids. As Mother often remarked, he always did seemingly childish things in a very adult way. With his "candy store" he made other children happy *and* turned a profit.

For the next three years the guys performed up to five shows a night almost every weekend, singing Top 40 pop and soul hits like "Who's Loving You" and "Tobacco Road." Most bookings were local, but some took them as far as Phoenix, Kansas City, Washington, D.C., and Philadelphia. Mother, having packed them plenty of food, and Randy, Janet, and I would wave good-bye from the front lawn as my father chauffeured them to another gig. Sometimes I cried, missing them already.

Though now semiprofessional entertainers, my brothers still had their everyday responsibilities and chores. On the road they brought along their schoolbooks, for homework had to be finished by Sunday night, or else. A few days later they were back, exhausted, but with fantastic stories about where they'd been and the great acts they'd opened for: Sam and Dave, Gladys Knight and the Pips, the Temptations, the Isley Brothers, the O'Jays, James Brown.

The Hardest Working Man in Show Business, Michael's biggest influence then, was a special favorite for his tornadolike spins, acrobatic deep splits, liquid glides across the stage, and, of course, soul.

James never performed in or around Chicago without visiting our home. I remember his rough, raspy voice and especially his flamboyant clothes and heavy, gaudy jewelry. I'd never seen a man dress like that. James spent many hours in our living room, warning Joseph and my brothers about the music business's pitfalls. It was the age-old advice veterans offer young hopefuls—who usually don't listen. But everyone listened to their idol, James Brown, the Godfather of Soul.

One time I got to see the guys sing at Chicago's Regal Theater, a grand old place with an ornate ceiling that reminded me of a wedding cake. The heavy velvet curtain opened, and . . . wow! There they were up on a big stage, bathed in colored lights, with hundreds of strangers on their feet, applauding the Jackson 5 and shouting, ''More!'' Even in these early days my brothers were so good, so polished, so exciting, people sometimes overlooked how young they were. You have to remember, in 1967 Jackie, the eldest, was just sixteen. And Michael, already the star, was only nine.

Onstage they stood in basically the same formation they would keep for years: Tito at stage right, hunched over his guitar; in the center, the tallest, Jackie, flanked by Marlon and Michael; and on the left, bassist Jermaine. Keyboardist Ronnie Rancifer and drummer Johnny Jackson (no relation) accompanied the group then and into the 1980s.

The real test of the Jackson 5's talent came the following year when they won first prize at the legendary Apollo Theater's Wednesday-night amateur show. By then they were fairly well known from their appearances at traditional black theaters such as Detroit's Fox and Philadelphia's Uptown. But for any black artist, the Apollo is the pinnacle, the proving ground that separates the pros from the amateurs. Located on West 125th Street in Harlem, New York City, it boasts the world's toughest audience, one that will mercilessly heckle a lame act until it's given the hook. Win amateur night at the Apollo, and you're on your way. My brothers did, and they were. Not long after, Joseph quit his job at the steel mill to devote all his time to their career.

You might think my father and mother sound like stereotypical stage parents, but they weren't. Later, after we moved to Hollywood and met other young entertainers and their folks, we saw what real stage mothers and stage fathers were like. I found that many stage parents pressure their kids into show business to gratify their own egos, living vicariously through their children's success.

Even though Joseph had abandoned his dream of becoming a professional musician, he encouraged my brothers as much for their sake as his own. You have to remember, quitting his job then was a tremendous risk financially. This was his way—probably his only way—to express his love for his sons. The guys' younger years may not have been as carefree as their friends', but they truly loved entertaining, and our parents supported them every step of the way. For that, my brothers are thankful. Considering how wildly famous they became, today they certainly don't regret Joseph's vigorous management, though we might all wish he'd done it differently.

The next step, my father decided, was to make a record. That year, the Jackson 5 released their first single, a ballad titled "Big Boy," backed with "You've Changed," on the independent hometown Steeltown Records. After "Big Boy," distributed by the major label Atco, became a marginal local hit, Joseph pursued a contract with the nationals. His goal was Motown Records, the biggest, most successful black-owned record company in America.

In April 1968 the guys played a campaign fund-raiser for Gary's Richard Hatcher, one of the country's first black mayors. Motown founder Berry Gordy, Jr., frequently offered his stars' services to Democratic and black causes then, and my brothers happened to share the bill with Berry's biggest, Diana Ross and the Supremes.

According to legend, this is where Diana "discovered" the Jackson 5, afterward tipping off Berry to their talent. Legends may make for dramatic reading, but they are not always true. While Diana was certainly impressed by them, so were Bobby Taylor of another Motown group, the Vancouvers, Sam Moore of Sam and Dave, and Gladys Knight. So many people have claimed to discover the Jackson 5, it's hard to say who really did. Gladys may have been the one. Earlier, the group had opened for her and the Pips at a Chicago club. Gladys urged Joseph excitedly, "You ought to try Motown Records."

Suffice to say, from the recommendations of Gladys, Diana Ross, and Bobby Taylor, Berry Gordy's curiosity was piqued. One day Joseph gathered everyone together and announced sorrowfully that the brothers' scheduled national television debut on *The David Frost Show* had been canceled. We were all crushed. Mischievously my father added, ". . . because Motown Records called."

He, Jackie, Tito, Jermaine, Marlon, and Michael piled in the van, drove the nearly three hundred miles to Detroit, spent the night in a hotel there, then showed up the next day at Motown's original offices, Hitsville, on West Grand Boulevard. Their audition was filmed and later shown to Berry. I suppose because they were my brothers, I didn't fully appreciate how good they were. But whenever I see clips from that black-and-white audition tape, I'm astounded by their maturity and technique. You can see that the Jackson 5 wasn't a kid act singing soul music, but an accomplished soul act that happened to be kids. Michael had such a commanding presence even then, some people actually suspected he was a midget!

I know they were nervous, but my father whispered, "Just do it the way you always do it." When they finished singing and dancing for the camera, Michael asked cockily, "How was that?" and Jermaine, mindful of Joseph's orders not to say anything, put a finger to his mouth and shushed him. After being thanked for coming by, the six of them made the long drive back to Gary, unsure whether they had a deal. They didn't know that the moment Berry Gordy saw the tape, he couldn't wait to sign them.

At times like this you really sensed the connection between the performing Jacksons and the family members back at home. Whenever Joseph and the brothers traveled, Mother, Randy, Janet, and I worried. Were they safe? Did their shows go over well? Waiting for them to return from this audition, we practically trembled with anticipation. The second they got home, we bombarded them with questions.

"Who did you see there?"

"What did it look like?"

"Did you see the Temptations? How 'bout the Supremes?"

And finally, "So? What did they say?"

Even had Motown not offered them a record contract, it was my family's custom to view a setback as a learning experience. If they'd been rejected, everyone would have just worked harder. As it turned out, we didn't have much time to dwell on that, because Motown soon called again. This time with an offer.

My brothers—and later my sisters—would accomplish many great things in show business. But I don't think anything really topped that moment. Motown was the once-in-a-lifetime break the guys had been tirelessly traveling toward all these years. Now here they stood at the end of one journey and the beginning of another. It's impossible to express the hope, the happiness, the pride we all felt. None of us could imagine what awaited our family and how dramatically our lives would change.

2

A NEW LIFE
IN CALIFORNIA

At home in Gary, one of our favorite toys was the
View-Master, a stereoscopic viewer that looked like
a flat pair of binoculars. You inserted a cardboard
disk with tiny square transparencies around the cir-
cumference, then changed scenes by pressing a plastic lever. *Click!* Michael, Rebbie, and I used to play
with it for hours, oohing and ahhing over colorful
panoramas of Paris, New York, London, Africa, and
other exotic, faraway places. Most magical of all was
Hollywood, its palm trees and pastel buildings seeming to beckon.

"Imagine all that sunshine!" I exclaimed.

"Yeah," said Michael, "and the ocean! Wouldn't
it be great to live there?"

"I can't wait to go there. I wish we could fly there
tomorrow."

With characteristic certainty, Michael said, "You
can always dream, La Toya, and your dreams will
come true. But you have to make them come true."

After the Jackson 5 auditioned for Motown, things
began happening so quickly we barely had time to

absorb it all. First Berry Gordy invited them to perform at an exclusive party in their honor at his spectacular European-style mansion in Detroit. Its three floors were filled with marble, frescoes, and statues, the likes of which my brothers had never seen. Even more incredible, their "audience" included many of the stars whose records they studied and loved. Afterward Diana Ross gave Jackie, Tito, Jermaine, Marlon, and Michael each a kiss on the cheek. Motown's brightest star would be leaving the Supremes for a solo career at year's end, and the label—wise in the ways of public relations—knew that linking her name with the Jackson 5 would draw attention to both.

The most enthusiastic member of the audience was none other than Berry himself. A Detroit songwriter with an uncanny ear for hits, he'd built one of America's largest black-owned companies from an $800 family loan and was a self-made millionaire by the early sixties. Like our father, Berry believed in hard work, discipline, loyalty, and the value of family, regarding his artists, producers, and writers more as his charges than as employees. It's a funny coincidence that the Jackson 5, a family who became an act, wound up with Motown, a business that acted like a family.

By early 1969 when the guys signed, however, much of the label's close-knit feeling was dying amid intragroup hostilities, financial inequities, and the personal problems that seem to especially afflict entertainers. In this atmosphere the guys—young, innocent, enthusiastic—were warmly welcomed. Perhaps they reminded Berry of how things used to be in the late 1950s and early 1960s, when he'd discovered and helped develop Smokey Robinson and the Miracles, Marvin Gaye, the Supremes, the Temptations, Stevie Wonder, Martha Reeves and the Vandellas, and countless other future legends. As it turned out, the Jackson 5 would be the last stars to emerge from the old Motown system.

Berry's secret of success was following his instincts passionately, with remarkable results. He took a personal, active interest in my brothers, vowing, "I'm going to make you the biggest thing in the world. You're going to be written about in history books." Berry also predicted they'd have three Number One records in a row and outlined his grand plans for making that happen. The first step was moving the guys to Los Angeles, where Motown was in the process of shifting its headquarters from Detroit. They alternated between living at Berry's and Diana's Beverly Hills homes, which were practically next door to each other. I'm not sure where our father stayed.

Mother, so used to having us all within arm's reach, was naturally worried, asking Joseph via long distance, "What are they doing? Who are they staying with? How do I know whether these people are nice or not?"

"They're okay," he reassured her. "They're not into anything bad."

That eased her anxiety for a while, but she was

never completely calm until we were all under one roof again. She still can't stand the idea of any of us living too far away from her.

Back in Indiana, we all missed the guys so much. Especially me—they were my best friends. I couldn't wait for their calls and letters. "It's beautiful out here!" one might read. "We've been to the ocean, and tomorrow we're going to the beach again. There's so much sunshine, you wouldn't believe it. And palm trees!" Just like in the View-Master.

The house in Gary sure seemed empty, and now Rebbie was gone too. For reasons I didn't fully understand then, she left home to live with a family friend. Then she wed Nathaniel Brown, a fellow Jehovah's Witness she'd known since she was eleven, and moved with him to Kentucky to spread the message of our faith. Just eighteen, Rebbie initiated what was to become a family pattern of tying the knot as soon as legally possible. While I'm sure she loved Nathaniel, still her husband today after twenty years, marriage also provided the only acceptable escape from a family situation Reebie could no longer tolerate. But as we'd all see, though you could leave my parents' house, you were never beyond their grasp.

While my brothers were in Los Angeles, Berry and Diana became their surrogate parents. The guys never called home without telling us how wonderfully they were being treated. Berry was the liberal dad they never had, telling them, "You can do whatever you want, you can have whatever you want, you can eat whatever you want, as long as you clean up behind yourselves.'' Diana monitored them with motherly concern, even tucking young Michael and Marlon into bed at night.

As you might imagine, it wasn't easy for Joseph to relinquish his absolute authority. Motown controlled virtually every aspect of its artists' careers to an extent that my father would never permit. While cooperative, Joseph didn't let the company forget the Jackson 5 might be Berry's prize new act, but they were *his sons,* and with attorney Richard Arons he continued managing their business affairs.

Motown dictated the creative course, deciding that the Jackson 5 needed to polish its sound and image. The label's world-renowned style was a unique hybrid of pop and soul. Everything about Motown's acts, from their records' dynamic production to their elegant stage costumes, reflected its high commercial standards and meticulous attention to detail. When Berry promised my brothers three Number One hits, he meant the top of the soul *and* the pop charts. His company lived up to its motto, ''The Sound of Young America,'' with an infectious sound that appealed to everyone. This was in stark contrast to Motown's rhythm-and-blues predecessors, who had a predominantly black following.

By 1969 Berry's much-heralded ''Motown U,'' where earlier artists learned everything from slick choreography to table manners, no longer existed. Instead he assigned his new assistant, Suzanne dePasse, an attractive brunette in her early twenties, to supervise the Jackson 5's development. She seemed to spend every waking moment with them. One of her first pieces of advice was, "You guys are kids, but you're living in an adult world. I want you to understand that." I think that pretty well summed up what the guys' childhoods would be like for the next decade or so.

Looking back, I'm amazed that such a young woman could handle five energetic adolescent boys so well, even as well behaved as my brothers were. Suzanne helped them perfect their dance routines and stage presentation. By then the guys had probably rehearsed and performed more hours than many entertainers twice their ages, but at Motown, like at home, there was always room for improvement.

In August 1969 Diana Ross officially introduced the Jackson 5 at one of Beverly Hills' swankest discos, The Daisy. Her invitation, delivered via telegram, read in part, "The Jackson 5, featuring sensational eight-year-old lead singer Michael Jackson [actually ten at the time], will perform live at the party. Please come and listen to this fabulous new Motown group." Next the guys opened for her and the Supremes at the Los Angeles Forum, and in October they appeared on the popular television variety show *The Hollywood Palace*. Yet again Diana presented them.

That month, Motown released the Jackson 5's label debut, "I Want You Back." The first time Mother and I heard it, I exclaimed how wonderful and professional they sounded, but she was disappointed, complaining, "My kids are more talented than that. Why did they produce them like that? They could sound so much better . . ." My mother the music critic. While Joseph gets the most credit for guiding the brothers' career, Mother always took a keen interest in everything from the fit of their costumes to the quality of their publicity photos. If she ever thought something wasn't right for them, she said so, and everyone listened.

Like most of my brothers' early Motown hits, "I Want You Back" was the product of Berry's newest creative brain trust: writer-producers Freddie Perren, Fonce Mizell, Deke Richards, and Berry himself, officially credited as The Corporation. Setting the formula for the Jackson 5's early records, it featured a multilayered sound anchored by a funky, percolating rhythm section, topped with satiny strings, and in the middle, the unmistakable Jackson vocals.

Each of the five voices had a distinctive color and either blended in harmony or popped out of the mix to solo a phrase, in the style of Sly and the Family Stone. There was Michael's piping lead, Jackie's angelic falsetto, Jermaine's raspy tenor, Tito's sonorous bass, and Marlon's youthful tenor. They especially shine on "I Want You Back," which rose steadily to Number One in January 1970.

Soon after, our whole Jackson family was reunited. It was wonderful to have the eight of us back together again. We first settled in a huge Hollywood Hills house across the street from the Dick Van Pattens, who became good friends. Mother worried about Hollywood's permissive attitudes toward sex and drugs. She also frowned on our socializing with white kids, an attitude I found hypocritical coming from a Christian. Besides, few black families lived in this exclusive area.

Both she and my father regarded the city and show business in general as other "bad neighborhoods" full of questionable influences from which to isolate us. So despite the drastic change in scenery, our family life resumed as it had been in Indiana and would continue to, no matter what house we lived in. The beatings and abuse became so routine, all I could do was try not to think about them.

With his promise of three consecutive Number One singles, Berry Gordy underestimated my brothers' appeal, as the group notched *four* in a row: "I Want You Back," "ABC," "The Love You Save," and its first ballad, "I'll Be There," then Motown's best-selling single to date. In just ten months, they'd sold a staggering six million records.

In the wake of Michael's stunning solo accomplishments since, I feel that many people have forgotten what a phenomenon the Jackson 5—Jackie, Tito, Jermaine, Marlon, and Michael—were. *Life* magazine hailed them as "a black teen breakthrough," and *Look* headlined its profile, "The Hottest New Group in the Record World Has to Be in Bed by Ten O'Clock." (True!) Because some of their songs had juvenile themes and Michael was so young, critics initially labeled them "bubblegum soul.'' But had Michael been older, with a deeper voice, he'd have been hailed as one of the most soulful singers of the time, and the J5, in turn, as rivaling the Temptations, the Four Tops, and other soul greats.

Within weeks of the release of ''I Want You Back,'' my brothers emerged as the first black teen (and preteen) idols since Frankie Lymon and the Teenagers in the mid-1950s. They practically became the *raison d'être* for several recently founded black-music fan magazines. Each month for several years, page after page—sometimes over half an issue—was devoted to articles on the guys' personal likes and dislikes, color pinups, their astrological charts, and helpful advice for the predominantly female readers, along the lines of ''How to Act When You Meet the Jackson 5.''

Like the Beatles, each Jackson was stamped with a distinct personality: Jackie, handsome and athletic; Tito, serious and quiet, an accomplished musician; Jermaine, the group's sex symbol; Marlon, the adorable younger brother; and Michael, the charismatic prodigy. Countless sacks bulging with fan letters, school pictures, and stuffed animals flooded Motown's offices. Our home phone rang constantly from morning to night. It was, as they said, Jacksonmania.

Their youthful rise to stardom made great copy and was the subject of articles in every major national magazine. Because the brothers were family, the media regarded *all* the Jacksons as part of the act. Reporters and photographers invaded our home all the time, trying to unlock the "secret" to the Jacksons' success. In an era of widespread drug use, promiscuity, and teenage rebellion, America wanted to know how Mr. and Mrs. Jackson raised such a wholesome bunch of kids. Not a single article of this time failed to mention my brothers' politeness, clean-cut living, and devotion to family. Our mother was portrayed as kind and gentle, a saint. And in every one, our father emerged as a benevolent mastermind, "exert[ing] a steadying hand," one scribe wrote, "in the exhilarating flush of the boys' new popularity." A steadying hand indeed.

Most of what was written then was essentially true, if glossed up. Though unadorned the Jacksons' story was the old-fashioned American Dream saga, Motown concocted a rags-to-riches fable about my family. Consequently, the public came to believe we'd grown up in a crime-infested ghetto (or worse). Since our parents had worked so hard to give us the best life they could then, Mother often complained, "Why do they say we lived in a ghetto, when we didn't?" But the label's publicists believed that stressing our humble origins would inspire other minority kids.

The brothers were even given and rehearsed answers to reporters' predictable inquiries. From the beginning, publicity chief Bob Jones warned journalists, "No questions about religion or politics." Not that my family had anything to hide, except the reality of an abusive household. And looking at the ten of us posing together happily in our lavish new home, who would have believed that?

Like Jackie, Tito, and Michael, I was naturally shy. In the harsh reflected glare of my brothers' fame I grew even more withdrawn. Making friends at my new school in California was suddenly complicated. I didn't want any special attention or treatment because I was *their* sister; I never have. And I hated to think that someone might pretend to be my friend just to meet the Jackson 5. So for quite a while I never told anyone I was one of *those* Jacksons. This wasn't easy, since Michael, Marlon, and I attended the same school. I remember other girls in my class squealing with excitement whenever they passed one of my brothers in the hall.

"Oh, did you see Marlon?"

"He's *so-ooo* cute!"

"I wish Michael would notice me!"

I played along, feigning enthusiasm, though if anyone asked suspiciously, "Aren't the Jacksons your brothers?" I replied, "No. I don't even know who they are." Eventually some girls found out I was their sister, and were they ever mad, beating me up one day after school! Before long it became too much of a hassle for us to attend public schools, so we were enrolled in private institutions instead.

When you're related to a celebrity—five of them, in this case—it's hard to truly comprehend the magnitude of their fame. To me, Jackie, Tito, Jermaine, Marlon, and Michael were just normal guys. At home we still sang songs together and played practical jokes on one another. And as much as I adored them, there were still times when I thought they were creeps, probably making me the only girl in America who felt that way. I went to see them headline the Los Angeles Forum in June 1970. Hearing eighteen thousand teenagers and preteens (some with their parents) screaming hysterically for the Jackson 5, I looked around awestruck and wondered, *This is for MY BROTHERS?*

The pandemonium started the second the five of them hit the stage and never let up. When they first came out, I was surprised by how much their act had changed since Motown's "refinement." Now the guys sported bushy Afros and the loudest, wildest costumes I'd ever seen: vests dripping fringe, shirts and bell-bottoms splashed with electric colors, knee-high boots, sashes, and a beret for Tito. Unlike, say, the Temptations, they rarely wore matching outfits. I liked that, because it gave each guy his own identity.

Together, they were dynamite. The chemistry between them and the huge crowd seemed to ignite the entire arena. Their dancing was fast, furious, and, judging by the girls' shrieks, very sexy. Every time they thrust their hips, or Michael dropped to his knees like a miniature James Brown, the shrill screams threatened to topple the auditorium. Harried medics hustled up and down the aisles, filling stretchers with unconscious or delirious girls. Toward the show's end, hundreds of kids rushed the stage, sending security into a momentary panic. But, as always, they got the guys offstage, out of the building, and into their limousines before most of the fans even realized they were gone.

Capitalizing on the Jackson 5's sudden popularity, Motown kept them on the road for the remainder of 1970, playing arenas and stadiums all over the country. Out of concern for my brothers' safety, security had to be strengthened. My family hired a former policeman named Bill Bray to head the staff.

Several days before each concert, Bill flew to that city and inspected the venue's security arrangements. He also contacted the police to find out about street-gang activity, racial unrest; anything that might put the brothers at risk. In one city, rival gangs threatened to stage a shoot-out in the auditorium because one gang liked the Jackson 5 and the other didn't! Fortunately the concert went on without incident.

But a Buffalo, New York show had to be canceled after telephoned death threats were made to my brothers' hotel rooms. Security had good reason to believe that the callers were local gang members. It was nerve-wracking, because the only way to dial the Jackson 5's rooms directly was from inside the building. Therefore whoever placed the calls obviously knew the guys' room numbers.

Joseph phoned home to tell us what was happening. "Just cancel the show," Mother pleaded. "Don't let the boys go onstage." There was no need to argue, and the show was called off. However, in years to come my brothers bravely performed in the face of such threats. I'm not exaggerating when I say that this was the first of hundreds of similar threats made against members of my family. Several of us probably owe our lives to our security staff.

That said, there was no way we could feel like "normal" people living under those conditions. At a time when most kids are learning to become independent, exploring the world, we were kept fenced in. Eventually you learn to deal with the fear and the isolation, but you never accept it. Before long the entire family could travel only if surrounded by security, burly men bearing walkie-talkies and perpetually suspicious expressions. Our lives had no spontaneity or privacy, which drove Michael and me crazy.

"They know everything we do, La Toya," he'd gripe, "everything we talk about."

"I know. They're *always* here. I wish they could at least walk several feet behind us."

Ironically, our restrictive upbringing probably helped my brothers adapt to the lonely life of touring, where every day follows a fixed routine, only in a different city. They were whisked directly from the plane to their hotel rooms, then to rehearsal, then back to their rooms, then to the show, then back to their rooms for the night, or what was left of it. Sadly, despite all their traveling, my brothers' reality barely broadened.

On days off, the guys hibernated in their rooms because venturing outside was just too complicated. I think most adults would have gotten cabin fever, so you can imagine what it was like for five adolescents. There's a limit to how many pillow fights, long-distance calls home, pranks, and other distractions you can dream up. (A favorite trick was to balance a bucket of ice-cold water on top of a door left ajar, drenching the unsuspecting victim who opened it.)

Out of sheer boredom, Michael used to dial room service knowing full well the kitchen didn't have what he was about to order. "I'll have some collard greens . . . some cornbread . . . and some black-eyed peas," he'd say, as if reading the items off a menu. "Send 'em up right now!" Then he'd hang up, snickering. And when no knock at the door came, he'd call again. *"I'm waiting for my collard greens . . ."*

Now, most male singers can easily entertain themselves in their rooms, with women. God knows, Jackie, Tito, Jermaine, Marlon, and Michael could have had their pick of willing young girls, but even Houdini couldn't have penetrated the barriers Motown and Joseph constructed around them. No one was allowed near unless preapproved by security. To elude resourceful fans, they made up code names for one another and a "Jackson knock." Standing outside one of their rooms, rapping on the door, you felt like you were entering a 1920s speakeasy.

In addition to the guards posted in the hotel hallways, Joseph checked each room himself to make sure that my brothers, and only my brothers, were inside. He also did a strange thing: at night while the guys were sleeping, he brought girls into their rooms to gawk at them. (I'd rather not speculate as to his reasons.) While Jermaine later suggested that he and Michael snuck girls in, that's not true.

If they had, Motown executives would have thrown a fit. Scandal and paternity suits, whether genuine or not, might have ruined the guys' squeaky-clean image, in itself a valuable asset. Truth was, the company had nothing to worry about. Though my parents never discussed sex with any of us, they communicated their values quite clearly: we were not to date unless serious about marriage.

Not surprisingly, my brothers dated very little until their late teens. At eighteen Jackie actually had a girlfriend, but he was allowed to see her only in our home. For one hour. Come eight o'clock, Joseph rudely ordered her to go home. My father was unhappy with several of the girls Jackie dated, and with Tito's girlfriend. He didn't like one because she wasn't black and assumed all the rest were only after his sons' money.

Joseph's suspicions weren't limited to gold-digging girlfriends. He and Mother distrusted all outsiders—to a certain extent, with good reason. The tragic downfall of many young entertainers is the greedy shortsightedness of the people directing their careers. I know of one instance where a popular teen group's manager introduced them to drugs because it made them easier to control. Others are deprived of proper guidance and education, so they lag far behind kids their age. The manager of one teen act we invited to dinner called ahead and requested we serve only finger food, like hot dogs and hamburgers, to spare his clients embarrassment. It seems they'd never learned how to use silverware! I hate to think what awaits these kids when their careers are over. Seeing things like this later made us appreciate the positive aspects of our parents' and Motown's protection during those crucial formative years.

Unlike many less fortunate kids in show business, the Jackson 5 always had the best education possible. Tutor Rose Fine accompanied them on the road, to television rehearsals and tapings, and anywhere their work took them. Later, in the mid-seventies, when Randy, Janet, and I joined the live act, she instructed us as well, preparing individual lessons, since we were all in different grades.

Every morning after breakfast we'd meet in her hotel room. A real Jewish Mother, Mrs. Fine always asked whether or not we'd eaten. Some of the brothers, usually Jermaine and Randy, took immediate advantage of this golden opportunity to avoid schoolwork. "Mrs. Fine," one of them would say coyly, "I didn't eat breakfast yet. Can I order something from room service?"

"Of course, dear," she always replied, while the rest of us rolled our eyes. Mrs. Fine couldn't imagine forcing a child to study on an empty stomach. As we worked on our lessons, she walked around the table, peering over our shoulders, offering suggestions and answering questions. She became such a second mom to all of us that every Mother's Day Michael makes sure someone from the family has sent Mrs. Fine flowers.

* * *

In just one year, the Jackson 5 had released four albums, three of which sold over one million copies each, appeared on dozens of television shows, and had become the new decade's preeminent black stars. The guys had exceeded their, and Joseph's, wildest dreams, with no end in sight. Soon after their fifth single, "Mama's Pearl," went to Number Two in early 1971, our family moved to Beverly Hills.

Frank Sinatra lived nearby, as did Michael's ultimate idol, Fred Astaire, to whom he'd later dedicate *Moonwalk.* One day we learned that the legendary dancer, then about seventy-two, wanted to meet Michael. My brother was speechless. "I see you jogging around the neighborhood all the time," Mr. Astaire told him. Michael floated back home. It took a while to adjust to having stars for next-door neighbors, but soon it seemed perfectly normal.

For me, meeting Diana Ross was like having an audience with a queen. I'd grown up watching the Supremes on television and thought she was the epitome of chic. The first time Diana visited our house, I couldn't get over how beautiful she was, but also how surprisingly small. Likewise, when Michael first met Smokey Robinson, all he could talk about afterward was Smokey's hands. "They were so *soft,* La Toya, I couldn't believe it," he marveled. We'd assumed all men's hands were calloused like our father's. It's funny how sometimes seemingly inconsequential details about people stick in your mind.

We loved the Beverly Hills house, which had a swimming pool and a large practice room for rehearsals. But the grounds were overrun by rattlesnakes that came down from the hills. One day a rattler snuck up on Michael by the pool. Fortunately, a visitor pushed my brother into the water just as it was about to strike, probably saving his life.

"That's it!" Mother declared. "We have to move! I can't take this anymore; it's too dangerous." Despite her outwardly meek demeanor, she can be firm. She instructed Joseph to find us another house, specifying only that it be spacious and located in Beverly Hills. My father, having his own ideas, ignored her. When he gruffly informed us that he'd bought a mansion in the San Fernando Valley suburb of Encino, Mother was disappointed. Over twenty years later, though, she and Joseph are still there, and that house on Hayvenhurst Avenue remains the family center.

What initially attracted my father to the rambling, modern ranch-style home were the orange trees that covered the two and a half acres. When we moved in, there were six bedrooms, yet we younger kids continued to double and triple up: Janet and I, and Michael, Randy, and Marlon. The expansive property had a separate guest house, a playhouse, servants' quarters, a pool, immaculately manicured grounds, and basketball and badminton courts. Over time we made many improvements, such as the recording studio my foresighted father had added on so his sons could practice composing and recording without incurring studio costs at Motown. Attached to the studio was what we called the Candy Store, filled with ice cream and snacks. It was a child's fantasy come true.

Outside, though, were constant reminders that this magnificent house's cost to our family wasn't measured solely in dollars and cents: a high fence bordered the acreage, an electric gate stood imposingly out front, and a team of security guards manned the gatehouse twenty-four hours a day, while surveillance cameras scanned the grounds, impassive voyeurs. Even with all these precautions, Mother and Joseph never felt truly safe.

My siblings and I went out even less than we had in Indiana. California's legal driving age is sixteen, but except for Jermaine, none of us was allowed to drive a car until much later. My father's obsession with keeping us isolated was to continue all our lives. Those of us who remained at home through the seventies, though adults, were still not allowed to have private phone lines.

The older brothers hung out with a group of kids nicknamed the Motown Babies, consisting of Berry Gordy's children, Diana Ross's younger brothers, and the teenaged offspring of other label executives and artists. Michael, Randy, Marlon, Janet, and I usually stayed home, clinging to one another more than ever.

Sometimes I considered inviting a classmate to the house but was always stopped by the thought, *What if Joseph comes home while they're there? What if he starts yelling and screaming? What if he hits one of us? What will they think of me?* The mere prospect of being embarrassed and humiliated in front of other kids was too painful to even consider, so I continued not having any friends. It was easy to convince myself I was better off that way.

Following a summer 1971 tour that took the Jackson 5 to more than forty cities, Motown released thirteen-year-old Michael's first solo single, the million-selling "Got to Be There." Undeniably Michael overshadowed his brothers, his cherubic face alone gracing the cover of magazines such as *Rolling Stone*.

In most families, that kind of individual attention would breed jealousy and rivalries, but not in the Jacksons. Tito, Jermaine, and especially Jackie all understood why Michael received a disproportionate share of attention. A wonderful singer himself, Jackie used to tell people matter-of-factly that even when Michael was five, it was obvious he should be the group's leader. Tito, the most dedicated musician of all the guys and the only one to study music formally, was secure in his role. So was Jermaine, who got to sing solos and duet with Michael onstage.

Marlon, however, seemed to get lost in the shuffle. Offstage, he loved to play practical jokes and show off. Like any normal kid, he just wanted attention. One problem was that he got compared a lot to Michael, probably because they were so close in age and even looked alike then. I guess it was inevitable that he feel competitive with his younger brother, but Mother used to reprimand him about it all the time.

Jackie, the most sensitive of us, would ask her, "Why are you always correcting Marlon?"

"Because he can't be so competitive, Jackie. It's a bad trait, and he's got to break himself of it before he gets older." Perhaps. But it did seem that she picked on Marlon the most, especially about his dancing onstage. I never understood that, because he was frequently singled out in reviews for his smoothness and precision. One writer remarked that of all the brothers, Marlon looked the best onstage and was "as visible as the corner of a polished diamond," which made us all feel good for him.

Mother further quelled any potential jealousy toward Michael by treating him like a regular kid. We all did. In the Jackson family, the country's biggest teen sensation was very much a typically pesky brother.

Make that more pesky than most. Since we spent so much time inside, my siblings and I played lots of board games like checkers, chess, and Scrabble. At least, we tried to. In the middle of a chess match, Michael would dash in and snatch one person's queen or drop an object onto the board, scattering pieces everywhere. He also liked to knock candy bars from people's hands and sprint off, laughing uproariously.

"*Michael!*" His full name was reserved for the many times he exasperated us, like when he was teasing Janet about her chubbiness or me about my obsessive neatness and round face. Moonface, he used to call me. That wasn't nearly as bad as his gibes of Rocky Road, directed at Jermaine, who suffered from acne in his early teens.

"Rocky Road!"

"Michael, cut it out!"

"Rocky Road, Rocky Road!" Michael shouted, running away from his older brother. "Why, look at your pimply old face!"

Mother always intervened, scolding, "Mike, now stop teasing Jermaine about his skin. One day you're going to have a bad complexion, just from doing this to Jermaine." It was a variation on the old saw parents tell smirking children about their faces one day freezing permanently in that expression.

Michael pretended to listen obediently, but I saw the mischief in his eyes. With mock sincerity, he said, "Okay, I'm sorry . . . *Rocky Road!*" Then he fell to the floor, laughing and holding his stomach.

Back then, Michael was extremely outgoing, and a flirt too, probably from always being around older musicians. We'd pass a pretty girl, and my brother would remark, "Boy, did you see the pair of cakes on her!" Or he'd steal peeks under dresses, then ask me with a giggle, "Guess what color panties she has on?"

"Michael!" I was hardly shocked; we'd come to expect that kind of thing from him.

Having trouble reconciling these stories with your image of the adult Michael Jackson? I have the same problem sometimes. They almost seem like two different people to me.

It wasn't long before Motown realized what a gold

mine it had in the Jackson 5. Besides the millions of records sold and the company's take from the concerts, there was merchandising, or licensing the guys' likenesses for items such as lunch boxes. And also for a Saturday-morning cartoon TV series that premiered in fall 1971. Like *The Beatles* cartoons, *The Jackson 5ive* featured the group's music, but my brothers' speaking voices were dubbed by actors. Of all the things success brought, this was probably Michael's and Marlon's favorite perk, watching their animated selves cavort onscreen.

How all our lives had been transformed in just under two years! Living behind guarded gates, seeing yourself portrayed as a cartoon figure, unable to go out alone—this was my brothers' life. What little we knew about the outside world was fleeting and distant. In Indiana, Joseph and Mother alone built the walls that cut us off from the "outside." Now the uncontrollable force of the Jackson 5's success reinforced and heightened these. Padding around Hayvenhurst, I had to really concentrate to remember what life had been like in Indiana. Before long everything except the way we were now faded into memory.

3

THE FAMILY ACT

"You all are *nuthin'*."

That's what my father used to tell the wealthiest, most famous, talented black teenagers in America, contempt dripping from every syllable. "You all are *weird*." We heard it almost daily our entire lives.

Tito confided to me that when they were on the road, Joseph didn't even want to be seen with them. "It's awful, La Toya," he said. "He treats us like we're invisible. If we ask him why, he just looks at us."

Did our father really think so little of his five sons? I believe that systemically destroying their self-worth was Joseph's twisted way of maintaining control over the Jackson 5, his sole source of financial support. He must have realized now that the guys were older and somewhat exposed to the outside world, they could break away. Certainly if we were still in Indiana and the group never took off, my brothers would have rebelled and tried leading their own lives. There was no way Joseph could have stopped that. But things were different now.

It saddens me to think of all we have missed. Just recently Tito said to me of his school days, "La Toya, whenever I was around kids at school, they always talked about how their fathers took them here and there. And I had nothing to say. I never had that opportunity. Joseph did nothing with us."

"I know," I said softly. "I love you guys."

"We love you too, La Toya. But I don't know how much more of this I can take." Like our father, Tito loved to fish. He added, "I've never even been fishing with him. And I always wanted to do those things with him."

"It's a shame we never had a father," I answered. All of us needed to feel our father's love, but we rarely if ever did. The only emotions Joseph seemed capable of expressing to us were his anger and disgust.

Jackie, who turned twenty in 1971, still lived at home and continued to receive the brunt of our father's hatred and cruelty. To this day, Joseph blames him for anything that goes wrong, in any situation. "Jackie Boy did it," he'll say scornfully. My father thought nothing of slapping Jackie and the others in public, shocking and repulsing onlookers. Joseph's battering was a well-known secret around Motown. Yet none of them ever fought back. One time, after Joseph threatened to smack Jackie, my older brother reflexively reared back as if to throw a punch.

"What?!" my father roared, striding closer to Jackie. "Did you raise a hand to me?!" With that he crushed his heavy fist into Jackie's face, nearly knocking him unconscious.

"Joseph!" Mother cried, "what are you doing?" There was no use trying to reason with him, for his temper was uncontrollable. At one point the brothers confronted Mother en masse and insisted, "Joseph's got to stop this, or next time we're gonna gang up on him." But it proved an empty threat; with the occasional exception of Michael, none of them ever gave Joseph anything to fear.

In my father's eyes, we were just a bunch of over-pampered kids. To friends and associates he referred to us as weirdos, and he seemed to resent our new life-style. "When I was your age," he often lectured us, "I didn't live in a big house with a pool, I had to work hard." As if the brothers didn't work hard, rehearsing, recording, and following a punishing schedule. Whatever luxuries we were fortunate enough to have, they earned. "You have a driver taking you to school every morning," Joseph continued. "Me, I had to walk ten miles to school. And these gadgets you have; why, these weren't even invented when I was young . . ."

We were all relieved, then, when our father began staying away from home more and more, leaving at daybreak and not returning until after midnight. His whereabouts were a mystery. We knew only that he'd opened an office in Motown's building on Sunset Boulevard in Hollywood. Where he went after office hours, no one could say.

Even in his absence, though, Joseph's presence

dominated the house and us. Unless you've dealt with a parent like him, it's probably hard to imagine living perpetually on edge, never knowing what to expect. When was he coming home? What mood would he be in? Any time the security guard announced over the intercom, ''Mr. Jackson has just arrived,'' we dropped whatever we were doing and hid, usually in one of our bedrooms; anything to stay out of his way. Maybe every other day we'd catch him storming through the house, ranting at us, usually heading out the door.

On more than one occasion some of us tried talking to Mother about the fact that we didn't know our own father. Her response was always a resigned, ''You're better off *not* knowing him.''

''But we want to have a father who's at home,'' I said. ''Why is Joseph like this? Why doesn't he want to be with us?''

''La Toya, it's better this way. If Joseph were at home, he'd just start confusion.''

''But Mother—''

''It's better this way,'' she repeated curtly, then walked away.

We never understood why she stayed with Joseph, a man by her own admission we were better off not knowing. But we didn't hold it against Mother or dwell on how much easier life would be if she left him. Then and for many years to come we considered Mother one of ''us'': another victim of Joseph's wrath.

Looking back, I suppose the obvious question is,

Why didn't we kids leave home once we were old enough? Certainly money wasn't an issue. That we never considered that option shows how sheltered and dominated we were. As much as I feared Joseph, the typical childhood fantasy of running away from home was literally unthinkable to me. We all felt so helpless, and the world "out there" seemed so daunting.

The only acceptable way to leave home was to marry, like Rebbie had. In 1971, seventeen-year-old Tito shocked the family by announcing his plans to wed his first and only girlfriend, Dee Dee, as soon as he graduated high school. Jermaine, Marlon, and Janet, too, would marry their first loves while in their teens. I've noticed a tendency toward early marriages in other large, strict families, like the Osmonds.

Motown wasn't pleased to learn of Tito's impending nuptials. Ever since "I Want You Back" earned the label the first of many millions from the Jackson 5, label executives warned Joseph against letting his sons take wives. They believed it could diminish the guys' teen popularity and decimate the bottom line. "If any of the boys gets married," they predicted, "the fans will drop them like hot potatoes. And after one gets married, they'll all want to get married. Then the wives start butting in, and before you know it, the group's finished. We've seen this happen before."

When one of my brothers (I'd rather not say who) was on the brink of marrying, we had our first encounter with the evil that exists in the record business, and probably any high-stakes industry. You've no doubt heard about payola, drugs, and other scandals, but believe me, that's barely half of it.

Joseph came home one day visibly shaken. We rarely, if ever, saw him unnerved. Gathering the family together, he related an incredible story: a well-known and powerful music-industry figure approached my father and told him of his "concerns" that a Jackson marrying would result in the group's ruination. "You cannot let this happen," he said. "*We* cannot let it happen." Then he added ominously, "I can stop this, you know."

"What do you mean, you can stop this? How? If he loves this girl, and they get married, that's their business. Not yours."

"Do you want it stopped?"

"Well," Joseph admitted, "I'd rather he didn't get involved, but—"

"But do you want it stopped?"

"What exactly are you saying?"

"She can . . . disappear."

In disbelief, my father asked, "How can she just disappear?"

"She can fall or drive off a cliff," the man replied coolly. "People won't know anything about it. They'll find her, and everyone will just assume she lost control and drove off the road. We could make it happen right off Mulholland Drive. That would be easy."

Even Joseph was appalled. "No! You can't do something like that! Don't even think about it!"

"Okay, it's up to you," the other man said, holding his palms apart. "Just trying to help."

Would a person actually murder someone for money? In the entertainment business, sorry to say, the answer is yes.

While my older brothers were dating, the opposite sex was the last thing on my mind. For one thing, Michael and I were very active in the Jehovah's Witness faith. By this time most of our siblings had basically given it up. Five days a week the two of us and Mother studied the Bible at home and attended the Kingdom Hall. (Randy always wanted to go to the meetings with us but could never seem to get dressed in time.)

Every morning Michael and I witnessed, knocking on doors around Los Angeles, spreading the word of Jehovah. As my brother's fame grew, he had to don convincing disguises, like a rubber fat suit he bought years later, around the time of *Thriller*. Adults were easily fooled by Michael incognito, but it was a rare child who didn't see through his costume in seconds.

"Good morning," my brother would say cheerily to whomever answered his knock. "We'd like to talk to you about the state of the world today and how man can cope with the problems we all face. May I have a minute of your time?" Reactions to this stranger differed, but invariably a youngster standing in the doorway pointed and blurted excitedly, "That's Michael Jackson!"

"Honey, don't be silly," the parent replied.

"But it is! It is!" the child insisted, staring wide-eyed at Michael, who desperately avoided eye contact.

"Sweetheart, what would Michael Jackson be doing here?" The parent would flash us one of those looks that say, *You know how kids are.* I can't tell you how many times this happened. Children seem to regard Michael as a sort of Pied Piper, and it never ceased to amaze me how easily they saw through his disguises, yet their parents never did.

My brother and I were oddly unconcerned about walking into unfamiliar homes where conceivably someone could recognize Michael and perhaps try to harm or kidnap him. (Security did, however, follow us in a car.) But the faith instructed this was what we had to do, so we did it. Even if a house had "Beware of Dog" signs posted, we were obligated to try reaching the people inside. As a precaution, though, we always rattled the gate or made some other noise just to see if there really was a dog.

Michael told me that one time when he went canvassing alone, he crept into a yard, wearing his fat suit, and from around the corner darted a huge, ferocious looking mongrel. Pamphlets and copies of *Watchtower* and *Awake* flew up in the air as my brother took off down the street, the snarling animal nipping at his ankles. It must have been a hilarious sight: Michael screaming for help, looking back over his shoulder, and discarding his heavy costume piece by piece. Accustomed to outrunning Joseph around the house as a kid, he eventually lost the dog, which trotted home exhausted.

By choosing to follow the religion, I accepted its rules. For example, Jehovah's Witnesses are forbidden from listening to music with sexually oriented lyrics; I didn't listen to much pop music, not even my own brothers' records! To this day I still don't know all their seventies hits. And because we were supposed to associate exclusively with other members, Michael and I made few friends at the private high school we, Randy, and Marlon then attended. A number of celebrities' children were enrolled there, including some of Marlon Brando's kids.

We did, however, become close with another Witness. Darles was my first and only friend outside the family, and I treasured the time we spent together. One of the few girls in our school not in awe of Michael, she treated him as just another kid, which he really appreciated. Each day at lunch the three of us studied the Bible together. She also joined us at the Kingdom Hall.

During a meeting, Darles bravely challenged one of the elders. "Why is it that I will be saved," she asked innocently, "but my parents won't be? They may not be Witnesses, but they're perfectly nice people." The elder's reply was typical. He cited the scripture, which supported his position but did not really address Darles's point. So she wrote a letter further explaining her feelings and doubts. This outraged the other elders. One day Rebbie's husband, Nathaniel, also an elder, cornered me. "La Toya," he said, "you're never allowed to speak to Darles again. Ever."

''But why?''

''She's been disfellowshipped.'' Cast out of the faith, to be shunned from then on.

''She's my best friend!'' I protested. ''How can you do this?'' It was so wrong, and I was angry and hurt, but I pushed aside my feelings. After that neither Michael nor I had anything to do with Darles. We missed her so much and for the first time began to privately reconsider some of the teachings. We felt that questions should be encouraged, not silenced through threats of disfellowship.

The elders are obliged to reprimand members who dress or behave immodestly. As an entertainer and idol of millions, Michael was always being reproached for such things as the length of his hair and for wearing widely flared bell-bottoms. My brother loves vivid colors, particularly red, prompting one elder to criticize, ''The colors you wear are too bright, and you're attracting attention to yourself. You must stick with brown and black.'' Some Witnesses refused to associate with us at all.

In many people's minds, the faith is too strict, but we had nothing to compare it to. All I really knew were home, school, and Kingdom Hall, three places that demanded obedience and discouraged free expression. The older we got, though, the more Michael and I started to wonder where we fit in society. Outsiders saw us as sheltered, naive squares, and I guess we were. In the religion, at least we were accepted.

Prohibited from seeing Darles, I grew closer to

Mother. She became my new best friend. It was the kind of relationship most mothers dream of. Besides going to Kingdom Hall together, most mornings she drove me to school, detouring for breakfast pastries and a chance to be alone together. Mother was devoted to all her children but always made me feel I was special. She confided in me and never let me forget how much alike we were. As I grew older, Joseph would often remark, "Kate, doesn't La Toya look just like you did when we first met? Look at that tiny waist—just like yours used to be." Mother would smile.

Whatever I wore or whatever I did, Mother seemed so happy and proud. And that made me happy. Unlike most teenage girls, I looked forward to spending time with her and couldn't imagine being with anyone else, least of all boys. I turned sweet sixteen without having been out on a date.

Our wonderful tutor, Mrs. Fine, always gave me the third degree on that score, asking sweetly, "La Toya dear, do you have a boyfriend? Please tell me yes."

"No, Mrs. Fine," I'd reply, slightly embarrassed.

"You don't know it, dear, but you're missing out on the best years of your life. You're going to look back on these days and regret it. A pretty girl like you should have a boyfriend. I really feel for you." Her well-intentioned questions continued for the next five years, as did my answer.

According to our faith, it was a sin to even "entertain thoughts" about a member of the opposite sex. If I even just looked at a guy and thought, *He's cute; I could really like him,* I immediately confessed to one of the elders. I felt so guilty and confused. Why was it wrong to like a boy? Also, my brothers, so protective of me, probably frightened away anyone who might have been interested in me. Any time Jermaine saw a guy so much as glance my way, he barked, "What are you lookin' at? I'll break your neck!"

Mother never seemed concerned that I didn't date; in fact, it pleased her, because it meant I wouldn't leave home like Rebbie and Tito had. Jermaine was seriously dating Berry Gordy's daughter Hazel, Marlon was carrying on a pen-pal romance with Carol Ann Parker, a girl from New Orleans he'd met when he was eleven or twelve, and all women seemed to be in love with Jackie, so it was only a matter of time before they would leave too.

Our parents wouldn't acknowledge that we were growing from children into young men and women. The facts of life were a taboo subject. Out of shyness, my mother never talked to me about "personal matters," making the normal physical changes of adolescence traumatic for me. As a preteen, I was so embarrassed about my developing bust that I walked around the house with my hands pressed against my chest in a futile attempt at suppressing the inevitable.

Adolescence proved awkward for Michael too. He sprouted from just over five feet to five feet ten. Overnight, it seemed, he went from a cute little boy to a gangly teenager. Certain body parts outgrew others, and now Michael was the object of merciless ribbing, especially from his father. "Look at that big nose on your face," Joseph used to taunt. "I don't know where you got that from . . . *Bignose.*" Given the opportunity for revenge at last, my brothers chipped in with their own insults, but none was so mean-spirited and cutting as Joseph's. Michael was terribly upset, always better at dishing out teasing than taking it.

Then, Mother's earlier prophecy came true: he developed a severe case of acne. Of course, most afflicted teenagers feel self-conscious, so just imagine being a star whose face adorns magazine covers, T-shirts, and lunch pails. My brother was devastated. Suzanne dePasse and her cousin Tony Jones, also a Motown staffer, took him from one high-priced dermatologist to another, but every new treatment only exacerbated the problem. For the next two and a half years Michael endured countless ineffective regimens.

His personality changed. Before, he'd been outgoing and comfortable with strangers; now he withdrew into himself. My brother wouldn't talk to outsiders, and if he did, he looked down or to the side, to hide his face. He didn't want his picture taken. During years when he should have been going out, meeting girls, he stayed at home. My heart ached for him. "Mike, you shouldn't let this bother you so much," I told him. "It will pass."

"I can't stand it, La Toya, I really can't." He was

in utter despair. "There's got to be a way to make it go away."

Michael changed his diet drastically, eating only pure, natural foods. Although he finally outgrew the skin condition by his sixteenth birthday, he never recovered from its effects. Once the most sociable and effervescent of my brothers, he was now painfully shy, something I don't think he'll ever overcome.

In 1972 Michael invaded the Top 20 seven times, four as a member of the Jackson 5 ("Sugar Daddy," "Little Bitty Pretty One," "Lookin' Through the Windows" and "Corner of the Sky") and three as a soloist: his spirited remake of Bobby Day's 1958 smash "Rockin' Robin," "I Wanna Be Where You Are," and the heartfelt ballad "Ben," which went to Number One. A lot of people thought "Ben"—an ode to a rat—bizarre, but not Michael. To him, no creature is repulsive, not even a rodent. (In fact, he used to come to dinner with his pet white mice tucked in his shirt pocket. I remember stuffing towels under my bedroom door at night to keep escapees from crawling onto my bed.)

That same year Motown launched Jermaine's solo career with a moderate hit, "That's How Love Goes," followed by his Top 10 cover of Shep and the Limelites' tender "Daddy's Home." But after that, the brothers' record sales, both individually and as a group, started slipping. "Hallelujah Day," released in 1973, was the Jackson 5's lowest-charting single to date; both it and the follow-up, "Get It

Together,'' ran out of steam at Number Twenty-eight. The *Get It Together* album barely struggled into the Top 100. Michael's only single of the year, ''With a Child's Heart,'' stopped at Number Fifty; Jermaine's ''You're in Good Hands,'' at Number Seventy-nine; and *Jackie Jackson,* my oldest brother's promising debut album disappeared without a trace.

What was happening to the Jackson 5? (Actually 6, as baby-faced eleven-year-old Randy now joined his brothers on stage, flailing away on congas.) The guys felt, and Joseph concurred, Motown wasn't giving them the right material. They wanted to record their own songs, which they'd been honing in the Hayvenhurst studio for two years, but the label forced the group to sing only what its staff writers churned out. Berry Gordy, the record industry's Henry Ford, had built his empire on assembly-line production, with writers writing and singers singing. Despite Stevie Wonder and Marvin Gaye having recently proved successful exceptions to this rule, Berry wouldn't grant the Jackson 5 that same opportunity.

It seemed inconceivable at the time, but my father and brothers considered following the lead of Gladys Knight and the Pips, and the Four Tops, and finding another label. The days of Motown's golden touch were clearly coming to an end, for a number of reasons, among them a gradual loss of industry clout and Berry's increased preoccupation with movie-making following the success of *Lady Sings the*

Blues. In 1969, the year the Jackson 5 signed to Motown, the company charted twelve singles in the Top 10; in 1972, four. Though frustrated, the guys would have to bide their time, as that contract still had two years left.

Despite slumping record sales, the Jackson 5 remained a top concert draw around the world, touring the United States, Japan, and Australia through 1973. Tito's first baby was due toward the tour's end, but Joseph wouldn't let him fly home to be with his wife. So I took my brother's place at her Lamaze childbirth-preparation classes. The guys were in Europe when Dee Dee's labor started. I coached her during the delivery, helping adorable Toriano Adaryll II into the world. I love all my nieces and nephews, but Taj, as he's nicknamed, has a special place in my heart.

The month after Taj's birth, Jermaine and Hazel's wedding invitations went out. The two had fallen in love almost at first sight in 1969. From then on, Hazel wrote him devotedly. About twice a week back in Indiana Joseph used to sort through the mail and yell upstairs in a singsong voice, "Oh, Jermaine! Looks like you got another letter from that Gordy girl!"

After we moved to California, where Hazel lived, she and Jermaine resumed their romance. I think my parents were relieved he was marrying Hazel, because she was from a good family. They always worried that the brothers would wind up with girls who wanted their money. It's safe to assume that Berry

Gordy had the same fears of gigolos going after his only daughter. Once Jermaine returned Hazel's interest, her father promoted the relationship aggressively, practically nudging them down the aisle.

On December 15, 1973, Berry threw Hazel and Jermaine one of the most extravagant weddings in Hollywood history. Though it was balmy outside, the affair had a winter theme, replete with fake snow, white camellias, live doves, and a towering eight-layer wedding cake. Hazel looked stunning in a mink- and pearl-trimmed white satin gown, while Jermaine wore a sequin-trimmed white tuxedo.

Marvin and Anna Gaye's son, Marvin, Jr., was the ring bearer, Marlon stood as Jermaine's best man, I was a bridesmaid, and the other brothers were ushers. Smokey Robinson sang a song he composed especially for the couple, "From This Time and Place." Among the six hundred invited guests were Los Angeles Mayor Tom Bradley and his wife; Diana Ross and her husband, Bob Silberstein; Billy Dee Williams; Diahann Carroll; Coretta Scott King; and Nicholas Ashford and Valerie Simpson. It was a dream wedding, touted in the press as the merging of two great black showbiz dynasties.

Some fans had reacted adversely when Tito married Dee Dee, but that was nothing compared to the flak Jermaine took for giving up bachelorhood. To some, he was the most beautiful of the brothers, blessed with Mother's kind eyes and seductive lips. Motown exploited his sex appeal from the start, having Jermaine pose shirtless for photos, giving him the romantic ballads to sing—and keeping his and Hazel's romance a secret. Thousands of girls were crushed to learn he'd "spurned" their affection. They expressed their outrage in writing, much of it malicious:

"If I could see you now, I'd slap your face . . . So you lied to us, huh? . . . Why did you have to do this to me? . . . I want you to know that now you make me sick. . . . I was counting on us getting together sometime." These fans sincerely believed that Jermaine belonged exclusively to them! Their letters upset my brother, and later it hurt him when some fans would refuse his autograph just because he was married.

In 1974 the Jackson 5 put out "Dancing Machine," which heralded a new, more mature direction—and revealed that Michael's voice had deepened appreciably into a soulful tenor. Driven by a funky electric keyboard and a bubbling undercurrent of bass and percussion, it was to be their last Top 10 single for nearly three years.

Immediately after the record's release, my brothers flew to the Republic of Senegal for a special performance. They'd never been to Africa before and were inspired by the people and the sights there. However, the trip was memorable for another reason. Joseph herded the six of them into a room and said, beaming, "I have something to tell you: you have a new little sister."

"What are you talking about?"

"Mother didn't have any new babies."

"No, but *I* have a new daughter," he continued, "born right around the same time as Tito's. Her name is Anna [not her real name], and she's about six months old." Our father had a second family! We'd always suspected he ran around on Mother—all those unexplained late nights out—but never this. The guys were understandably sickened. But amazingly, Joseph acted as if this were perfectly normal, acceptable behavior; if he'd had some cigars, he would have passed them out.

The minute my brothers returned home, they told me about our father's shameful confession.

"He's got another *family*, La Toya, with some woman."

"I hate him!" one of the guys hissed.

Jermaine asked, "Should we tell Mother?"

"Are you crazy?" said Michael. "We can't tell her this. She can never know."

"It would kill her," I added, wondering aloud, "why does he do these things?"

"I don't know, but you should have seen him, La Toya; so proud, like we should be happy for him." Michael was filled with loathing. "It made me sick."

Teeth clenched, Jermaine spat angrily, "To be so proud of that—"

"—and he's not even proud of us!" Tears welled in Michael's eyes.

For months we kept Joseph's secret from our mother. It pained us bitterly to know he was deceiving her, staying out nights with his "second family." My father was so blatant that eventually people in his office and at Motown knew what was going on. Finally, one of the brothers couldn't take it anymore and blurted the truth to Mother. I think subconsciously some of us believed—even hoped—that if she knew this about her husband, she'd divorce him.

Of course Mother felt utterly humiliated, and when Joseph refused to end the affair, she was purple with anger. Yet she issued no threats, no overtures of divorce. Her way of dealing with his philandering was to deny that anything was wrong inside our home, and, incredibly, life went on as before. When I was very young, I interpreted this ability of hers as a strength. Now I see that Mother's denial was actually a weakness, a way to avoid confrontation and responsibility. Rather than direct her justified anger at the true source, she obsessed about Joseph's illegitimate daughter and spoke of her with uncharacteristic meanness.

"That bastard child!" she muttered once, her voice choked with rage. "You're never to speak to her. Do you understand me? Never!"

"Mother, she's not a bastard," Michael said softly.

"Look it up in the dictionary! She is!"

"But she can't help it," I said. "She didn't ask to be brought into the world. Maybe one day we would like to meet her, talk to her. I don't mean be close to her, but isn't it wrong to hate her like this?

She's just a little girl." When Mother moodily turned away, Michael shot me a look of resignation. We felt torn between the innate compassion we all have for children and our loyalty to our mother.

Later, we learned that Joseph's mistress was a woman who'd once had an unrequited crush on Jackie. For a while she and Anna lived miles away, but I guess Joseph got tired of "commuting," so he set them up in their own home just minutes from Hayvenhurst. Shopping in a local mall with their children, some of my brothers spotted Joseph holding hands with his girlfriend and daughter. Mortified, and to avoid hearing the innocent question, "What's Grandpa doing with that lady and little girl?" they distracted their kids and quickly ducked into a store.

Most of my siblings refused to have anything to do with Anna, but Michael and I were curious about her. We often wondered aloud to each other, "What do you think she looks like? What sort of personality do you think she has?" Frankly, we felt sorry for her, considering the kind of father Joseph was to us. But as we discovered, he displayed to her a completely different side of himself, catering to Anna and treating her like a princess.

Though my father never said it outright, I always suspected that he wanted us to get to know his "other" daughter. Years later Joseph once said to me, "There's a little girl that has all your pictures and admires you very much. She wants to speak to you. Will you just say hi to her?"

Thinking he was talking about some fan, I asked, "What's her name?"

"Anna."

That Anna? He didn't say, he just dialed the number and handed me the receiver.

It was a pleasant, if brief, conversation, consisting mostly of her excited, girlish squeals. "Oh, I love you so much!" she said. "I want to be just like you!"

"Oh, that's nice . . ."

"I'm so happy you called to talk to me."

"Oh, that's okay, it's no trouble." The whole time I wondered, *Is this my half-sister I'm talking to?* Something told me it was.

It became increasingly clear that Joseph considered Anna and her mother his "real" family. One afternoon an assistant of my father's delivered his Rolls-Royce to Hayvenhurst. Strangely, an hour or so later he returned, climbed in the car, and drove off. As we eventually learned, what had happened was that when ordered to take the car "home," the assistant naturally thought Joseph meant Hayvenhurst. Sadly, he did not. *Home* was a few miles away, with another woman and their child.

Around the same time my father started his second family, he created a second Jackson family act that included the six guys, Janet, and me. With the hits not coming as consistently as before, he felt the brothers should branch out into playing Las Vegas showrooms. No one was exactly thrilled about that, because back then you had to tailor your act to Vegas standards, singing only your most popular songs and fewer of them, and adding more dancing, middle-of-the-road standards, and between-song patter. It bordered on corny, but we were a family, and this was after all a family act.

Though I loved music and had sung in the school choir, I had no interest whatsoever in show business—one reason being that I associated performing with getting beaten. I was scared to death of Joseph. When he told me I would be singing and dancing, I knew from his stern tone of voice that I had no choice.

As it turned out, appearing with my brothers and my sister Janet as the Jacksons was so much fun, one of the happiest times of my life. There's really nothing like a family working together. I know many musical acts feel like a family after a while, but when it's really your own blood, it's something special.

Audiences truly loved this show, but, frankly, the scene backstage was even more entertaining. Janet and I would be waiting in the wings, all ready to go, but the guys had to hurry off the stage after their regular opening set and change into their sequined white satin costumes with ''J5'' emblazoned across the front. A typical night sounded something like this:

Jermaine: ''Gimme my jockstrap!''

Randy: ''Where're my pants?''

Jackie: ''Who took my shoes?''

Then Jermaine noticed with alarm, ''Uh-oh! Marlon's in line, you guys!''

Standing at the edge of the stage, grinning devil-ishly, was Marlon. My brother thought it was the funniest thing to step out early, cueing the band to start playing and forcing us to hustle into line, ready or not. One night I nearly rushed onstage with my costume on backward.

Onstage the blare of the music is so loud, you can hold entire conversations out of microphone range, and the audience can't hear you. During one of the tap-dancing numbers, some of the guys clapped and shouted encouragement—"Yeah, get it!" "Great!"—while Jermaine and Marlon, the two jokers, offered running commentary:

"Look at Tito, he can't even do the move right!"

"Hey, you crazy, stupid idiots! You're out there tappin' for these people! Look at ya's!"

Performers are supposed to smile on stage, but with us it was usually because we were about to burst out laughing.

One night Michael and I were tap-tap-tapping along to a routine he'd choreographed, smiling away, when all of a sudden Jermaine called out, "Yeah, get it, Mike! Go, Mike! Yeah, yeah! Go, La Toya, *your zipper's wide open!* Yeah, go!" He didn't miss a beat or change inflection, which made it even funnier. I stopped in mid-tap, glanced down, and quickly tapped off the stage, leaving poor Michael up there alone, not knowing what was going on.

Randy and Janet parodied famous duos like Nel-son Eddy and Jeanette MacDonald, Sonny and Cher, and Mickey and Sylvia. At home the two of them argued about anything and everything, and it was no different on the road. They squabbled before shows, after shows, and even between songs, turning their backs on the audience and fussing and tugging at each other's costumes. The crowd usually assumed this was part of the act and laughed all the more loudly.

Mother, our biggest fan, never missed a single show, sitting among the audience and critiquing us. She's still that way, accompanying Michael or my brothers on tour. Afterward, we'd run up to her and ask, "How was the show, Mother?"

"Well," she'd say, "this song started a little too slow. Mike, maybe next time you shouldn't do that this way. Tito, your guitar solo was great, but try to keep a more relaxed facial expression." And so on. Oddly, she never complimented any of us. One time Michael and I observed a mother backstage with her young performer son, urging him to do whatever it was that he did, then asking of everyone, "Isn't he great? Isn't he wonderful?"

My brother and I nodded and smiled. "Mother would never say that about us," I remarked.

"I know. But lots of parents do." We didn't understand then that it was our father's and mother's attitudes that were unusual, not the other way around. Mother once explained her philosophy by saying, "You children always knew you were talented. There was no need for me to tell you." I don't think she and Joseph will ever understand that all the applause in the world doesn't add up to a parent's "I love you" or "I'm so proud of you." Today my siblings and I go out of our way to praise our children, nieces, and nephews.

While we were in Las Vegas, Randy developed a facial tic, and Mother wanted him to see a doctor. Everyone we spoke to recommended one of Elvis Presley's personal physicians. We weren't aware of their reputations for overprescribing drugs. Security chief Bill Bray, however, knew all too well. When the doctor came to see Randy, Bill told him firmly, "Listen, I don't want you giving this kid things he doesn't need."

We had no idea what he was referring to, because not one of the Jacksons had ever tried drugs. I think our having seen so many great artists destroyed by substance abuse had as much to do with our personal abstinence as did our strict upbringing. Certainly seeing its effect on Elvis made a strong impression.

One night all of us went to see his show at the Sahara in Lake Tahoe and could tell right away something was wrong with him. Elvis moved heavily and awkwardly, sometimes slurring his words. After the final encore we went backstage, and what we witnessed was incredibly sad: the great singer pacing back and forth manically, like he had too much energy pulsating through his body. As soon as he saw us, though, he stopped, and his face lit up.

"You guys are incredible," he said kindly. "You started so young, it's really somethin'." Elvis spoke knowledgeably about the guys' records, obviously having listened to them. At one point he remarked,

"You know, all this rock and roll, it started with the blacks." Having heard rumors that Elvis was racist, my siblings and I were pleased to discover otherwise.

But when we all shook his hand good-bye and left the backstage area, we looked at one another. "My God, he's a legend, and everybody loves him, but look at how drugged he is," Jermaine observed. Two-plus years later, Elvis was dead. We were all saddened, naturally, but not shocked. Unfortunately, backstage scenes like this replayed themselves countless times over the years with too many other performers, among them the great Marvin Gaye. It was hard for us to understand why anyone would waste their talent with drugs. For the Jackson kids, no lesson in prevention could have been more effective.

Our family act was completed when my oldest sibling, Rebbie, joined. Slim and pretty, she was talented too, having won a dance contest when she was just four. For years Rebbie claimed to have no desire to enter the "family business." Her abrupt change of heart surprised Michael and me, and provided us with some chuckles as well, because when I became a singing Jackson, my devout sister had taken me to task. "How can you do this?" she had asked, a bit self-righteously. "You know you're not supposed to perform; the Jehovah's Witness teachings forbid it." But since joining us, Rebbie has stayed in show business.

During a run in Las Vegas, our security staff informed us they'd received an anonymous threat on Michael's life. We'd received so many before, but this one was chillingly different. The would-be assassin specified the night he planned to strike, and security took this very seriously. After weighing the risks, it was decided the show would go on. Or, I should say, it was decided for us. Performers are contractually bound to perform. Promoters and hotel owners don't want to hear about entertainers' problems, not even if they concern possible assassinations. All we could do was hire the best security and pray. Though the place crawled with security, everyone was gravely concerned about Michael's safety.

That night while my brother was singing, Rebbie suddenly declared to me in the dressing room, "I am not going on that stage. Do you realize I can get shot?"

I rarely get angry at my brothers and sisters, but this made me furious. "Rebbie, how can you be so selfish? Michael's going to be out there two hours straight and could be killed any minute. You'll be out there for four minutes, tops. And *you're* worried? Come on."

"But what if they decide to get him while I'm right next to him?" she retorted in panic. I thought to myself, *Maybe Rebbie isn't as ready for show business as she thinks.* These terrifying threats had become a way of life for the rest of us.

During our last Vegas engagement of 1974, that November, Jackie married Enid Spann. What we didn't know at the time was that he wasn't the third Jackson son to wed, but the fourth. Marlon, always one of the more independent brothers, already had secretly married his sweetheart, Carol Ann Parker.

Jackie had been dating comedian Redd Foxx's daughter Debra for some time and seemed to be pretty serious about her. But while they were going out, Jackie met Enid, and they fell in love. Her family background was radically different from ours or Debra's: Enid was an adopted child of mixed parentage, which everyone believed had left some emotional scars. She was sweet but highly emotional. My brother felt torn between the two women.

"I love Debra," he said, "but she comes from a good family and has everything she wants. What can I do for her? Enid, she needs a lot of attention and love, and I know that I can help her." As he would learn, this was not the best reason to marry, but he truly did love her, and Mother gave her consent.

As busy as my brothers were, performing both as the Jackson 5 and with the family act, they were growing increasingly restless. Motown still wouldn't let them release their own material as singles. Besides feeling creatively stifled, they had financial concerns, for in the music business the lion's share of record-sales income derives from publishing, or owning the rights to a composition. Thus the writer of a hit song can earn many times more money than its performer. The rare times the guys did get to record one of their songs, Berry Gordy insisted it be published by his company, Jobete.

Michael appealed to Berry, who regarded him as something of a son, for more creative freedom and the rights to their own publishing, but Berry wouldn't be swayed. You'll probably be surprised to know that even with fourteen Top 20 hits, my brothers had not earned as much money over the years as they might have. For a group of their stature, the Jackson 5's royalty rate was substandard, though fortunately Joseph and partner Richard Arons invested wisely. Since the group was unknown at the time of its signing to Motown, the pact was fair then. But the company rarely renegotiated contracts, no matter how much money an act generated.

When 1975's *Moving Violation* failed to produce one hit single or rekindle the group's popularity, my father announced at a family meeting, ''That's it, we're leaving Motown! Berry's taking everything. You boys are all talented, and he won't let you write your own songs; he won't let you keep your own publishing. You can't do this, and you can't do that. I'm sick of it. I'm going to take you to a company that will let you do whatever you want.''

After a brief honeymoon, Joseph's rapport with Motown had deteriorated. Unlike those managers the label itself handpicked and assigned its artists (an interesting conflict of interest), my father never hesitated to question Motown's creative and marketing strategies, demanding copies of important documents, financial breakdowns, and so on, and in general acting as a thorn in its side to protect his and his sons' interests. Motown did not take kindly to this. However, executives there knew they had no choice but to deal with him, since as far as outsiders could see, the brothers were completely devoted to Joseph.

Many Motown acts, my brothers' included, have complained of how the company undermined internal unity by pushing individuals out front, as it did with Diana Ross and the Supremes, and Smokey Robinson and the Miracles. This was a way to keep performers bickering among themselves and not against the label. In awarding Michael, Jermaine, and Jackie solo careers, the company was creating a potentially ticklish situation, as intragroup competition can rip acts—and families—apart. Motown didn't care: it made money no matter which Jackson's name was on the label.

All the brothers agreed with their father—except for Jermaine, who didn't think much of Joseph's managerial skills in the first place and was now a member of Berry Gordy's family, too. Everyone respected Jermaine's conflicting loyalties, but it disturbed us that he couldn't seem to see anything but what Motown had done for the Jackson 5 in the past. As Michael asked him, "What's happening *now,* Jermaine? And what's going to happen in the future?" If the guys didn't regain their chart-topping form soon, they could well wind up stranded in Las Vegas or on the oldies circuit for the rest of their career.

They all felt they were too young to stop growing artistically.

Despite Jermaine's dissent, Joseph started label shopping, and once the Motown contract expired in March 1975 he inked a deal with Epic Records, a division of CBS. The lucrative new deal included provisions for full creative control and publishing rights. Many of my father's managerial moves would be subject to second-guessing, but of all the things he did for the guys, this was by far the most savvy. I sincerely believe that had the Jackson 5 stuck with Motown, their and Michael's stories would have turned out drastically different.

The Epic deal was announced that summer at a press conference at Manhattan's Rainbow Grill. Most of the family was present, with the glaring exception of Jermaine. When a reporter asked Joseph about his son's conspicuous absence, my father replied that he was confident Jermaine would continue with the group. Jermaine has always been Joseph's favorite child; I doubt that in his heart he could have possibly believed otherwise.

One night backstage Jermaine announced, "I'm sticking with Motown. We started there, and I'm staying there." Everyone was shocked. But we let him know we understood he had to consider the feelings of two families now, not just ours. Nonetheless, Jermaine remained adamant and defensive, listing his reasons for staying. "Berry groomed us. He introduced us to the world. You guys are wrong for leaving him, because if it wasn't for Berry, we wouldn't be known today.''

"That's all fine, Jermaine," Joseph said evenly, "but do you want to not have a penny in your pocket for the rest of your life?"

Jermaine turned to Jackie, Tito, Marlon, Michael, and Randy. "How can you guys do this to Berry? It's so wrong."

"We have to have the freedom to do what we want," Michael spoke up. "At Motown we were like robots, we were being controlled. We want to express ourselves and our music. We're beyond listening to Berry and Suzanne dePasse and doing every little thing they say whether we like it or not."

Jermaine appeared unmoved. After an uncomfortable silence, Tito said softly, "Jermaine, we're *brothers.*"

"Yeah, let's stick together," Jackie pleaded.

"Well, then you guys come my way," Jermaine replied stubbornly, "because I'm not leaving Berry."

It was an emotional evening, especially when Jermaine walked out before the second show. We finished the engagement without him. No one took his quitting harder than Michael, who depended on looking to his left and seeing Jermaine singing and playing his bass. Michael felt it was up to him alone to compensate for his missing brother.

Beginning that night, he seemed to reach within himself and draw out talents even he didn't know he had. Michael danced harder, sang harder, did everything with a sharper edge. Mother grew concerned that he now shouted the lyrics in a thinner, higher-pitched, almost strained voice. "Mike," she warned, "you're singing too hard."

"Well, Jermaine's gone," was his reply, "and we have to keep it rolling. We have to be complete."

Though Randy did a fine job stepping into Jermaine's shoes, Michael never stopped trying to fill the void left by his older brother's defection. It was fantastic to watch, but sad, too. Oddly enough, outside of the group's hard-core fans, few people really noticed: they were still the Jackson 5; count 'em.

Motown's conduct following the guys' signing to Epic Records was, in a word, deplorable. The label went to court to bar them from using the Jackson 5 name, which my brothers had coined years before going to Motown. Unfortunately, like so many acts, they'd signed away their rights to the name as a condition of their contract. Berry Gordy even claimed that *he'd* dreamed up the name. The whole thing was absurd. I thought, *What do you mean my brothers can't call themselves the Jackson 5? They ARE the Jackson 5!*

The label's motive? Vindictiveness, to punish them for leaving. This suspicion was confirmed when many disc jockeys told us privately they were being pressured not to play Jackson 5 records anymore. Motown even went so far as to claim it was going to assemble another quintet and name it the Jackson 5, which legally it could have done. One company executive actually remarked that there were plenty of black kids surnamed Jackson from which to choose.

Joseph, though angry, was pragmatic. "The best thing we can do," he said, "is get the legal rights to the name *the Jacksons* and forget it."

Jermaine wasn't exactly an innocent bystander in all of this. When the Jacksons wanted to record a song written with Jermaine prior to his leaving and contacted him for his permission, he claimed he would sue if they released it. We all thought he was kidding—until a letter from Jermaine's attorneys arrived. The brothers suspected that he was being overly influenced by his wife and father-in-law.

Yet no one held it against him personally. One thing about the Jacksons is that we've usually been able to separate our professional and private lives. Jermaine's quitting certainly had no effect on his status as Joseph's favorite. "That's Jermaine," he continued to say proudly, "that's my boy."

Personally, I believe Jermaine felt a twinge of guilt over leaving and the subsequent legal skirmishes. (The various lawsuits and countersuits between the Jacksons and Motown continued until finally settled out of court in 1980.) Though he'll never admit it, I could see it in his face. Years later, when Jermaine's career didn't blossom as Berry had promised, I think he realized he'd made a dreadful mistake.

Nearly a year and a half would pass between the last Motown single, "Forever Came Today," a remake of the Supremes' 1968 hit, and the Jacksons'

Epic debut, "Enjoy Yourself." For the first time since they were little, my brothers were able to take a break from work and from one another. Those who were married spent time with their families, while the others caught up on the kinds of everyday pleasures most people take for granted.

Michael went to Disneyland.

4

ON OUR OWN TOGETHER

Perhaps because Michael lost his childhood to his career, he's always loved fantasy and make-believe, counting among his favorite films *E.T.*, *The Wizard of Oz*, and Walt Disney's *Peter Pan*. So he jumped at the chance to play the Scarecrow in the all-black remake of the second film, based on the recent hit Broadway play. Ironically, Motown had purchased the movie rights.

Diana Ross was already cast in the lead as Dorothy, while my brother beat out several actors, including Jimmie Walker from the TV series *Good Times*, for the part of the insecure, philosophical Scarecrow. He was absolutely thrilled. Michael and I had seen the play several times and adored it and its score. The song "Home," a poignant paean to family and, of course, home, held special meaning for us.

In summer 1977 he and I flew to New York City, where shooting was taking place. Mother came along to help us get settled in our Sutton Place apartment before returning to Encino. We were both old enough to vote, yet this was our first time living away from home! It was a little frightening, especially because of the many horrible things you hear about New York—the crime, the grime, the unfriendly people— but a great adventure.

When not accompanying Michael to the set I hung around with our friend Stephanie Mills, the Broadway production's Dorothy. She was understandably miffed that Diana Ross was playing the role she'd created. Other times I went to the movies with Diana's younger brother, Chico. I'd been to only a handful of movie theaters in my life, and once, in Indiana, to a drive-in with my family. These outings were so rare, I even remember the film we saw at the drive-in: *Goldfinger,* starring Sean Connery as James Bond.

Chico apparently developed a crush on me, leading Diana to speculate about us becoming a couple. I really liked him but thought of him more as a brother. Back in our apartment after a day's filming, Michael would tease, "Guess what Diana said today: 'La Toya is so right for Chico. I wish those two would get together, because he's a little wild. He needs somebody like her.' " Michael, a brilliant mimic, imitated Diana's voice and manner, which was always hilarious to watch.

Mother visited us for a few days every now and then. Once when she was in town we watched them shoot the scene where the Scarecrow is lashed to a table in the wicked witch Evillene's sweat factory, and a buzzsaw is poised to slice him in half. The second the circular metal blade started whirring, Mother screamed, "Get my son off that table! You're not going to do this to my son!"

"Cut!"

Michael walked over and tried comforting her. "Mother," he said, laughing, "it's just a movie. It's perfectly safe."

But she was adamant. "Mike, that thing could slip; there could be an accident. Please don't do it."

"Mother, the blade goes through a dummy, not me."

"I don't care, Mike. Anything can happen."

The scene was later finished without Mother present. No matter what anyone said, her fears weren't assuaged a bit. When my brother was seriously burned while filming a TV commercial six years later, her suspicions that special effects could go awry were confirmed.

Michael and I became friends with other people working on the film: Dick Gregory, Nipsey Russell, Quincy Jones. I think they and everyone else saw we were babes in the woods, so to speak, and took an avuncular interest in us. Dick taught us all about metaphysics, mental telepathy, and nutrition, starting us on a daily vitamin regimen. Each morning Michael gulped down his fifty pills in one swallow, then stood around laughing at me as I spent an hour taking mine one or two at a time.

Michael and I, surrounded by our security people and servants brought from home with us, weren't completely on our own. But we did go out more than we ever did in Los Angeles. The Studio 54 disco was then *the* hippest night spot in New York, and we maneuvered our way through the dancing throng there several times, meeting regulars like Halston, Andy Warhol, Bob Mackie, Truman Capote, Bianca Jagger, and Liza Minnelli.

It was all very eye-opening. Despite our family's many years in entertainment, Michael and I were both ridiculously naive about drugs. Returning home after one late night out with Liza, one of the nicest, most genuine people I know, Michael remarked to me, "These New Yorkers are so amazing; they never seem to get tired."

"Yeah, they don't, do they?"

"Can you believe them, eating breakfast at five o'clock in the morning?" We, who led pretty unorthodox lives ourselves, found that really strange. "And they're always laughing and so cheerful!"

"I guess it's just the New York life-style, Mike."

Little did we know. The first few times we went to Studio 54, co-owner Steve Rubell escorted us into the private back room reserved for VIPs. Everywhere you looked, dancers paused to sniff from tiny colored vials that hung from chains around their necks. I just assumed these were the latest fashion accessories; it never occurred to me they contained cocaine.

"Want some?" someone inevitably whispered in my ear.

"No, thank you."

"How about you?"

"No, no thanks," Michael answered.

It's hard to believe, but we didn't even know what cocaine was, what it looked like, or how you used it. But we both sensed something was wrong, and it made us uncomfortable. The laughter seemed artificial, the conversation forced. I've since learned that people who use drugs or alcohol like being around other users. It's really no different than the peer pressure young kids deal with.

Because at home we could rarely have a private conversation—fearful that our father might be eavesdropping or that security guards were within earshot—Michael and I developed a degree of mental telepathy with each other. Between us, a single glance was worth a thousand words, and we always knew what the other was thinking.

While in New York we had a very strange experience. I enjoyed playing practical jokes on Michael, just as he did on me. One evening I attended some function with Dick Gregory, and Michael stayed home to relax watching television. He became absorbed in a *Twilight Zone* episode about a man who loses his identity. Everyone he thinks he knows treats him like a total stranger, until he begins questioning whether he exists at all. For some reason this story made an impression on Michael, blessed with an active imagination. At the same moment I was inserting the key into the door of our apartment, he was sitting in front of the TV asking himself, *Who am I? Am I really real?*

Why I did this, I don't know, but on the spur of

the moment I pretended I didn't recognize Michael, staring at him blank-faced and asking, "Who are you? And what are you doing in my house?"

Michael jumped on the sofa, aghast. "What do you mean? I'm Mike!"

"But who are you?"

"I'm Mike!"

"But who are you?" I asked him over and over again.

"Don't do this to me, La Toya!" he pleaded.

I burst out laughing. "I'm just kidding, you creep," I said, wondering why he looked so agitated.

"No, you don't understand." He gulped for air. "I saw this *Twilight Zone* episode where a guy loses his identity. And I said to myself, 'If La Toya comes in here and asks me who I am, I am going to die.' You almost gave me a heart attack."

In October 1978 all the Jacksons attended the Los Angeles premiere of *The Wiz*. It was so exciting to see the finished movie, and everyone thought Michael made a fantastic Scarecrow. But *The Wiz* elicited only lukewarm reviews and proved a box-office fiasco. This upset Michael, because he knew the film industry viewed it as a litmus test to determine whether big-budget black pictures were worthwhile. Its poor reception disappointed him, but, typical of my brother, he shrugged and said, "That's okay. I'll be in another film one day, and it will be better."

By then Michael was immersed in his first solo

album in four years, *Off the Wall.* At the same time, he, Randy, Marlon, Tito, and Jackie were readying the Jacksons' first totally self-composed, self-produced LP. This was the creative freedom for which Joseph had fought, and as *Destiny's* mammoth success confirmed, they were right to have left Motown. The guys already had a number of hit singles from their first two Epic LPs ("Enjoy Yourself," "Show You the Way to Go," and "Goin' Places"), but the Top 10 "Shake Your Body (Down to the Ground)" helped make *Destiny* their highest-charting album since 1972 and fueled a mini-revival of Jacksonmania a full decade and ninety million records after the first wave.

With his new partners Ron Weisner and Freddy DeMann, Joseph still managed the Jacksons, and on his own oversaw Janet and me. (Hazel managed Jermaine.) Even the most insignificant career decision was subject to family discussion. While mapping out *Off the Wall,* Michael told us he wanted to work with Quincy Jones. This would prove to be the pairing of the decade, but back then it seemed a mismatch, as Quincy was known mainly for jazz and scoring films.

Almost everyone objected, no one more so than Joseph. Oddly enough, in the 1950s my father had been one of Quincy's biggest fans. Staffers at Michael's label, too, reacted negatively when he told them, "I want Quincy Jones to produce my album." But Michael felt he and Quincy had a special rapport, and he followed his instincts.

People often misread Michael's soft-spoken, shy demeanor as lack of confidence. Hardly. My brother is the most self-assured person I know. Once he decides to do something, it's as if he makes an unbreakable pact with himself. Michael has incredible powers of concentration, and when he puts together a tour, a record, or a video, it consumes him. He focused his energy on *Off the Wall* to the exclusion of almost all else.

Fans know that Quincy nicknamed Michael Smelly, ostensibly because of my brother's talent for writing funky music. "Man, that's *smelly,* Smelly," he'll say after a hot take in the studio. (To translate, that's a compliment.) Anything's possible, but we at home thought Smelly meant something else. Inexplicably, when he was twenty, Michael decided deodorant was unhealthy and daily showering excessive. He wore the same jeans and socks for days, perplexing his brothers, who appealed to me, "La Toya, you're closest to Mike. Talk to him."

"What do you want me to do? He's not going to change. It's just his personality; maybe a stage he's going through."

"But La Toya, you're not in the studio with him," one of the guys said, wrinkling his nose. "It's, um, musky in there."

Randy was more direct. "The whole studio *stinks!*" he exclaimed.

When Mother picked up Michael's shoes one day, she noticed gaping holes in the soles and brought him a new pair. He refused to wear them. I had to plead with him to discard the old shoes and, really tempting fate, to change his socks. Forget about it.

"La Toya, these things are not important," he said, turning suddenly profound. "Why do people care about clothes? Music is what's important to me, how it sounds, that I get it right. And why do we care about having new shoes? What about the man who has no shoes? Or the man who has no feet?"

Hoo boy. "Mike, really. You look awful."

"These are great shoes," he said resolutely, "and I'm going to keep wearing them." Michael is nothing if not true to his word.

My brother has since repeated this behavior for every album since, and, considering the brilliance of his music, I'm sure at least a few of us have considered following suit. Before the Jacksons' 1984 *Victory* tour, though, the others confronted Michael, telling him he couldn't continue venturing out in public looking so unkempt. "Okay," he said quietly, "I'll change. You'll see." The next thing we knew, whenever Michael went out he dressed to the nines in fifty-pound sequined military jackets, pants with creases so sharp you could slice onions on them—the works.

But at home, it was back to wrinkled jeans and old sweaters. Michael's sloppiness extended to his room, for which our family employed a special maid. Sometimes I couldn't refrain from tiptoeing in and organizing some of the papers that were strewn all over the bed and floor, occasionally getting caught in the act.

"Don't touch that!" he'd scream.

"Mike, look at this mess. You can't even walk in here. How can you find your papers?"

"I know where everything is," he assured me. "Leave it."

He doesn't keep just papers and books lying around. Michael saves everything, and I do mean everything. Sweetly sentimental, he keeps family members' photographs and mementos such as all my report cards, and his young nieces' and nephews' first shoes, first outfits, even their first soiled diapers. Among his very personal souvenirs is his own nose cartilage, extracted during surgery.

Once again, when my siblings and I made enough racket about the slovenly state of his room, Michael vowed, "Okay, you guys, tomorrow I'm going to clean my room, and it will stay perfectly clean for a whole year." Sure enough, the next day his room was immaculate and remained that way for 365 days. The day after the "anniversary," however, promise fulfilled, it resembled a war zone once again.

What with Michael, me, Randy, and Janet the only kids left at home, Hayvenhurst seemed comparatively quiet. The latter two enjoyed somewhat happier childhoods than the rest of us. It seems that often in large families, parents slacken the reins with their youngest children. But even with what the rest of us considered looser rules, most outsiders would consider their upbringings very strict. Having not witnessed our father's physical abuse as much as the older siblings, Randy and Janet weren't as fearful, though that's not to say they didn't suffer their share of beatings; they did. We were all still terrified of our father, but not nearly as much as Michael, who'd long outgrown fighting back. By his teens, he finally accepted that Joseph would always win.

One time Mother, Janet, and I were sitting around the kitchen table listening to Michael pour out a tirade against his father.

"How could you marry him?" he asked her from the pantry, his back toward us.

Mother smiled. "Oh, I don't know . . ."

"Well, I can't stand him! What did you like about him," Michael half-kidded, "his green eyes?"

My father came ambling into the kitchen just in time to catch an earful: ". . . ugly old rotten bulldog . . . [grumble grumble] . . . can't stand him [grumble grumble]." I was sure Michael would sense from our frozen silence that Joseph was standing right behind him, but he kept ranting and raving, oblivious. Finally, he found what he wanted and, still muttering insults, emerged from the pantry to find himself face to face with Joseph.

"So-ooooo, I'm an ugly old rotten bulldog, huh?"

Uh-oh, I thought, *what's Michael going to do now?*

Blame me, that's what. "La Toya said it first!" he blurted, pointing my way.

"Michael! I did not!"

"Yes you did! You said it in your room!"

Joseph turned to me. "Yes you did!" he snapped.

Michael wasn't off the hook, though. "So, that's what you think of me?" He must have repeated the rhetorical question five or six times. Surprisingly, my father didn't strike Michael or chase him, and, thankfully, the situation diffused.

As we grew older, Joseph's terror tactics turned more psychological than physical. Hundreds of times I was lying sound asleep in my room only to be startled awake by him pounding on my door and shouting, "Open this door, or I'll break it down!" I scurried out of bed, ran to the door, and flung it open. There stood my father, absolutely wild with rage. Over what, I've lost track; it could be everything or nothing.

An avid gun collector, Joseph kept a cache of loaded weapons under his bed and in closets. Mother objected strongly, especially since he'd once accidentally shot out her brother-in-law's eye during a hunting trip. "Joseph," she used to say, "aren't you tired of those guns? Haven't you had enough?" He ignored her, taking perverse pleasure in aiming at one of us and squeezing the trigger. *Click.* What if he'd forgotten to empty the chamber?

"Joseph," Mother would scold, "suppose something's in it?"

"Kate, I checked; nothing's in it," he'd reply, then laugh out loud.

Another of my father's games was to burst in our rooms without knocking, making it impossible for us to relax. He also lurked around the hallways, standing mute outside our doors eavesdropping, and listened in on phone conversations too. "I am the Jo Jo," he liked to proclaim. "I am the hawk, and I've got eyes in the back of my head." Every time "the Jo Jo" came in my bedroom, my stomach knotted up, and I eventually developed ulcers from the incessant pressure.

I coped as best I could by refusing to interact with my father. Whenever he screamed at me, I barely acknowledged him, answering with only a distant yes or no. This drove him crazy. Michael used to watch our confrontations awestruck, marveling later, "La Toya, Joseph was right up in your face, and you just stared off into space like he wasn't there!" Seeing its effectiveness, my brother learned to perfect the same studied detachment.

"Talk to me! Don't you hear me?" Joseph would shout.

"Yes," I'd reply in a calm, affectless monotone. When addressing my father, you had to be careful. He was sensitive to every little nuance. You had to be polite, but if you were "too" polite, Joseph took it as sarcasm or a challenge.

Did this behavior change anything? Not really, but it gave us a wisp of control—or, should I say, the *illusion* of exerting control—over our lives. For better or worse, my brother and I came to suppress our emotions, including the positive ones. Even today, I don't let myself get overly excited or depressed about anything.

Being a public family generated a constant tension between the real-life Jacksons and the facade we presented to the world. I can't tell you how many times Michael and I have smiled courteously when someone remarked, "Boy, your father did such a great job of raising you. I really admire him. You must be so proud to have a father like that!" They thought we were the ideal family. "If only they knew," we whispered to each other afterward.

Joseph can be charming and gregarious when he wants, and in front of company he staged a real show, which repulsed me and my siblings. Not only was it so hypocritical of him, but we couldn't figure out how not to play along. From the head of the great dining room table—where he never joined us unless we had guests—my father portrayed the affectionate patriarch, asking me playfully, "So, Toy-Toy, how ya doin'?"

Toy-Toy? "All right," I mumbled, barely glancing up from my plate.

"Mikus! What's happenin'? How ya doin', Mikus?"

Michael murmured, "Okay," shot me a look of disgust, then averted his eyes.

The minute we were excused from the table, Janet, Michael, and I gathered in one of our bedrooms.

"Do you *believe* him?" Michael asked.

"He makes me so sick," Janet hissed.

"I know," I said. "But he's our father."

As in most large families, certain siblings grew closer to others for periods of time. Strangely, it seemed that whichever brother I was tightest with got married: Tito, Jermaine, Marlon, and Jackie. Now Michael and I were best buddies.

My brother is talented both with a camera and a pencil, and repeatedly had me model for his photos and sketches. He also enlisted me as his assistant for his magic act. Michael loves watching magicians and learned how to perform many tricks and illusions. At home we put on magic shows for the family. We had everything we needed, but we never got around to practicing Michael's ultimate tricks: levitating me and sawing me in half. Thank goodness.

The two of us shared many mutual interests and traits, but above all else an insatiable curiosity about the world of which we saw so little. We made a game of learning several new words each day and then using them as often as possible, which drove everyone else crazy. Fascinated by history, the two of us ferreted out films about significant global events, particularly anything having to do with black history, and screened them at home in the thirty-five-seat theater Michael built.

Both of us were voracious readers. Michael often asked me, "La Toya, if this house burned down, what would you grab first?" Before I could answer, he always teased, "Your diamonds and furs, right? Well, I'd take my books before anything else, because you can never replace knowledge."

Michael's bedroom walls were filled with hundreds of books on different subjects, but especially philosophy and biographies. He's probably read about every great artist, businessman, and inventor that ever was, posing questions afterward. He'll finish a biography of, say, Henry Ford, then ponder, "Why did he make *that* car? What made him think of it?" Most of all, my brother is intrigued by success stories and why it is that success leads some to self-destruct.

People often refer to Michael as childlike. I disagree. He is, however, unusually in touch with the child inside him, full of wonderment and a positive outlook on life. Just gazing at a stately tree could inspire a conversation between us about how that tree is visible proof of God's existence, the way it grows and changes, provides food and shelter, and so on.

What I'm trying to say is that Michael's perspective is unusually pure, which leads others to misinterpret some of the things he does. For example, another of my brother's favorite subjects is human anatomy. Do you remember from biology class those plastic models of the torso with the snapable organs? Well, Michael kept one in his room, studying it all the time. "We have vocal cords, but why can we talk and a dog can't?" he'd wonder aloud. "What makes humans different? Or a monkey. La Toya, do you think there's some way a monkey could be taught to talk?"

"I don't know. Anything's possible."

"Well, I'm going to find out." He asked a doctor he knew to order him a full medical library. "But Michael," the man replied, a little taken aback, "these are professional books, meant only for physicians."

"Then order yourself another set at my expense, and let me have these."

Those medical books, however, paled next to what another doctor gave my brother.

I was in a hurry to leave the house one afternoon, when Michael waved at me. *"Pssst!* La Toya, come here! I've got something to show you!"

I told him I couldn't, that I was running late for an appointment, but he persisted.

"Please, come to my room. I've got to show you this. You'll really appreciate it when you see it." He led me into his bathroom and closed the door behind us. There on a table in a giant glass jar was a brain! He picked up the jar, then turned it around so that I could get a better look.

"Ta-da!"

"Oh my God, Mike, where did you get that?"

"Shhhhhh!" He peeked out the door to make sure no one overheard us.

I must admit to being curious—having never seen a brain before—and looked at the pickled gray mass floating in formaldehyde. It seemed . . . quite large.

"Is it a human brain?"

Michael wouldn't say, but somehow I knew it was. "Where did you get it?"

"Oh, a doctor gave it to me," he answered nonchalantly.

I'm willing to bet that right now many of you are cupping a hand to your mouth, thinking, *Gross!* But to Michael, the brain and the body are simply miraculous creations and not revolting at all. Following his recovery from a badly burned scalp in 1984, he grew fascinated with how the body heals itself and received permission from some doctors to don surgical gown and mask and observe several operations.

In the course of reading his medical books, Michael developed a fascination with freaks of nature. He devoured information about every conceivable condition and could talk for hours about the lives of Siamese twins, the famed Alligator Man, and other sideshow celebrities. Because of his interest in these poor creatures, the press has gleefully depicted Michael as some sort of morbid creep. But as with so many facets of my brother's personality, all I can say is, if you knew him like I do, you'd see that it's not macabre at all.

An extremely sensitive soul, like Mother, Michael becomes emotional over any form of human suffering. The sight of a starving African child on TV moves him to tears. He was overcome with sympathy for freaks such as the Elephant Man, crying no matter how many times he sees David Lynch's film about John Merrick.

"Imagine what life was like for them," he'd say sadly. "How hard it must have been to be stared at wherever they went, taunted, and to be considered so different from normal people, even though they probably had the same feelings . . ." Why Michael empathized with them is pretty obvious, considering how celebrityhood turns you into a bit of a freak (in other people's eyes, that is). I get angry when Michael's curiosity in this field is made fun of. It's not out of mockery that he takes an interest, but caring. The public really doesn't know—and maybe this is partially Michael's own fault, for being so reclusive—what a wonderful, generous human being he is.

You really see these qualities observing him with animals, which all the Jacksons, including our father, absolutely love. Besides your usual domestic pets, like dogs, cats, mice, and hamsters, at one time or another someone in the family has owned lion cubs, swans, ducks, chimpanzees, llamas, and snakes. The first time I came face to face with a thirty-foot python, I was apprehensive, but I've since come to enjoy snakes as pets. They're magnificent creatures, not at all slimy as people assume, and are fascinating to observe.

Now, snakes are intellectually limited, they don't come when you call, and they can't really be trained. But once you've been around one and get to know his ways, you can tell whether he likes you. If he doesn't, keep your distance. The types of snakes we owned could easily squeeze the breath out of you, or open their jaws wide and swallow your head. Anytime a snake coiled itself too tightly around me, I knew to stay calm, for these reptiles will instinctively squeeze harder if they sense you resisting.

Llamas, too, make great pets, gentle and meek. The two we had, Lola (who died) and Louis, used to kiss us all the time. At first, about the only pet my siblings and I weren't allowed to keep were chimpanzees. Mother believed they were dirty and "too human," whatever that means. Michael, who adored them, lobbied to change her mind, even borrowing a couple every now and then, and pointing out to her how cute they were. After a few years of this, she relented, and we got Bubbles.

This is going to sound odd, but we knew Bubbles's parents; they'd been to the house as part of the campaign to sway Mother. Everyone anxiously awaited Bubbles's birth, and when he was old enough, we adopted him. Though he belonged to all of us, Michael was his master.

I can't imagine anyone spending some time with Bubbles and not coming away head over heels in love. This chimp is such a character, you can't help but think of him as a small child. My brother, who never shopped for himself, used to buy Bubbles clothes, returning home from kids' stores (I've never heard of a Chimps 'R' Us chain, have you?) with piles of outfits that were so nice, Rebbie asked if she could have Bubbles's hand-me-downs.

Every night, at Michael's command, Bubbles slipped into his little pajamas, kneeled at his bedside, and pretended to say his prayers, then crawled under the covers. In the morning, he hated to get up. Many times Michael woke him, saying softly, "Bubbles, it's time to get up . . ." But the sleepy chimp yawned, stretched, turned away, and pulled the covers up over his head. My brother snatched them away; Bubbles grabbed them right back, and before you knew it, there was a tug-of-war underway.

When he finally did get up, Bubbles went into the bathroom to brush his teeth (honest!) and comb his fur: on his head and then on his arms. After that he laced up his sneakers and joined us at the breakfast table. Michael took him everywhere, including on airplanes, where Bubbles sat beside him—in the first-class section, of course.

Like any "child," Bubbles could be a discipline problem, getting into all kinds of mischief. He often snuck into my bedroom, helping himself to a can of soda, then tossing the empty across the room. If he felt frisky, he slapped people, and several times smacked me so hard that he left bright red paw prints on my face. Another time we looked up to see Bubbles descending the stairs with Jermaine's infant son wrapped in his arms. It was such a cute, if heart-stopping, sight. After Bubbles tore up a couple of rooms and swung from one too many chandeliers, we decided he needed professional discipline training.

So we hired an animal trainer, who on his first visit to Hayvenhurst was shocked by how humanized our pet was. "This is ridiculous!" he observed, realizing he faced the challenge of his career. "This chimpanzee eats Häagen-Dazs ice cream from a dish, drinks Evian water out of the bottle, and eats health food, when he should be eating only monkey chow." Monkey chow? We'd never heard of it. Somehow the trainer worked a miracle, and Bubbles completed training as sweet as before, but well behaved. Any time family members dropped by Hayvenhurst, the first words out of their mouths were always, "Where's Bubbles?"

While working on *Off the Wall,* Michael suffered a breathlessness attack. "Take me to the doctor," he gasped. "I'm gonna die!"

At first Mother thought he was merely hyperventilating, but when my brother kept insisting we get medical help, we rushed him to the hospital. Although everything checked out normally, the doctors there discovered Michael has an extraordinarily small chest cavity that sometimes presses in on his lungs. They sent him home with some medication, which Mother had to order him to take.

My brother had never ingested any pill before that wasn't a vitamin. He panicked, complaining of not being able to breathe again, so we had to drive him right back to the hospital. It turned out to be nothing more than a stress reaction to the sedative's relaxing effect. Remember, not only had Michael never taken a drug in his life, he'd never tasted alcohol, or caffeine, for that matter. He's continued to have these stress-induced breathing attacks sporadically ever since, and has been hospitalized many times—always under the strictest secrecy, until one episode in spring 1990.

Off the Wall came out in late summer 1979, producing two Number Ten hits, the title track and

"She's Out of My Life," and the Number Ones "Don't Stop 'til You Get Enough" and "Rock with You." Released in the midst of a severe industry-wide record-sales drought, it rained down into the hands of seven million consumers. My brother was so proud. The music business buzzed with predictions that he was a sure bet to sweep the 1980 Grammy Awards.

Michael, Mother, Janet, and I watched the ceremony on television that February night. To our dismay, he won only one of two awards he'd been nominated for: Best R&B Vocal Performance, Male. I'll never forget the sight of him sitting in a chair, staring forlornly at the screen, tears streaming down his cheeks after the winner of the other category was announced.

"How can they do this?" my brother cried. "This is so wrong!"

We felt so badly for him. Very competitive when it comes to his craft, Michael was crushed. He believed he'd been passed over for reasons other than artistry. The music industry is as political as any other, with Grammys sometimes bestowed in recognition of power rather than talent. Michael suspected some in the business felt that at twenty-one he was too young to receive such a prestigious honor. And, as much as it hurt to admit it, there was the issue of color. The creative fields may have been less racist than most professions, but they weren't completely color-blind yet.

Michael cried for several minutes, then snapped

up in his chair, wiped his eyes, and vowed, "This will never happen to me again. I'm going to make the biggest-selling album in history. And I'm going to win every award. You watch."

Mother, Janet, and I just nodded, never doubting him for a second.

5

STARTIN'
SOMETHING

"La Toya, *come on*. Let's go out for a drive."

"I can't, Mike. And you shouldn't go either. There's a family meeting today."

"I know, La Toya, but please don't go."

"No, Mike, if there's a family meeting, we should all be there," I insisted.

"Okay, but I don't think you're going to like it," he warned, shaking his head. "One of the wives is calling it, and it's about you."

"Not again," I groaned.

These meetings are a Jackson tradition. Anyone, including in-laws, could convene a family meeting to discuss issues that ranged from what to buy Mother for Mother's Day, to whether Randy went out too much, to whether the nephews should visit one another more often. Of the brothers, Jermaine called the most meetings by far. Since marrying Hazel Gordy, a sweet but headstrong woman, he'd become increasingly domineering, making everyone's business his own. Even if he wasn't the instigator,

In the beginning. The Jackson 5's first photograph after signing with Motown Records in 1969. CLOCKWISE, FROM LEFT: *Tito, Jermaine, Jackie, Michael, and Marlon.* (PICTORIAL PRESS/ STARFILE)

ABOVE: *Still very much children, in California. Left to right: Michael, Randy, Marlon, and Janet.* (GEORGE RODRIQUEZ/ GLOBE PHOTOS) BELOW: *Joseph and his youngest son, Randy, soon after moving to California.* (ROLAND CHARLES)

LEFT: *A love of animals was one of the very few things we children shared with Joseph. Here he is with our pet German shepherd Heavy.* (ROLAND CHARLES) BELOW: *Even at this tender age, Michael knew what he wanted from life. This is an outtake from a* Rolling Stone *cover shoot.* (HENRY DILTZ)

The Jackson 5 with one of dozens of gold records to come. Left to right: Jermaine, Tito, Marlon, Mother, Michael, Joseph, and Jackie. (BOB MOORE/GLOBE PHOTOS)

ABOVE: *All of my earliest memories are here, in our first house, on Jackson Street in Gary, Indiana. Here, I was beaten and abused at the age of six. Here is where I shuddered as my brothers were beaten during each rehearsal. Here is where I watched my siblings being tortured by the man we all called Joseph.* (POST-TRIBUNE) BELOW: *The dream home that became our sanctuary and our prison: Hayvenhurst, in Encino, California* (DAVID NUSSBAUM/GLOBE PHOTOS)

The Jackson 5 during the Motown days, in the classic formation. Left to right: Tito, Marlon, Jackie, Michael, and Jermaine. (NBC/GLOBE PHOTOS)

ABOVE: *The show-business marriage of the 1970s: Hazel Joy Gordy and Jermaine on their wedding day, December 15, 1973. (GLOBE PHOTOS)* BELOW: *Onstage doing the Jackson Family act in the mid-1970s. Left to right: me, Randy, Janet, and Rebbie. (CHRIS WALTER/RETNA LTD.)*

The Jacksons, *our family musical variety program, aired during the summer of 1976 and in early 1977. Here's the whole family, except Jermaine, who had left the group. Left to right: (back) Jackie, Michael, Tito, and Marlon; (front) Janet, Randy, me, and Rebbie.* (PHOTOFEST)

ABOVE: *In front of a camera, we were one big happy family. Left to right: (back) Rebbie, Jackie, Marlon, and Tito; (front) Michael, Janet, Randy, and me.* (NEAL PRESTON) BELOW: *At home in Encino, Mother and Michael were my two best friends in the world. We were very, very close (I thought).* (NEAL PETERS COLLECTION)

ABOVE: *This is one of my favorite pictures. (*AAD SPANJAARD/
RETNA LTD.*) BELOW: On a promotional tour for my second
album,* Heart Don't Lie. (JANET MACOSKA/STARFILE)

ABOVE: *The Jackson 5 and Randy not long before the split with Motown Records. Left to right: (back) Michael, Jackie, and Jermaine; (front) Marlon, Randy, and Tito. (FIN COSTELLO/ RETNA LTD.)* BELOW: *Me, Michael, and Joan Collins on the set of her television series,* Dynasty. *(JACK GORDON, LA TOYA JACKSON)*

ABOVE: *I am congratulating my brother, Michael, on receiving one of his eight record-breaking Grammy awards, 1984.* (AP/WIDE WORLD PHOTOS) BELOW: *At the 1984 Grammy Awards ceremony with (left to right) Brooke Shields, Michael, and actor Emmanuel Lewis. You can see Mother and Joseph sitting behind us.* (SAM EMERSON/SYGMA)

RIGHT: *Appearing in Washington, D.C. on the Fourth of July with the Beach Boys and Julio Iglesias at the Lincoln Memorial.* (*RICHARD SANDLER/ CAMERA PRESS LONDON/GLOBE PHOTOS*) BELOW: *Announcing the* Victory *tour at New York City's Tavern on the Green restaurant, 1984. Left to right: Marlon, Michael, Tito, Randy, Jackie, and Jermaine.* (*JAMES COLBURN/PHOTOREPORTERS*)

ABOVE AND LEFT: *Janet, Mother, and I were always close. It was quite a shock for us when Janet eloped with James De Barge during the Victory tour. The marriage ended less than a year later.* (VINNIE ZUFFANTE/STARFILE), (KEVIN WINTER/DMI) *As copromoter of the* Victory *tour, Mother finally got more involved in the business and gave her first press conference outside the Hayvenhurst gates. Here, she is flanked by Joseph, Don King, and the Reverend Al Sharpton.* (UPI/BETTMAN)

The Victory *tour wasn't the only thing happening that summer of 1984. At a New York City party to celebrate Jermaine's Arista Records debut are* ABOVE: *Arista's Clive Davis with Jermaine and Randy, and* BELOW: *Rebbie, Mother, and Joseph.* (DAVID MCGOUGH/DMI)

ABOVE: *Michael and I at home, relaxing and enjoying a private joke, during a photo shoot in 1984.* (AP/WIDE WORLD PHOTOS) BELOW: *Our pet chimpanzee, Bubbles, at the piano.* (THIERRY CAMPION/SYGMA)

Jermaine ended up taking over the meeting. More and more he reminded me of Joseph.

Most married children gradually grow away from their parents as they become involved in their own families. That never happened to my siblings. As far as Joseph was concerned, the Jackson family—*his* Jackson family—came first. Jermaine used to phone my parents every morning just after sunup, which made my father quite happy. Jackie, Tito, Jermaine, and Marlon all lived within minutes of Hayvenhurst and dropped by or called almost daily, usually to speak to Mother.

A large, close family can be wonderful, but to outsiders I imagine it would be intimidating. I know that for the brothers' wives, Hazel, Enid, Dee Dee, and Carol, blending into the Jackson family took time. They all hailed from families not nearly as tightknit as ours and so had a hard time adapting. In addition to the difficult but routine adjustments all newlyweds experience, the guys and their wives had several other hurdles: their youth, the brothers' fame, the wives' feeling left out.

I'd initially welcomed having sisters-in-law around, thinking we'd become girlfriends, but it was never to be. Instead, I became the target of whatever dissatisfaction they felt toward any and all Jacksons. Unbeknown to me, they were actually jealous of my closeness with my brothers.

At first I refused to see it for what it was, not believing that anyone could be so insecure as to resent her husband's sister. But after a while the evidence was hard to ignore. One time in Lake Tahoe the guys planned a small birthday celebration for me. Their wives objected; why, I can't tell you. So the four schemed to tell Tito I'd made the outrageous, untrue allegation that my nephew Taj wasn't really his child. What they said about me was a vicious, hurtful lie.

Fortunately, Marlon happened to overhear them and told the brothers, who each confronted his wife. The incident upset me so, I became violently ill, and a doctor was summoned to our hotel. Diagnosing my problem as a nervous stomach, he forbade me from performing with the family act that evening.

"But I have to," I said weakly. He gave me some medicine and that night, like most nights, seconds before my onstage introduction, I heard a couple of the wives hiss at me, "You little bitch . . ."

"You're going to do a bad show . . ."

In a rare open moment, Carol once confessed, "La Toya, do you know why the wives hate you?"

I shook my head.

"Do you know what I hear from Marlon every single day? 'La Toya doesn't do it that way; La Toya does it this way. La Toya does it better.' Dee Dee hears the same thing from Tito. And Enid from Jackie. We get so tired of it."

"But that's not my fault," I protested.

"Well, that's why we all get together and talk about you. We're sick of hearing your name." Later I learned that Dee Dee once told Tito, "You didn't marry your sister, you married *me*.'' And she was right.

Remember, my brothers hardly dated before marriage. I was the only girl they knew well while growing up, and they probably couldn't help but subconsciously compare their wives to my mother, my sisters, and me. I think it was all quite innocent on the guys' parts; they truly didn't understand how this would hurt their wives. Understandably, this got on my sisters-in-law's nerves.

I thanked Carol for telling me, but the lies and nastiness persisted. That was why I never looked forward to family meetings, especially this one. Against Michael's warnings and my better judgment, I went anyway, and sure enough, no sooner had it begun than an irate Hazel was pointing at me angrily.

''I've got a bone to pick with you!'' *Here we go again*. ''You're never to see or speak to my kids again,'' she said. ''Ever!''

''I-I don't understand,'' I stammered, shocked. Hazel knew how much I loved her children and that this was the cruelest punishment she could inflict. ''What did I do?''

''You know what you did!'' she said accusingly.

''What?'' I asked, bewildered.

''As if she doesn't know!''

''But Hazel—''

''Well, you know what you said,'' Jermaine chimed in, shaking his head gravely, ''and you're not seeing our kids anymore. That's it!''

With no idea of what they were talking about, I pleaded for them to at least tell me what crime I'd supposedly committed, but to no avail. I ran up to my room. Later Michael knocked on my door. "I told you not to go, La Toya," he said, trying to comfort me. "Look at you, all crying and sad. You're just letting them get to you. You know the wives talk about the way you walk, the way you talk, the way you act. Don't bring yourself down to their level."

"Yes, but it's so upsetting. The brothers believe whatever they say. And I didn't do anything."

"I know you didn't," he said sympathetically. "I know they're lying. But you have to remember, these girls they married don't want to see peace and harmony in our family. They hate that we all get along so well. That's why they make up the lies they do."

One day he stopped me and said, "I want you to hear a song I wrote for you, because I feel so bad about what's been happening with you and the wives." The song was "Wanna Be Startin' Something," which would appear on his *Thriller* album. Reading some music critics' interpretations of its lyrics, I had to laugh. One surmised that the song betrayed Michael's alleged persecution complex and paranoia. In fact, it's not about Michael at all, it's about the friction between me and my sisters-in-law: "Someone's always tryin' to start my baby cryin'/ talkin', squealin', lyin'/Sayin' you just wanna be startin' somethin'."

My brothers are so sweet and accommodating,

their wives swiftly assumed control of their marriages. Whenever the guys visited Hayvenhurst, they compliantly called home to say they'd arrived and later phoned again to say they were leaving. Observing his sons' submissiveness, Joseph growled to Mother, "Kate, it's a real shame. All these boys took after you. None of them took after me. Every last one of 'em, they're all easygoing, lettin' their wives run over 'em."

As might be expected of young marrieds, Jackie, Tito, Jermaine, and Marlon all endured periods of strife at home, subsequently turning to Mother for advice. Her daughters-in-law disparaged her behind her back, but my mother, as is her way, always played the Great Conciliator. No matter what his wife had said or done, she advised each son, "You should go back to her. Be more understanding. Think of the children. Try to make it work." Just as she had bent over backward to make her marriage work, she tried to convince the guys that giving in was always the right thing to do.

My brothers' marital troubles became our troubles, a new crisis arising each week, it seemed. The phone rang at all hours, and Mother would rise, get dressed, and drive to whichever home was aflame with conflict, a firefighter off to extinguish a four-alarm blaze. Joseph, not surprisingly, wanted nothing to do with any of the wives and resented it whenever one of them meddled in family business.

Marlon and Carol separated at one stage, during which she came to Hayvenhurst practically every day, crying to Mother about how much she loved her husband. Now, I say this realizing that as Marlon's sister I'm not entirely objective. During the separation Marlon moved back home, as my parents expect any of their married offspring to do in times of marital turmoil, and Carol went back to Louisiana.

Carol was absurdly suspicious of Marlon, a homebody who likes to be in bed before ten o'clock. In fact, at one time or another each of the wives suspected her husband of cheating. I think it takes very secure, mature women to marry celebrities, especially handsome singing stars like my brothers. Girls are always after them; it comes with the territory.

She admitted to me, "La Toya, I used to get so jealous when you kissed Marlon hello. We'd argue about it afterward."

"But Carol, Marlon's my *brother*."

"I know. I can't help myself; I'm just that way." She went on to tell us, "If there's an *Ebony* or *Jet* magazine in the house, I rip out the centerfold girl so Marlon can't see it. Or if I get a copy of *Vogue*, I always rip out the pages with girls on them."

"But . . . that's the entire magazine."

"I know. I just don't want him to look at other girls."

It was impossible not to feel sorry for Carol and to see that she truly did love my brother. Marlon refused to return home, but my sister-in-law was determined. And strangely confident, as if she had glimpsed the future or knew voodoo. Carol told my mother calmly, "Marlon's going to come back to me, I'm not worried. I even know on what date and at what time . . .'' Mother thought she'd gone slightly cuckoo. But sure enough, on that day, ten minutes before the exact time, Marlon left Hayvenhurst, moved back home, and has been with Carol ever since.

Jackie's marriage, too, was tempestuous from the start and, unfortunately, the first to end in divorce. In 1975, less than a year after he and Enid married, Jackie filed for divorce, but they reconciled, and it was on and off until 1984.

It seemed inevitable that he should fall into someone else's arms. An avid Los Angeles Lakers basketball fan, my brother used to take me with him to the L.A. Forum. At a game I noticed one of the team's cheerleaders staring fixedly at Jackie. Nudging him in the side, I asked, ''Why does that girl keep looking at you like that?''

''She likes me,'' he confided proudly.

''Obviously.'' Afterward Jackie introduced me to her, a pretty, petite brunette with exotic features. ''La Toya, this is Paula Abdul.''

We'd all been invited to an aftergame get-together with some of the Lakers, but I asked my brother to drop me off at home. To my amazement, Paula climbed into the car with us.

''*Jackie,*'' I whispered in his ear, *''what are you doing?* You can't take her in the car! What if Enid sees us? I don't want to be caught in the middle of this.''

''She's just a friend, La Toya.''

"Come on, Jackie, be honest. I saw what was going on before."

The next day Jackie asked me, "She's nice, isn't she?"

"I found her sweet and charming." Which Paula truly was. At the time I still had a pretty sheltered outlook on things of this nature. I've changed my attitudes a lot since, but then I could only wonder what a single woman was doing with a married man who had children.

I understood that Jackie was rightfully unhappy with his home life. But I just could not accept his affair with Paula, which lasted over eight years—not at all the brief fling or friendship it's been reported to be. They were madly in love with each other. In fact, there was serious talk of marriage, but that broke off abruptly when Paula's recording career took off in 1988. They used to meet secretly at Hayvenhurst, making everyone uncomfortable.

Because Paula was around so much, she and I talked a lot and went shopping together. She told me about her problems with Enid. Jackie bestowed extravagant gifts on Paula, including a sleek sports car.

Enid's anger and hurt were probably justified. Paula brazenly called Jackie at home, which I thought was very disrespectful, no matter what she or he thought of Enid. Finally Paula went too far, actually showing up at Jackie's front door. She sure was surprised when Enid opened it and, what's more, greeted her warmly and invited her in.

As Paula later told me, the moment the door

slammed, she realized she'd made a mistake. Enid roughly shoved her into a chair, brandished some rope, and tied her to it! "Enid was screaming, 'I oughta do this to you' and 'I oughta to do that.' But I talked my way out of it by pretending I had no idea that Jackie was married," Paula remembered. Luckily for her, Enid bought her story.

Jackie's kids also knew exactly what was going on. While having dinner, my darling niece asked me, "Do you know Paula?"

"Who's Paula?" I replied, trying to play dumb.

"You know who Paula is!"

"No, I don't. Who's Paula?"

I was shocked!

"Paula's nice," my little nephew said.

"She's not nice, and you know it," the girl snapped. "She's taking Daddy away from Mommy." It was so sad to see innocent children caught up in their parents' bitterness.

Practically all the models of marriage around us were fraught with turmoil. Just looking at my parents' marriage alone was enough to lead both Michael and me to conclude that we would never wed. Who needed the grief?

As I've mentioned, one problem was my brothers' marrying so young. Making it a doubly difficult adjustment, I'm sure, was their never having lived apart from the family before. (Jackie had lived on his own briefly before wedding Enid.) When eighteen-year-old Randy, one of the most strong-willed Jacksons, announced that he wanted to live with a woman ten years his senior, my parents were totally shocked.

"This is against our rules," Mother said, appalled. "You know that you should live at home until you get married."

"Then I'd like to be the first one to break the rules," Randy replied coolly. His girlfriend, Julie Harris, was a pretty background singer with an act that had opened for the Jacksons on tour.

"Randy, you're still in school," Mother continued. Then she added nastily, "This girl's an old lady. Why should you move out to support her?"

"Because I love her. And I want my independence."

Michael and I overheard Mother, Joseph, and Randy as they talked into the next day. Finally Mother surrendered. "Joseph, let him go," we heard her say. "Don't hang on to him. If he wants to go, then let him be. He's going to do it his way." We were surprised Mother gave in like that. Randy and Julie moved into a fabulous condominium in Encino.

Not long after our brother left, Michael, Janet, and I were sitting in my room late one evening. We sometimes stayed up talking or playing games, then falling asleep in one of our rooms. The phone rang, but I didn't answer it, thinking it must be a fan who'd somehow gotten our home number. When it rang again, Michael looked concerned. "La Toya," he said, "I think you should answer it."

I lifted the receiver. "Hello?"

A stranger's voice said, "I think I just saw your

brother Randy in a car accident. A really bad accident." Mother and Joseph had also picked up and were on the line.

"What kind of car did you see?" Joseph asked.

"A Mercedes 450SL."

Oh my God. It was the correct make and model. Somehow we all sensed the caller wasn't mistaken. I dialed a local hospital and was told that yes, Randy Jackson had been admitted in extremely serious condition. "Please come down right away," the nurse said. "I don't think your brother has much longer."

I fell to my knees crying, "Randy! Why Randy? Why did this happen to him?" But my brother and sister quickly hushed me. "La Toya, don't do this," Michael said sternly. "You'll only get Mother upset." After the two of them helped me get dressed, we hurried out to the car. The trip to the hospital was torturous; Joseph is a very cautious driver, and Michael, Janet, and I, sitting together in back, thought we'd never get there in time. It was hard not to just leap out and run the rest of the way. The whole time, the dreadful thought *What if Randy dies?* repeated in my mind.

Los Angeles had been caught in a drenching rain that night. Randy, cruising along Cahuenga Boulevard in his Mercedes, skidded on a treacherous curve and slammed into a concrete light pole. The force of the crash was so great that the car's hood crumpled as if made of tin foil, collapsing the roof and propelling the engine into the driver's compartment, crushing my youngest brother. Police and paramedics at the scene took one look at the wreckage and presumed the driver dead. Using the Jaws of Life, it took them an hour to free Randy from the twisted metal. Both his legs were broken in several places, but the greatest damage was to his left ankle, which one doctor described to us as "demolished."

We raced into the hospital emergency area, where Randy was lying in shock. "Please," a doctor cautioned the five of us, "if you have to see him, pretend that nothing is wrong. In fact, I strongly suggest that you not look at his legs at all. They're all torn apart, with flesh hanging off. Please try to remain calm, for his sake."

"I'm in so much pain," we heard Randy moan.

On our way in to see him, a policeman commented to the doctor, "He's not going to make it. You know, it's a miracle he's even made it this far."

"If he does," came the hushed reply, "we'll probably have to amputate both legs."

Knowing I'd probably break down crying, Michael took me aside and repeated the doctor's instructions. "La Toya, don't say one word; don't show any emotion." I tried to stay calm, but as soon as I saw Randy, I gasped. Nothing the doctor said could have prepared us for this. "Please help me," my brother sobbed, though he had no idea how severe his injuries were. Tears trickled down my cheeks; I just couldn't help it. Michael, exasperated, led me out by the arm and tried comforting me. Meanwhile, Joseph, in a typical display of compassion, lectured his suffering son, "None of this would have happened if you'd stayed home where you belong."

We kept vigil at the hospital the entire night. The doctors wanted to amputate one or both of Randy's legs, but he told them no over and over. The next morning they explained that although Randy's life was now out of danger, he would probably never walk again. Several times over the next few weeks, my brother's condition deteriorated so drastically that amputation seemed the only choice, but each time he courageously, miraculously rallied.

Throughout Randy's lengthy hospitalization, Julie was right beside him, forcing my parents to reexamine their feelings toward her. Once he was finally released, confined to a wheelchair, Mother suggested hiring him a full-time nurse, but Julie wouldn't hear of it. "I *am* his nurse," she said, and indeed she was, making sure Randy took his medicine, preparing him health food, changing his bandages, and wheeling him wherever he wanted to go. It was apparent to all that Julie was no gold-digger and that she truly loved him.

Randy refused to accept any painkillers or the doctors' gloomy prognosis, insisting, "I'm going to walk again. I believe in myself, and I know I can do it." It took years of operations, excruciating physical therapy, and sheer willpower, but my brother indeed proved them wrong.

In 1980 I launched my solo career. Or, I should say, my father-manager launched it for me. In Joseph's mind there was simply no question that I would enter show business. For a while I studied business law, but he discouraged me at every opportunity, asking, "Why are you doing that? You don't need that." I disagreed, knowing how complex the business could be.

Having spent the last ten years in Hollywood, I was aware of its seamy underside, but I'd never experienced it myself. I was so naive then, I have to laugh. For instance, one famous entertainer's comely wife kept inviting me to their home. As she barely knew me and was a good deal older, I couldn't understand her persistence and . . . *overly friendly* manner. Later I learned she and her husband were notorious for hosting orgies and that her predilection for young girls was well known in certain circles.

I quickly learned that a woman in show business had to be on guard with practically everyone, even family friends. An older, popular actor who had known the Jacksons for years asked me to come to his office one afternoon to read for a part in a new program he was casting.

Every summer my family vacationed in Hawaii, and the plan was for Mother and me to join the others as soon as the audition ended. When we pulled up to his impressive office complex, an aide told us, "He would like to see La Toya alone." Mother stayed in the car.

A secretary showed me into the star's office, lavishly appointed with fine furniture, rich wood paneling, and a heavy marble desk, behind which he sat. I lowered myself into a chair opposite him. As soon as she closed the door behind her, he surreptitiously reached under his desk and pressed a button. I heard a sharp *click!* behind me.

Cordially he asked, "How are you doing?"

"Fine, thank you."

"Would you like anything?"

"No thank you."

"I'll bet you're the spoiled one in your family," he teased.

"No, I'm not."

"You know, I've been following your career. I think you're a very beautiful girl . . ."

An hour of small talk and suggestive innuendos later, he moved out from behind his desk and stood over me. "Why don't you come to Las Vegas with me and have dinner?" he asked.

"I can't."

"Why not?"

"I don't have dinner with people that I don't know." Which was true.

"You know me," he answered. "We've been talking for over an hour."

"Well, yes. But I really *don't* know you, sir. And besides, I have to go to Hawaii with my mother later tonight."

"I have a show tonight. Come with me," he implored. "I'll give you whatever you want. I'll take you shopping. I'll buy you whatever you want."

"I don't need you to take me shopping; I can buy whatever I want myself."

I'd heard about the casting couch before but couldn't believe this was happening to me. Not with a family friend. Not with a man old enough to be my grandfather. In my best businesslike tone, I said, "I think I'm here to read for a part. Can we please get started? My mother is waiting for me downstairs in the car."

"Well, you know the part is yours, La Toya," he said, smiling wickedly.

"But I haven't read for it."

"It's yours, honey—providing you have dinner with me tonight."

He started circling my chair like a shark. I nervously jumped up and took a seat on a long couch. While I debated what to do next, he walked over to a turntable and put on a record. "Do you know what your eyes remind me of?" he asked charmingly. The song contained the answer: ". . . When I look into your big brown eyes, it does things to me . . ." Oh, brother. As the music filled the room, my mind raced. *How can I get out of this place?*

"You have to let me go. I can't stay here. I can't go to dinner with you," I finally said with surprising forcefulness. "What you're suggesting is not going to happen; I'm not that kind of girl. I'm not desperate for a part. I came down here only because you called and my father asked me to. Now please let me go."

"No!" His tone changed abruptly from seductive to demanding. I bolted from the couch and ran for the door, but as I suspected, it was locked. The next

thing I knew, his gnarled hand was on top of mine. "You're not going anywhere! Now sit down!" he ordered, as if commanding a pet. "You're going to dinner with me. And we're going shopping for clothes on Rodeo Drive. And from there I'm taking you straight to Vegas."

Since a show of force only seemed to make him more determined, I tried a different tack: surrender. "Okay," I said meekly, "I do want the part. I want it very badly. You win."

The old man smiled. "The part is right for you, and you know it. You also know that I'm in love with you. I've always been in love with you."

Changing the subject, I feigned enthusiasm for our upcoming illicit weekend together, asking him where we'd be staying, where we'd be dining. "Oh!" I suddenly exclaimed. "I have to get a few things from home first. What time do you want me to meet you back here?"

That bit of acting alone should have won me the role, for apparently I convinced the old man I couldn't wait to rush back to him. Finally, he let me out of his office. As I calmly exited, I gave him my sweetest smile, then ran to the car, very upset. When I told Mother what happened, she murmured, "Next time I'll go upstairs with you." I think she was as shocked as I was, but that was all she said. We never discussed the matter again. At the time, I just wanted to put the episode behind me, but as I got older I thought about how peculiar Mother's reaction was. Imagining how I would feel if that had happened to my daughter, I found her passive response incomprehensible.

Later that year I recorded my first album, *La Toya Jackson*. To guide the project, Joseph selected a producer with no professional credits whatsoever. This was illustrative of my father's drawback as a manager. He was good at getting the ball rolling but eventually found himself out of his depth, which is why every one of his children eventually left his managership.

Though fancying himself a savvy businessman, Joseph was comparatively unsophisticated, making vital decisions based on personalities. If he liked a person, he hired that person, irrespective of his qualifications or lack thereof. Inevitably, my father got swindled by shysters, and his clients (us) suffered. Shaking her head, Mother often said of him, "He always walks around with a 'Kick Me' sign on his back."

Joseph tried to pressure Michael into producing me, but my brother resisted. While Michael's largesse to strangers is well known, he believes that family members should make it on their own. I agree with him one hundred percent. I've always wanted to earn my own success, as La Toya, and not have it hinge on my famous last name. Michael may be treated like the rest of us within the family, but in the public's eye he casts a mighty long shadow, one nobody would willingly choose to be judged under. In fact, I didn't even want *Jackson* to appear anywhere on the album, but Joseph insisted.

My father harped on Michael until he reluctantly agreed to produce and cowrite with me the song "Night Time Lover." It was fascinating to watch my brother at work. Neither he nor I plays the piano expertly, but we can peck out a song when necessary. Usually Michael sings the melodies he hears in his head to a pianist, or into a multitrack tape machine, then scats each instrument's lines, one on top of the other:

"*Dat, da-da-dat, dat, da-da-dat*—okay, that's what the drums are going to do, while the bass is going, *a-dum, dum, dum, dum, a-dum, dum, dum, dum* . . .'' Guitar parts, keyboard parts, horn parts, he hears and can vocally reproduce them all. It's uncanny. When everything is played back mixed together, it sounds like a full band, but with the human voice in place of musical instruments. Other times, he'll simply "dictate" a song into a regular tape recorder, narrating when the drums enter, where the hook starts, and so on. You have to hear it to believe it.

I expected we'd joke around a bit while recording, but to Michael making music is Serious Business. "You ready?" he asked intently over the studio intercom, as if talking to a complete stranger. "Now, I want you to sing it this way . . ." And Michael demonstrated exactly how the phrase should go. After we finished the track, he confided that the only reason he hadn't wanted to produce me was "because Joseph wanted me to." Nothing more needed to be said.

When I heard Michael's final mix, I was very pleased. But after reconsidering, he remixed it again. It was still a great track, I thought, just different. I trusted Michael and believed he did what he thought was best. Mother, however, saw it differently. "Michael's jealous," she said to me. "He's scared that somebody in the family will be bigger than him, so he had to go back in the studio, make it different, and now it isn't as good."

It was the most absurd thing I'd ever heard. "Mother, I don't know if he made it worse, or if I just liked it better before," I replied. "But maybe he felt that it sounds better this way."

Mother's expression said, "Sure."

"I just cannot believe Michael is jealous or that he would do something like that." I walked away wondering, *What is she trying to do? She knows Michael. How could she say such a thing?*

I was initially ambivalent about a recording career not only because Joseph thrust it upon me but because of my religion. Until I was twenty-four, I listened only to Frank Sinatra. Putting on something as innocent as a Peter Frampton record, I worried that I was sinning, and if an overtly sexual song like K. C. and the Sunshine Band's "(Shake, Shake, Shake) Shake Your Booty" came on the radio, as a Jehovah's Witness I was obligated to turn it off at once.

So you can imagine my dismay when presented with my first single, "If You Feel the Funk," which contained the line, "If you feel the funk, shake your rump." I firmly told my father I wouldn't—couldn't—record it.

"It's a good song," he argued. And it was, becoming a top dance hit. "There's nothing wrong with singing that."

"There is," I protested. "I just don't feel comfortable singing things like that. I can't do it."

My father prevailed, enlisting Mother's support. Frankly, I was surprised at her. As a fellow Witness, she certainly understood my misgivings. But she urged, "Go ahead and do it." Reasoning that if she felt it was all right then the song couldn't be as bad as I thought, I recorded it.

From day one my mother's attitude toward my solo career baffled me. She constantly contradicted herself. In her eyes, nothing offered me was worth pursuing. When Mother dissuaded me from project after project, I assumed it was because she had my best interests at heart. From the way she repeatedly criticized Joseph's management, I believed she was behind me. I didn't know that while she was talking me out of things, she was telling my father and Michael that I refused to do them because of the religion. Why would she make up such lies? In fact, I wanted to work very badly, but she always convinced me not to, saying it was against our faith.

Loving Mother so, I overlooked her faults and always managed to justify her behavior. When Michael wasn't home, she and I spent whole days together. In the morning, she'd call my room from hers. "Are you up? What do you want to do today?"

Usually we went out to lunch, shopped a bit, studied the Bible together, read, watched afternoon talk shows, discussed family goings-on, and so forth. We were like a pair of Beverly Hills matrons! The older I got, the closer we became. I couldn't imagine going anywhere without her and was sure I'd feel guilty if I left her alone. Mother always told me lovingly, "You're my best friend," and mused aloud, "What would I do if you ever left me?"

Without friends or any life outside Hayvenhurst, I'd grown so emotionally dependent on Mother that my brother Jackie semi-jokingly remarked, "La Toya, what would you do if Mother died? You'd probably die too. You're with her every minute of the day. I can't believe you. Don't you want a boyfriend or something?"

Jackie was trying to be funny, but I thought, *He's probably right. If Mother died, I don't know what I would do. I'd lose everything.* Whereas before the pull that kept me by her side calmed my fears, I slowly began to feel a hopeless despair. There had to be more to life, but I'd never find out unless I left her. And leaving her was the worst thing I could ever do. Before long it became unthinkable. Without my realizing it, I'd turned into a real Mommy's Girl.

Oddly enough, Joseph's infidelities played a part in our closeness. It's funny: Mother had always tried to shield me from the outside world. As an adult, I felt compelled to protect her as well. It killed me to know that my father's running around on her was common knowledge within the music industry. In fact, the word around town about the Jackson patriarch was, ''If you want to get to any of the kids, just get Joe a woman.''

It reached the point where Mother opted to stay at home rather than attend public functions. She felt, correctly, that people whispered and snickered behind her back. ''I'm not going to sit at a table full of women Joseph's been with smiling in my face,'' she said quietly. ''I just can't go.''

Poor Mother. The things she had to put up with. All my father's girlfriends were always *so* nice to her when they saw her—patronizing is the word—kissing her cheek, hugging her warmly, cooing over her like a flock of pigeons. Seeing how sweet and kind my mother was to them made this charade even more unbearable to watch.

Any time Joseph hurt Mother, it hardened our hearts against him. I'll never forget how back in Gary, Indiana, she had to walk nine blocks to Broadway to catch a bus to work at Sears, Roebuck. After the department store closed, Mother frequently stayed behind to count the day's receipts, rarely getting home before ten o'clock and often past eleven. Gary's winters are bitter cold, the wind whipping off Lake Michigan, and the slippery sidewalks were especially hazardous for someone with a limp. And at that time of night, no woman should have been forced to make her way home alone.

But Joseph refused to pick up his wife in the family car, remaining slumped in front of the television, watching professional wrestling. My brothers bundled up against the cold and, defying the city curfew, escorted Mother home safely. There were countless other times when she and I went to and from the market in a taxi because Joseph wouldn't drive us. Maybe to some people these seem like little things, but they troubled all of us.

I doubt that many children truly ever know all the facets of their parents' marriage or its chemistry. We certainly have never understood why Mother has stuck with Joseph for over forty years. He never did the things I now know husbands are supposed to do. Wedding anniversaries went unacknowledged. He never took Mother anywhere socially. Flowers? Forget it. But no matter what, the minute Joseph walked in the door, Mother cooed, "Oh, Joseph!" and went off with him.

As much an enigma as our father was to us, we had almost as many unanswered questions about our mother. How could she stay with a child-batterer and philanderer? How could she witness such violence against her own children and do nothing to stop it? Why didn't she protect us? Naturally I can't answer for Mother other than to say that she loves Joseph madly. I would guess that the options open to a woman with nine children back then were severely limited. Maybe because of her polio she felt lucky to have a husband at all. Perhaps she was as afraid of him as we were. To this day, I don't know for sure.

Gradually, in the early 1980s, Mother's long-smoldering resentment toward Joseph and his other women began to flare. In the past she never responded to Michael's prying questions about her marriage. "We're all accidents, right?" he used to tease. "You planned Rebbie and Jackie, but the rest of us are all mistakes!" Now she revealed bits and pieces about their life together. The two of us were stunned when she told us matter-of-factly, "Someday I will divorce Joseph. I'm just waiting until you all get older. Maybe when Janet graduates."

Then Mother started snooping on Joseph. For years, as soon as she left the house, I would catch him whispering into the telephone. Certain that he was up to no good, I told Mother so. One afternoon she announced as usual, "I'm going shopping" and walked out the front door, but instead of getting into her car she snuck back into the recording studio and eavesdropped on our unsuspecting father's call to his mistress. They were making plans to meet. When Joseph drove off to the woman's house, Mother tailed him in her car and confronted the mother of his illegitimate daughter right there in her driveway.

"I don't know what came over me," she told me and Michael the following morning. "I saw him with her, and a feeling just came all over me. Before I knew it, I'd grabbed her and slapped her!"

This was incredible. "You did?"

"Yes, I did."

We were torn between feeling glad she'd finally asserted herself and sad that Joseph had driven her to lower herself like that.

"Mother," one of us said gently, "why fight over trash?"

"I can't take it anymore!" she exclaimed with surprising firmness. To say we were shocked when she consulted a lawyer and set in motion a divorce is an understatement. But our reaction was mild compared to Joseph's. After all those years of doing whatever he pleased, he felt like his world had shattered.

Practically overnight Mother turned into a new person. Before, she always denied herself material things, but now she treated herself to grand shopping sprees, her car groaning with boxes and boxes of expensive clothes. Sorting through them, I held up a matching outfit of leopard hat, shoes, and coat. "Mother!" I said, flabbergasted. "This is not you! Why did you buy all this stuff?"

"Because I'm leaving your father. I'm going to stay with my mother."

Her mother, Mama, and stepfather, Papa, had retired to Alabama. Somehow I couldn't picture Mother down in tiny Hurtsboro, population one thousand, in her leopard-skin ensemble. Apparently, neither could she; she never wore any of the clothes she bought on that binge.

For the next two weeks, Joseph was distraught without Mother, calling her constantly, begging her to come back home. Every day Mother called me from Alabama to say, "La Toya, he's been crying on the phone, begging me to come back."

"Mother, are you going to get a divorce or not? You're not really sure, are you?"

"Well, you should hear him. He's crying like a baby." I detected a measure of satisfaction in her voice.

"That doesn't sound like Joseph to me, Mother."

"Well, he loves me and wants me back," she said firmly. Apparently Joseph touched her heart, because a week or two later she was back. We'd never seen him so desperate or so contrite. He stopped seeing his girlfriends and wouldn't go to the office, staying around the house instead. I couldn't remember the last time he'd been home so much.

But soon my father was back to his old ways. Only now instead of merely rubbing his affairs in his wife's face, he felt compelled to telegraph his sordid activities to his children as well. I recall sitting in Joseph's offices with Janet once, opposite one of his girlfriends; "Judy," we'll call her, a secretary. She made a big show of thumbing through a mail-order catalog, ordering expensive items over the phone.

". . . Ooh! That dress is only nine hundred dollars? Okay, I'll take that too . . .

". . . Uh-huh, the name on the credit card is—" she raised her voice deliberately—"*Joseph Jackson.*" She must have ordered more than a thousand dollars' worth of merchandise while we sat right there. After hanging up, she sashayed into my father's private inner office and in a shrewish voice demanded, "Gimme the other credit card!"

"Shhhh!" we heard Joseph say. "They can hear you!"

"Can you believe how she's talking to him, ordering him around?" I whispered to my sister.

Before Janet could respond, Judy was back in her chair, dialing another number. ". . . Yes, you know those shoes in your window? The ones with the rhinestones? Well, I'd like a pair of those, charged to Joseph Jackson and delivered to my address, which is . . ."

What really made us angry were her repeated phone calls to Joseph at home. It was disrespectful to Mother, who sometimes answered. When she couldn't stand it anymore, my mother told Judy, "Out of respect to me, do not ever call my home again, and get out of my husband's office."

"You don't tell me what to do!" the girl retorted.

Then Mother issued Joseph an ultimatum, that if he didn't fire Judy immediately, she'd file for divorce again, and this time for good.

"Don't worry," my father assured her, "I'll take care of it."

But of course he didn't, as Mother discovered upon dialing Joseph's office and hearing Judy's unmistakable "Hello, Joe Jackson Productions . . ."

"That's it!" Mother shouted, slamming down the receiver. "I cannot take this another minute!" She, Randy, and his girlfriend, Julie, hopped in the car and sped to Joseph's office. Judy looked up from her desk to find Mother glowering down at her.

"I want you to leave this place right now!"

"No," she said snidely. "You can't tell me what to do."

"Then we should talk. Let's go out in the hallway." Judy accompanied Mother, all right, but not voluntarily: my demure mother actually grabbed her by the hair and dragged her screaming out the door. Onlookers didn't know whether to intervene or to laugh.

When she got as far as the staircase, Mother let go and ordered, "You leave my husband alone, do you hear me? I'm sick of you!"

Regrettably, the story made all the music-industry trade papers. Judy wasn't hurt as much as scared. And surprised.

Now here's the truly amazing part of the story: even following the assault, Judy and my father remained an item for a number of years. But while Mother was unsuccessful in quashing the affair, she'd demonstrated to my father and to her children that she was no longer the same meek, forgiving, long-suffering woman. She would never again stand by silently and tolerate anything that threatened her marriage or her family. Mother began to change, in ways that weren't entirely becoming.

6

INSIDE THE
GILDED CAGE

Reflecting on the early eighties, I sometimes find it difficult to fix certain events. Perhaps that's because life at home changed so little from year to year. The personal points of reference most young women use to mark time, like friendships and romances, didn't exist for me.

Mother loved us all so much, but today I have to wonder, Didn't she worry about me never knowing the pleasure of a man's company or love? Didn't she have the same hopes all mothers have to one day see their daughter walk down the aisle in a white gown? Didn't she wish for me to have children, having said so often that motherhood brought her the greatest joy in life?

Between the rigid, Puritanical views about dating and sex extolled at home and in the Kingdom Hall, my attitudes toward both were pretty well set. I believed dating could lead only to marriage and that sex without the benefit of matrimony was sinful. I continued believing that until only quite recently. They say that you don't miss what you never had, and for most of my life, I didn't. By the time I was in my twenties I just didn't think about guys much, perhaps because I knew it would kill Mother if I left home to marry. Furthermore, any time one showed genuine interest in me, I usually didn't even realize it. Having grown up surrounded by so many brothers, I liked men as friends but was totally unversed in deciphering the nonverbal cues between men and women.

Shortly after Prince released "Soft and Wet," he shyly introduced himself to me at a roller-skating party. "Hi."

"Hi," I said nonchalantly.

"I'm Prince."

"Yes, I know." There was no mistaking his large brown eyes, downy moustache, and straight black hair. Although I was sitting down to put on my skates, he was barely my height.

"I just want you to know that I'm madly in love with you," he whispered passionately.

"Oh." I thought this was his way of complimenting someone. I had no idea of his real intentions until he said, "I have all your pictures and everything, and I like everything about you." His voice trailed off as if he had run out of words.

"Oh . . . that's nice."

Most girls would have kissed him or slapped him. Me? I stood up, offered a cheery "Well, hope you have a nice time tonight!" and skated off.

In fall 1980 my brothers released their second self-produced album, *Triumph,* which surpassed *Destiny* in sales and carried two major hits, "Lovely One" and "Heartbreak Hotel." One of its songs, "Can You Feel It," was made into a fantastic video that in my opinion stands as one of the genre's most creative. In it Jackie, Tito, Marlon, Michael, and Randy appear as omnipotent, benevolent creators, dispersing joy, wisdom, and enlightenment in showers of celestial dust. Arising from an exploding sun, towering over a city skyline, hoisting a rainbow, and creating a comet with a clap of Michael's hands, they seem godlike. The theme of "Can You Feel It," like several of the brothers' and Michael's later songs, expressed how we Jacksons all feel about the state of the world and our responsibilities to it. The notions of a saving message, eternal grace, and nonviolence all derive from our beliefs.

The guys never fell out of love with music, but touring gradually became a burden, especially for those with children. At every opportunity during the 1981 tour they jetted home, even if only for a day or two. Their shows were as energetic and exciting as ever, but watching them from the wings I could tell that sometimes a couple of them wanted to be someplace else. When the Jacksons took a short hiatus following the final date, our manager-father turned his attention to his youngest daughters. I recorded a second album that year, *My Special Love*. Because it was another of Joseph's projects, I had no control and wasn't satisfied with it. I vowed I wouldn't let that happen again. I wanted everything I did to reflect my best, and I knew that couldn't happen as long as my father managed me.

Janet and I no longer toured as part of a family act, yet we were always busy. I appeared on television shows in Europe and met a lot of entertainers, some established, some just on the way up. George Michael and I were part of a show together, he with his duo, Wham. In the morning all the acts on the bill had to straggle to the airport for the flight to the next town. Everyone was sleepy and grumpy, but not George.

Even at that hour, he had on his headphones, singing at the top of his lungs, finger-popping, and dancing in his seat. He had soul to spare. And he was so cute! We got to talking, and he mentioned he lived in a big house in London with his partner, Andrew Ridgley, and a singer who called himself Boy George.

"Boy George?"

"Yeah," he said. "I'm sure that one day he's going to be popular."

I felt wonderful when George rhapsodized about black music like the Jacksons'. It had obviously been a great influence on him. In fact, he reminded me of my brothers in the way he totally immersed himself in music, always trying to learn. You could tell music meant everything to him.

Besides touring and recording, I was volunteered by my father for various public functions. Whether I felt they were or were not in my career's best interest never concerned him, for he knew I would never dare refuse any of his orders.

One of these obligations was to act as presenter at the American Music Awards. The day of the live broadcast, I fell ill with severe stomach pains. While I lay in bed in agony, my parents stood around wondering what to do. Joseph grumbled, "I know what can cure this," left the room, and returned with a prescription bottle containing a very mild tranquilizer.

Turning to Janet, who'd wandered in from her room, he said, "Get dressed and be ready, because if La Toya's sick, you'll have to stand in for her."

My sister was all heart. "You'd better get well real quick," she warned, "because I am not going on-stage for you. Now, get up!"

Joseph handed her the small plastic bottle, instructing, "Give La Toya this medicine every two hours, you hear me?" The limo soon arrived, and before I knew it, she and I were on our way.

The hours of preparation, rehearsals, and waiting dragged on and on. Every time I emitted the tiniest groan, Janet brandished the pill bottle, chirping merrily, "Here, it's time to take more!" I'd never taken any kind of drug before, and even though this was quite mild, I was soon very . . . very . . . *relaxed.*

"I don't want any more, Jan," I said groggily, feeling the words mush in my mouth. "I feel so drowsy, and I'm tired . . . so tired . . ."

"La Toya," she commanded, determined to see me up on that stage, "open your mouth!"

Soon I was feeling no pain whatsoever, and not much of anything else. We sat in the audience during the live show, me in a long white beaded gown, waiting for my turn. Janet maintained a running commentary, whispering that she thought the host, singer Teddy Pendergrass, liked me. "Can't you tell he's looking at you?"

"Janet . . . I don't care about . . . anything."

Finally the call came. "Okay, La Toya," my sister piped up, "it's time for you to go onstage."

"Onstage? Where am I?"

"You're at the American Music Awards!" Janet gripped me by the shoulders and shook me. "Now, get up there!"

Somehow I made it to the podium, gave my speech, and presented the award as planned. That night I slept like a baby.

Janet and I were like my mother and her sister Hattie growing up in East Chicago, she as tomboyish and aggressive as I was feminine and soft-spoken. Jan wasn't one to care about appearances. At least several times a week Michael invited famous guests to Hayvenhurst: Marlon Brando, Sophia Loren, Muhammad Ali, Elizabeth Taylor. Since household help was on the premises at all times, and you never knew which celebrity you might encounter downstairs, we were never completely relaxed in our own home. You couldn't dress sloppily or pad around in your bathrobe. As much as it irritated most of us, we tried dressing neatly all the time.

Janet, though, didn't think twice about bounding downstairs clad in only a wrinkled T-shirt and a baseball cap. As guests looked on in disbelief, she'd offer a chipper "Hi!" and go about her business. Michael was mortified and as close to furious as he ever got. "Don't come downstairs unless you're dressed, Janet!" he scolded afterward. "You never know who's going to be here, and it's embarrassing. Please."

"I can't stand this house!" Janet grumbled. "You can never walk around the way you want. First, there's too much help, and you always have to put on clothes because of them. Then you can't go downstairs and look the way you want. It makes me so mad!"

I understood how she felt, but diplomatically pointed out, "Jan, your T-shirt is up to there and—"

Ever the tease, Michael had to crack, "And look at your fat, funky thighs!" sending our sister storming into her room and slamming the door. From the hall we could hear her angrily shoo her dogs off the bed.

Michael is the consummate host, anxious to make everything absolutely perfect for his guests. If we have someone over, he'll corner me a dozen times to inquire, "Are you sure she has enough to drink? Are you sure she doesn't want something else to eat? Are you sure everything's okay?"

"Mike, I've asked her, and everything is fine."

"Are you sure?"

"Yes, I'm sure."

My brother's sweetness can be exasperating after a while. I was dressed to go out one day when I got the idea to play a practical joke on him. I snuck into my father's room and on a second phone line called my brother. In my best New York accent, I said, "Hello, Michael?"

"Yes?"

"This is Sidney Lumet's secretary."

"Oh, hi!" Michael, having admired the director since working with him on *The Wiz*, was thrilled.

"Mr. Lumet's in town and would like to see you."

"Really?" I heard the phone drop and then Michael's footsteps as he ran toward my room, shouting, "La Toya! La Toya!"

I hid the receiver under a pillow. "I'm in here!"

His head popped in the doorway. "Guess who's on the phone! Sidney Lumet's secretary! And guess what?" Michael was so beside himself with excitement I almost fell out laughing right then. "Sidney Lumet wants to see me!"

"He does?"

"Yes. I gotta go back. She's waiting for me." A few seconds later I heard a breathless "Hello?"

"Yes, Michael," I said in the New York accent, "Mr. Lumet would like to see you at your home. In fact, he's not too far from there right now. May he come over?"

"You're kidding! Hold on!"

Michael rushed back to Joseph's room. "La Toya,

what are we gonna do? He's on his way over now! I wanna see him, but . . ." My brother surveyed the house, which was always immaculate. "Clean the house!" he cried, then ran back and told the "secretary" he'd be ready. I couldn't resist laying it on thick. "You know, Michael," I said, "Mr. Lumet really thinks you're incredibly talented, and he always talks about what a wonderful job you did on *The Wiz*."

"Oh, that's very nice. But I've got to go and get ready. Bye!"

"Mother!" Michael shouted. "Sidney Lumet's on his way over! Sidney Lumet's on his way over! Everybody hurry up! Close the garage! Clean the house!" He was barking orders like a staff sergeant.

Michael was frantic, pulling out clothes and asking, "But what should I wear? How should I fix my hair?" I played along, even as he stood out by the gate waiting for his esteemed guest. Finally, unable to bear it any longer, I strolled out to the driveway and casually inquired, "So, Mike, are you camping out here?"

"I don't understand, La Toya," he replied distractedly, peering through the gate.

"Well, what did his secretary say to you?" I asked coyly, "Did she *tawk* like this?"

Michael spun around. "Yeah . . ."

"Did she say, 'Mr. Lumet thinks yawr incredibly talented'?"

"Yeah!" He thought for a moment. "Wait a minute," he said suspiciously, "you were listening to my phone call!"

"No I wasn't, Mike," I replied innocently.

"Yeah? Then how do you know what she said?"

"Because it was me!"

His jaw dropped. "Now you're going to get it!" I laughed so hard I didn't realize he'd picked up the garden hose. My brother drenched my suede outfit, laughing vengefully, while I screamed for Mother to rescue me.

What most girls wouldn't give to have a brother like Michael. Whenever I was upset, he went out of his way to cheer me up, driving to the store and bringing me back a stack of magazines or a Three Stooges video that we'd watch together. Or he'd do something special, like surprising me with an autographed picture of Frank Sinatra, or inviting one of my favorite authors, the inspiring Og Mandino, over to the house. I'll never forget that.

Knowing Cary Grant was my idol, Michael surprised me one evening by inviting the legendary actor to dinner. Over the years I've met so many celebrities, but what a thrill! This was not long before he passed away, but even at age eighty-two Mr. Grant was as suave, sophisticated, and handsome as I'd imagined; in a word, the consummate gentleman. When I entered the dining room, he said in his glorious English accent, "Please stay. Won't you sit down?" as if I were the guest and he the host. It was truly a memorable evening for me.

Our strangest guest was a popular musician. Living in Los Angeles, you hear a lot of record-industry gossip, but you never really know about a person until you meet them. Rumor had it that this man was into the black arts and practiced witchcraft. (We'd heard similar tales about other entertainers whose names you would never guess.) Jehovah's Witnesses are prohibited from believing in the occult or having anything to do with it. However, it's my personal feeling that merely acknowledging the existence of such things as voodoo and the black arts doesn't make you either a believer or a practitioner.

Dinner was uneventful. As this person was getting ready to leave, he handed Michael a large unwrapped cardboard box. Later my brother, Janet, and I carried it up to Mother's room, and Michael cautiously removed the lid. Inside were several smaller boxes, each containing strange items: a small twig, dried leaves, a cassette tape. We looked at the boxes, then at one another, all three of us thinking, *Maybe those rumors are true* . . . There was no note or anything to explain the unusual present.

"Play the tape! Play the tape!" Janet urged, but Michael shook his head no. "For one thing," he explained, "I don't want to be accused of stealing anybody's songs. And I really don't want to hear it." Later we gave it to one of the household employees. He listened to it and reported back to us, "It's a song and some talking, all recorded backward."

Michael and I discussed the significance of the boxes and the tape. Later we learned through an assistant that somehow one of Michael's heavy rhinestone socks had come into this musician's possession as well. We couldn't help wondering if our guest was trying to cast a spell on him. My brother said, "If you're strong religiously, these things won't affect you, no matter how hard somebody tries." I knew he was right, but just thinking about it, even today, gives me chills.

Our favorite guests at Hayvenhurst were children. The public knows that my siblings and I do a lot of charity work with youngsters, perhaps in reaction to the way we were raised. Through organizations such as the Make a Wish Foundation, kids begged to meet Michael, and he never let them down. For countless terminally ill children, getting to meet Michael Jackson was a final wish. He traveled to their homes or hospitals and invited them to Hayvenhurst for as long as they liked. The best part was seeing the looks on kids' faces when they realized they could watch any movie they wanted in our home theater, or choose any candy they wanted from our Candy Store. Michael did whatever they wanted, showing them his exotic pets, playing the latest arcade and video games in our game room, anything to make them happy.

Most of these visits were not publicized; nor was the fact that many of the youngsters kept in touch after their stay. One boy suffering from cancer died just two days after leaving Hayvenhurst. Whenever Michael learned of a child's passing, he broke down sobbing. He really loved each of them, including Ryan White, the brave young boy with AIDS who did so much to combat ignorance of the disease. Michael had Ryan and his family out to his Santa Ynez ranch many times. When the boy passed away in 1990, Michael attended the funeral, which was very unusual for him.

No matter who visited, Michael insisted I stay at his side. We'd always done so much together, but now whenever guests were expected, Michael pestered me, "Come on, let's go downstairs. Please come."

"No, Mike, just go by yourself for once."

"*Please,* La Toya?"

"Okay, later."

"No, now."

It was as if being Michael Jackson was just too much for one individual to handle, and he needed some kind of support. Michael is extremely interested in people but shy, so I often wound up filling the lulls in the conversation. Once Yul Brynner was over, and my brother barely said a word to him, so to be polite I bombarded the famous actor with questions about *The King and I,* his children, and so on.

I'm sure that some people thought this a little odd. The fact that Michael and I often dressed alike, a habit we got into while he was making *The Wiz,* probably made them wonder too. I can't say exactly why we did it, but each day one of us suggested, "Let's wear the pink sweaters and black pants," the other said "Great!" and that's what we wore. What a sight we were together.

By early 1983 the album my brother claimed would be the biggest seller in history was on its way to becoming just that. *Thriller* sold nearly 50 million copies, spawned two Number Ones ("Billie Jean" and "Beat It"), five Top 10 hits ("Thriller," "Wanna Be Startin' Something," "Human Nature," "P.Y.T. [Pretty Young Thing]," and, with Paul McCartney, "The Girl Is Mine"), and captured an unprecedented eight Grammy awards.

Not as quantifiable but more important to Michael, however, was *Thriller*'s demonstrating that music can break down barriers. He had predicted, "I'm going to make sure that people of all colors accept me as an individual and say, 'This is Michael, I like his record, I don't care what color he is.' " And indeed, his dazzling videos for "Billie Jean" and "Beat It" hurdled the de facto color line that had virtually barred black artists from the influential music-video cable channel MTV, paving the way for an entire generation of black talent.

Historians cite Michael's performance of "Billie Jean" on that spring's Motown twenty-fifth anniversary TV special as one of the transcendent moments in music history. Moonwalking across the stage in a black sequined jacket (which I'd originally bought for Mother!), Michael cast a wondrous spell from which the world will probably never awaken. He came home that night absolutely ecstatic. And, of course, full of gossip about who was there, who said what, and who did what to whom, especially Diana Ross's and Mary Wilson's onstage spat during the Supremes reunion.

When Motown contacted Michael about appearing on *Motown 25: Yesterday, Today, Forever* with the rest of the Jacksons, he initially refused, but not because of any lingering animosity toward the label or Berry Gordy. Ever since *The Jacksons,* our light mid-seventies musical-comedy series for CBS, he was unenthusiastic about television in general. People tend to remember it as the night that Michael rejoined his brothers, when in fact, it was Jermaine who returned to the fold. Despite his acclaim as a solo artist, Michael technically remains one fifth of the Jacksons to this day.

I hesitate to say that Jermaine was jealous of his younger brother, but he had not exactly been supportive while Michael was laboring on his new album. During a family meeting Jermaine remarked sourly, ''He's wasting all this time on *Thriller,* and it's not gonna do anything. The music industry is in a slump, it's all going down. Besides, I think this album sounds like a buncha junk.''

''Don't say things like that,'' I protested. ''It's a great album, and Mike predicts it's going to be the biggest seller in the world. Can't you have some faith in him?''

''Aw, he's always dreaming, just like in the Peter Pan story.'' Jermaine waved his hand dismissively. ''And all you do is take up for him. You two stick together like glue.'' Sometimes when my brother talked to me like this, he grabbed my shoulders and pushed me down in a chair and commanded, ''Now you listen to me.''

Except for Jermaine, all the Jacksons were overjoyed for Michael when *Thriller* rocketed to astronomical success. It was certainly understandable for any of the brothers to feel overshadowed that year by Michael. To illustrate what a phenomenon *Thriller* was, if you tallied up the 1983 sales figures for six of that year's biggest acts (the Police, Duran Duran, David Bowie, Quiet Riot, Culture Club, and the Rolling Stones), then *doubled* the sum, it still didn't equal Michael's total.

We all loved both Michael and Jermaine, so it hurt us to read the latter's vicious comments in the press about his younger brother, like his opinion that Michael was trying to "be white." How could Jermaine say that? Yet in the next breath he'd claim he wasn't at all jealous of Michael, and that the entire family "shared" in his success. Jermaine may genuinely feel that way, but the fact is that Michael's success is his alone. Typically, none of us had the courage to tell Jermaine he was wrong.

Interestingly, at the same time he was discrediting Michael publicly, Jermaine was pushing hard to reunite all six brothers. In 1983 Jermaine left Motown Records, with Berry Gordy's promise to make him a huge solo star unfulfilled. In the eight years since he'd opted to stay with his father-in-law's company, Jermaine had released seven albums and eleven singles. Of those, only 1980's *Let's Get Serious* and its title track (coproduced by another onetime Motown teen star, Stevie Wonder) made the Top 10. Frustrated, Jermaine belatedly reached the same conclusion as had Joseph and the others years before. Simply, the label had lost its ability to catapult artists to the top of the charts. With the blessings of both Berry and Hazel, he signed with Arista Records.

I know that Jermaine's reuniting with Michael, Marlon, Randy, Tito, and Jackie for the *Motown 25* special was one of their happiest moments. Seeing all six guys together again at home rehearsing "I Want You Back," "The Love You Save," "Never Can Say Goodbye," and "I'll Be There" . . . God, it was so touching and so exciting.

Jermaine proposed, and almost everyone more or less agreed, that the reunion be permanent, while still enabling each brother to record additionally on his own. "We should all stick together like brothers, do a tour, and make a comeback as a family," Jermaine said emotionally at a Jacksons meeting. Then he scowled. "But the problem is You-Know-Who," a bitter reference to Michael, "because he's got his head so far up in the air." We all rolled our eyes. Why was Jermaine like this?

My father supported Jermaine's idea wholeheartedly. Having all six of his sons together again, it would be just like the old days, but with one major difference: Joseph was no longer actively managing their careers and hadn't for a couple of years. From the beginning, he'd involved the guys in a number of bad deals, incurred needless lawsuits, alienated important industry people, and in general created more problems than he solved. For their own protection, my brothers finally confronted him and told him that from then on he was manager in title only.

Michael had been among the first to find fault with our father's handling of his career, complaining constantly. Countless times Michael said, "Uh-oh. Here comes Joseph, and I know he's going to ask me to do something I don't want to do. God, I hate going through this." When I'd laugh and ask him if he weren't overreacting, Michael replied, "You'll see someday, La Toya. It's not so funny. When he starts managing you, and you don't want him to; when you want to do something, and you're not able to do it, you'll know what I'm feeling right now." As usual, he was right.

From the time he was eighteen, Michael essentially managed himself anyway. I'd overhear him on the phone ordering my father's associates, Freddy DeMann and Ron Weisner, "This is the way it has to be done. You listening to me? Okay, and we should come out with this and that . . ." My brother may be mild-mannered, but his business savvy is legendary, and entertainers in all areas call him constantly for advice.

In early 1983 Michael and the others officially fired Joseph and Weisner/DeMann, leaving our father shocked, hurt, and angry that he'd be deprived of his percentage of their earnings. For the first time Joe Jackson wasn't "calling all the shots," as he liked to say, and he was at a loss. He still managed Janet and me, and had a client list of other acts, most of whom you've never heard of. It wasn't the same.

When word of his firing reached the press, my father reacted as if it weren't true. He was widely quoted as saying, "There are a lot of leeches trying to break up the group. A lot of people are whispering in Michael's ear. But we know who they are. They're only in it for the money. I was there before it started, and I'll be there after it ends." Joseph told reporters that he'd signed the guys to Weisner/DeMann because "There was a time when I felt I needed white help in dealing with the corporate structure at CBS and thought they'd be able to help. But they never gave me the respect you expect from a business partner."

We were all shocked and embarrassed by Joseph's racist comments, Michael stating publicly, "I happen to be color-blind. I don't hire color; I hire competence. The individual can be of any race or creed as long as I get the best." He added, "Racism is not my motto. One day I expect every color to love as one family." My brother attempted some additional damage control by saying, "I don't know what would make him say something like that."

But in fact we all knew the truth, not only about our father but Mother, too. I'm ashamed to admit that both my parents harbor racist attitudes, particularly against Jews, who happen to fill a large number of influential positions in the entertainment industry.

"Wherever you go, whatever you do in this business, you find a Jew," Mother used to complain bitterly all the time, "I can't stand it." That wasn't the end of it. She'd go on and on. "They're always on top. Jews are so nosy. They like controlling you. I hate 'em all." To their faces, however, my mother was as sweet as could be.

Ironically, whenever Joseph got into any kind of legal or business trouble, my mother's first suggestion was always, "I think you need a Jew right now, to get where you're going. Because they control the world." I'm sorry to say her offensive views rubbed off on Janet, who'd respond to one of Mother's venomous diatribes by saying that she also hated Jews. From the way Janet often spoke, it seemed that she felt it was best to pretend you liked them, get what you could, then drop them.

Hearing talk like this turned my stomach, especially when it came from my mother's mouth. How could a religious woman be so hateful? Whenever anyone made an anti-Semitic remark in our presence, Michael and I immediately took them to task. We'd attended a predominantly Jewish school and knew our parents' attitudes were disgraceful.

"You can't say one race is better or worse than another," I argued. "We're all the same."

"Mother, look at it this way," Michael implored. "We're a minority, and so are the Jews. Look what they've done. They've suffered so much, but they pulled together and made so much progress. Why can't we as a race do the same thing?"

But whenever either of us tried pointing out that you can't condemn an entire people based on one person's conduct, she'd snap, "Don't tell me that!

They're all alike. I've lived longer than you. I've experienced more. *I know.*''

Some of my other brothers were equally appalled by Mother's and Joseph's remarks. ''We're so tired of hearing this,'' one said. Another commented, ''Every time I come over all I hear is 'Jews this' and 'Jews that.' It makes me sick. Is that all they talk about?''

The depth of Mother's loathing was expressed in one of her oft-repeated opinions: ''There's one mistake Hitler made in his life—he didn't kill all those Jews. He left too many damn Jews on this earth, and they multiplied,'' to which Joseph usually added an amen: ''Those damn Jews.''

The less control my father wielded over the guys, the more suspicious of outsiders he and my mother became. For years he'd told her to stay out of the business, and she obeyed. But especially after Michael's *Thriller,* things really changed. On one hand, I don't blame Mother. It seemed like people were robbing him and her other sons blind, something easily accomplished in the music industry. Employees hired to handle your business can handily skim a few thousand dollars here and a few thousand dollars there, secretly award themselves monetary ''gifts,'' and rig contracts to conceal under-the-table kickbacks that comprise their actual ''commissions.'' It wasn't unusual for Michael to hire a person with no personal assets to speak of, and a few weeks later he or she was driving a shiny new BMW.

When business demands became overwhelming,

Michael took on Frank Dileo as his manager in 1984, though in reality my brother continued to direct his own career. Michael knew Dileo from Epic Records, where as vice-president he'd been integral in promoting *Thriller* (which many executives there had predicted privately would flop). He became what I call the "No" Man, more a buffer than an active manager, because my brother found it so hard to turn down anyone. A rotund little man with a receding hairline and baby-fat cheeks, Dileo could be arrogant, but he did Michael's bidding.

To no one's surprise, Joseph didn't like his son's new manager at all, and the feeling was mutual. In fact, my father disapproved of anyone who worked for Michael, and he made his feelings well known. My brother often held business meetings at Hayvenhurst, and when Joseph came in, naturally the guests cordially extended their hands. My father used to regard them coldly and sneer, "Why would I want to shake your hand? All you're doing is stealing from my son." Needless to say, this upset and embarrassed Michael terribly. Even as adults we still couldn't have company over.

On January 27, 1984, I was home with Mother when we received a phone call alerting us that Michael had been badly injured in an accident at the Shrine Auditorium, where he and the brothers were filming a commercial for Pepsi. The caller wasn't very specific, saying only that he'd been rushed to the hospital. We raced to Cedars-Sinai Medical Center and met Jackie, Tito, Jermaine, Marlon, and Randy, all badly shaken, in the waiting area.

The auditorium had been packed with screaming fans as the guys performed for the cameras time and again. Michael was to make his entrance dancing down a large staircase to a revised version of "Billie Jean." When he appeared at the top, a single explosion was timed to go off and illuminate him. But for this take the director asked him to hold his pose a few seconds longer. When he did, the device detonated too early, setting his hair ablaze.

For a couple of seconds, Michael didn't realize what had happened, but as he went into a choreographed spin at the bottom of the stairs, he suddenly screamed, "Tito!" Fortunately, Marlon Brando's son Miko, who worked for our family, thought quickly and furiously rubbed his hands through my brother's hair to smother the flames. Someone else had the presence of mind to apply ice to the wound and keep him warm and calm until the paramedics arrived.

I went directly to Michael's private hospital room. He was lying in bed, and I remember thinking how small he looked. Like a child.

"Mike, are you okay?" I asked tenderly.

Though he was in tremendous pain, he answered, "Yes, I'm fine, La Toya." But he was very anxious about his skin and how badly he'd been disfigured. Since the burns were on the back of his head, he didn't know how severe they were. "How does it look?" my brother asked. "Does it look like it will be okay?"

The wound was an angry-looking mass of scorched tissue about the diameter of your palm. It was hard not to wince. But I said, "I'm sure it will be okay," and quickly changed the subject.

He was transferred to Brotman Medical Center, where the wound was operated on. (Coincidentally, in the past Michael had visited the burn center at Brotman to cheer up patients.) Within a few days Michael was back home, and after several subsequent operations over the next few months, the area healed back to near-normal. It was a terrible accident, but we all were grateful, realizing it could have been far worse. No one knows the exact cause of the accident, but it's safe to say that pressures to complete the commercial played a role.

Around the same time Michael was recuperating, the press was linking him romantically with Brooke Shields, the actress and model. My brother had been as sheltered from the opposite sex as I was. He too believed that sex came after marriage, and marriage was the goal of dating. Up till then he'd had only one close friendship, with Tatum O'Neal in the late 1970s. Tatum, just fifteen then, was in some ways more sophisticated than Michael, running with an older, faster crowd. We always found it so strange that her father, actor Ryan O'Neal, regularly left her and her younger brother Griffin unsupervised for days at a time, but for them, and many kids in Hollywood, that was considered normal.

I recall so many times when I've seen famous children, sometimes not even in their teens, in the company of adults known to drink, use drugs, and who knows what else. Perhaps some of my siblings lost their childhoods, but it was to work, not drugs or alcohol. Very few Hollywood children ever really get to be kids.

Despite the press's portrayal, Michael and Brooke's relationship was a friendship, plain and simple—at least in Michael's mind. It was obvious to Janet and me that she had other ideas. About to watch a movie with us at home, Brooke would declare, *"I'm* going to sit by Michael," grabbing his hand. "Michael, where are *we* going to sit?"

Janet and I concurred that she was a bit forward, especially when she started making plans for them as a couple. Brooke longed to accompany Michael to the two upcoming music awards shows, the 1984 American Music Awards and the Grammys, and pestered him about it every chance she got.

"Michael, I'm going to be your date, right?" For a supposed question, it sure had a ring of finality to it. "It's going to be you and me."

"Well . . ." Michael laughed nervously. Just like when it came to business, he could never say no. He turned to me and whispered urgently, "La Toya, *say something.*"

"It's your problem," I hissed out of the side of my mouth.

". . . Uh, I don't know if I'm going to take anybody or not," he replied at last, though to no avail.

"Sure you are," Brooke said happily. "The two of us are going."

Later Michael cornered me and asked, "La Toya, how can I tell her no?"

"You just have to tell her, Mike."

Janet, who really couldn't stand Brooke, calling her "Giraffe Butt" behind her back, eagerly offered, "Let me tell her!"

Michael surrendered. "No," he sighed, "I guess I'll take her. But you know"—he lowered his voice—"she tried to kiss me!"

"She did?"

"Yeah, she's more aggressive than she looks."

This was a common scenario. Other women, probably attracted to Michael's relative innocence, approached him even more directly. But other women were simply friends, and he received many gifts from them, which he took as thoughtful tokens of their affection. One famous actress gave him a set of beautiful gray silk sheets monogrammed with her initials, ET. We thought they were so sumptuous and pretty; we never thought there was anything untoward about the gesture.

Michael, Brooke, and I went to the American Music Awards together. It was one of the longest nights of my life. First of all, I was seated next to Brooke. Farther down the row sat singer Julio Iglesias, whose voice I love. I listened to his records all the time, thought he was extremely handsome, and kept his calendar resting on the fireplace mantel in my bedroom.

Throughout the show, Brooke whispered excitedly in my ear, "La Toya, Julio is staring at you."

"No, he isn't." If she said it once, she said it a dozen times that night. I wondered if Michael had told her how much I liked Julio, because she seemed to do it just to bother me. If so, she was succeeding.

Then there was Michael's behavior. It was one of those times when I wanted to kick my brother in the behind. Every few minutes he whipped out a mirror and stared at himself in it, twirling his curls and cocking his head to check every conceivable angle. After the twentieth time, I leaned close and threatened, "If you take that thing out one more time, I'm going to snatch it and throw it under the seat!"

"I've got to look good when I go up on stage," he answered, never taking his eyes from the mirror. "They're going to call me up any minute. How do I look, Brooke?"

"Oh, Michael," she cooed, "you look great!"

I can't believe these two, I thought to myself. Glancing around, I caught Julio Iglesias's eye, and sure enough, he was winking at me! What an evening.

Michael received his awards, and after the ceremony we attended an exclusive party thrown by CBS Records. I was meandering through the room when I heard a loud gasp. "Oh my God! La Toya! Look at you! Look at you!" Before I could react, Julio grabbed me and started kissing me, and I mean really kissing me, not just little pecks on the lips. Everyone was staring as Julio held me at arm's length and exclaimed. "Look at this waist! You're just like a little doll!'' Julio is very physical—too physical for me.

I've got to get away from him, I thought, *but how?* Julio plopped into a chair, pulled me onto his lap, and kept kissing me. I felt like a big baby sitting there. I was really out of my depth, with no idea how to get out gracefully. Moments like this reminded me how little I knew about life. Finally I politely excused myself and slipped away.

Julio soon became a good friend of the family's. Once he came right out and asked Mother, ''What would you think if I married your daughter?''

''Don't even pay attention to him,'' I said, ''he's just kidding.''

''You know, Michael,'' Julio continued seriously, ''one day I could be your brother-in-law.''

Later Michael said to me, ''La Toya, he really likes you. He told me so.''

''Well, whatever you do, Mike, please don't show Julio the picture of him in my room. Please don't.'' I should have known better. My brother escorted Julio into my bedroom the next time he was over, and before long everyone in town seemed to know about my ''crush.'' Which wasn't a crush; I just happened to like Julio's music. I had no interest in a romance with him. Quincy Jones called one day just to tell me he'd purchased Julio's house. ''So,'' he teased, ''does this mean you'll like me as much as you like him?''

We ran into each other some time later in Atlantic City, New Jersey, and once again Julio tried kissing me, but I pressed my lips tightly together. "La Toya," he scolded me in his Spanish accent, "you kiss like a grandmother!" He kept embracing me and touching me in places that I guess are okay for some people, but not for me. But that's just Julio. Finally, thank goodness, the whole business died down.

From this time on, Michael's superstardom attracted more and more women who wanted to exploit him for his position, his money, and what he could do for their career. One of my biggest fears is that my brother will never get to know if a woman really loves him for who he is rather than what he is. This is a problem for all celebrities, but because his experiences with the opposite sex are so limited, I think it's a little tougher for Michael. I've often said that if he ever does marry, it will have to be either to someone equally famous or to someone who's never heard of him.

By then Michael had been in the public eye for a decade and a half, but after *Thriller* the media treated him as if he'd just landed from another planet. He wasn't merely famous, he was a *phenomenon* now, and the repercussions were on a grander scale than anyone could have imagined.

At home the contingent of fans loitering outside the Hayvenhurst gates swelled. Some had been standing there for years; my family and I have literally watched kids grow up in front of our house. I recall one youngster whose mother permitted him to wait for a glimpse of Michael on the condition that he make straight A's in school, which he did. I also remember the young girls who tore off all their clothes and ran around naked, hoping to attract my brothers' attention. If nothing else, it certainly brightened the guards' days.

All the Jacksons love our fans. But not all gawkers and autograph seekers are harmless. Some are unstable, to say the least, and have some pretty bizarre ideas about their relationships to the Jacksons, Michael in particular. One ubiquitous woman told security, "Jesus sent me here for Michael. I belong with him." When she threatened to harm us if not allowed to see my brother, police arrested her and held her overnight. The next day she was back at the gates, pleading, crying, threatening.

While making their regular afternoon rounds, security guards found another woman sleeping on a couch in our home recording studio. Apparently she'd been living there undetected for days, subsisting on sweets and snacks from the adjacent Candy Store. The police carted her off to a detention cell, but the next day—you guessed it—there she was again.

Not long after, Michael and I were watching videos in his bedroom, which is several stories high and has a balcony. Hearing a strange noise, we both glanced up the upper railing to see a figure peering down at us. It was her! As she descended the stairs, we both screamed, bolted to our feet, and ran for the exit in such a panic that we got stuck in the doorway! It was like being in a Keystone Kops movie. Finally we squeezed past, rushed down the hall, locked ourselves in my room, and called security, who came and took her away yet again.

Another morning the entire family was awakened by a heavy *crash!* and ran outside to investigate. We saw a tiny young woman tramping along the perimeter of the swimming pool, shrieking at the top of her lungs, and toppling these solid-marble statues it had taken four brawny men to move into place. When all the statues were lying on their sides, she commenced turning on the gas valves that feed the heating units in the pool, the Jacuzzi, and the gas lamps.

"I'm going to kill all of you!" she screamed hysterically. "Every last one of you!"

My father managed to calm down the woman while waiting for security to arrive. They brought her in the house, and he demanded, "Okay, what's your name? How did you get in here? Why are you doing these things?"

She glared at Joseph, Mother, Michael, Janet, Randy, and me, lifted her skirt, and in a deranged voice declared, "My name is Pussy, and I'm gonna give it to all of you! All of you! And I hate you! Because you're close to Michael!"

"What are you talking about?"

"I hate you!" she said, looking at me. "And I'm gonna make sure you don't live. God's gonna strike you dead!" When I'd heard about enough, I walked out of the room.

We subsequently tightened our security, but even so, you never really stop worrying. What's truly sad is that you grow fearful of all strangers, no matter how nice they seem. One of the scariest incidents for me involved a young man hired to wallpaper a section of my bedroom. He was polite and charming, and while he worked we struck up a casual conversation. It didn't make an impression on me that he took an entire day to complete a relatively small job. *He must be a perfectionist,* I thought. *That's nice.* Nor did it seem odd to me when he wanted to return the next day to reinspect his handiwork.

He came back, again we chatted amiably, he asked for an autographed picture and a recommendation, which I gladly gave him, and he left. The next thing I know, this guy is hanging out by the front gate babbling to the guards that he loves me and that unless they let him see me, he'll kill me! "I know where her room is," he said sinisterly, "I studied it, and I know how to get in there."

Security will keep threats from you as much as they can, but this was deemed serious enough for me to be informed. A chill ran down my spine: *He was right here in my room.* And he'd seemed so . . . normal.

That wasn't the end of it. After pulling my car out of the gate one afternoon, I noticed a red car following me. It was him, shaking his fist and screaming red-faced, "I'm gonna kill you! Because you don't love me! You don't acknowledge me! No girl does that to me and gets away with it! You know I'm madly in love with you!"

My hands shook on the steering wheel, and tears

blurred my vision as I frantically thought about how to lose him. Instead of continuing on to my destination, I headed back for Hayvenhurst. Fortunately, one of the security guards happened to see me racing down the street and opened the gate in time for me to zoom past, then closed it just as the red car screeched to a halt a few feet in front of it.

Whenever something like this happened, or I received a crazed letter from someone claiming to be my husband and the father of my children (news to me!) it further convinced me that I was safer at Hayvenhurst than *out there* in that hostile, dangerous world.

One morning I was alone in the house, sleeping in my room, when I heard a commotion out in the hallway. I ran out to see several security guards wrestling with a man who kept screaming ''La Toya! La Toya!'' and brandishing a knife. I found out later he'd come there on a mission to kill me, because I ''belonged'' to him. It really got to me.

And Michael too. He appreciated his bodyguards, but there were times when he snapped at them in frustration, ''Get off my back! You're too close to me! Give me my space!'' One day my brother decided he couldn't take it anymore. ''That's it!'' he declared. ''No more security. I don't care if I get killed, I'm going a whole week without security.''

''Mike,'' I said, shocked, ''you can't do that!''

''Oh yes I can. You just watch me!''

He set out on his own, driving to the Kingdom Hall, the guys' homes, and a few other safe places—

unaware that our security chief Bill Bray was following him everywhere he went. Michael is not a very good motorist, driving up onto curbs and nearly spinning off freeways, and his week sans security was less than a total success. One time his car broke down a few miles from home. Not knowing what to do, my brother abandoned the vehicle in the middle of the street and ran to a pay phone to call security to pick him up!

Another time several cars full of fans staked Michael out, tailed him down our street, and blocked his car with theirs, forcing him to stop. They jumped out and ran up to him, yelling, "Hi, we just want to touch you and say hello."

"Sure, sure," Michael answered, relieved. He'd been petrified they were a bunch of crazies out to harm him. Not only does he have to worry about harassment from civilians but policemen as well, which I find especially scary. Several times local cops have stopped my brother's car and demanded to see his license and registration—anything to detain him, even though he'd done nothing illegal and there was no question as to his identity. Later we found out from a front-gate regular that one officer had been bragging, "One day I'm gonna pull over Michael Jackson and beat him up!" Why? Because he was Michael Jackson.

Trouble seemed to stalk him. Ironically, my brother's most terrifying encounter was with someone who didn't even know who he was. He and Mother were visiting her mother and stepfather in Alabama, accompanied by Bill Bray. Michael and Bill went driving one afternoon, and stopped at a gas station. While Bill used the restroom, Michael browsed in a small shop next door. When Bill came out, he was surprised to find Michael gone. "Where are you, Joker?" he called out, using his pet name for my brother.

Suddenly he heard "Help! Help!" It was Michael, yelling from inside the store. Bursting through the door, Bill saw my brother curled up on the floor and a white man kicking him viciously in the head and stomach, screaming with blood-curdling venom, "I hate all of you! I hate you!" Over and over he called Michael a nigger.

Bill, a tall, middle-aged black, subdued the attacker and helped up Michael, who was crying and bleeding from several deep cuts. "What's going on?" he demanded.

"He tried to steal a candy bar!" the man claimed, pointing at my brother. "I saw him put something in his pocket!"

"No I didn't!" Michael protested.

"Yes you did."

"Wait a minute," Bill said skeptically. "He doesn't even like candy, and he doesn't steal. Why would he steal a candy bar?"

It was obvious then that Michael's attacker had no idea who he was. As far as he was concerned, this was just another black person—another nigger—to abuse. Bill rushed Michael to a local hospital to have his cuts and bruises tended to.

Mother called us from Alabama to tell us what had happened, and we all cried in anger and sadness. How could this kind of thing still happen? If Bill hadn't been with Michael, he might have been killed. Jermaine was livid, threatening to fly to Alabama and take the law into his own hands. It took some time to persuade him that vigilantism was no way to handle the matter.

Instead, a lawsuit was filed against the store owner. Two girls standing outside had witnessed the beating, and one offered to testify on Michael's behalf. We felt very strongly that racial violence must be stopped, but, unfortunately, justice did not prevail in this case. The racist harbored no regrets. In fact, discovering that the black man he'd assaulted was a celebrity only inflamed his hatred. Now he threatened to *kill* Michael. Bill convinced us that this person was mad, that the threat was quite serious, and that it was better for everyone to drop the action. None of us was happy about this, but there really was no other choice.

Not only did the fans outside the gates make me feel like a prisoner, I felt like a prisoner *within* our own home. Joseph had always eavesdropped on my and my siblings' conversations. Now he listened over the intercom or by way of high-tech bugging devices he'd planted throughout the house.

His temper was as volatile as ever. I lived in total fear of him. If for some reason he and I happened to be home alone together, I got in my car and drove aimlessly for hours. I knew that even armed security guards couldn't have saved me if Joseph ever came after me.

Glancing out Janet's bedroom window one day, I spied a stranger coming through the front gate. I walked down the hall to my parents' room, and asked innocently, "Someone's coming into the yard. Do you know who it is?"

My father looked up from where he sat and burst into an incendiary rage. "Who are you to call the shots around here?"

"I didn't do anything," I replied in the deferential tone I used to placate him, then turned and started back down the hall to the suite containing Janet's and my bedrooms. Joseph stalked angrily behind me, screaming, "I'm the man of the house! Who are you to ask who invited him over? *I* invited him over. And what are you gonna do about it?"

This went on for fifteen minutes. ". . . I'll throw you out the window!" he shouted. "I'll throw you out the window!"

"But all I said was—"

Michael, standing behind Joseph, put a finger to his lips and vigorously shook his head no. Trying to defend oneself to my father was pointless, not to mention dangerous. I stood there absorbing the rest of his insane tirade until, finally exhausted, he left the room. My heart and head were pounding. I was overcome with despair, feeling as if my life were withering away. *Isn't this ever going to stop?* I wondered. *Is this how I'm going to live the rest of my life, as frightened as I was when I was eight? Clutched with fear?*

I didn't know where I would go or what I would do, but I was leaving.

7

MINDING THE FAMILY BUSINESS

My bags were half-packed when Mother walked into my bedroom. Without her saying a word, I knew she was confused and surprised.

"I'm moving out," I said. "I'm leaving."

She looked at me for a moment, then at my suitcases, as if she couldn't believe what she saw. "You can't go, La Toya," my mother pleaded. As she'd done so many times before and would do again, she tried scaring me into staying. "It's dangerous out there. People know who you are. Men will follow you. Someone might kidnap you."

"But I *have* to go. I can't take this anymore," I replied, collecting my things.

Janet, hearing what was going on from her bedroom across the hall, joined in. "La Toya, stay! Don't go!"

I adamantly shook my head no and with a suitcase in each hand started for the door. I was at the threshold when suddenly Joseph's imposing frame blocked my way. "Put those bags down!" he snarled. "Now!"

I don't know where my courage to stand up to him at long last came from. "No!" I said forcefully. "I'm leaving!"

"You come on past me, La Toya," he dared. "Just see if you can get past me."

I might have tried, had he not grabbed my shoulders and shoved me back into the room. How could this be happening to an adult woman? I might as well have been six years old again, getting the switch. I always felt so powerless against him.

"I can't take you anymore!" I screamed. "Don't you see you're ruining everybody's lives?"

My sister, fearing a brutal battering for me any second, clasped my arm, crying, "It's not worth it, La Toya! It's not worth it! Just stay!"

Amid all the shouting came Mother's soothing voice. "Now just sit down and relax," she said. "Just calm down." Joseph, satisfied that the crisis had passed, turned on his heel and sauntered out of the room.

Sitting on my bed, my bags strewn across the white carpet, I sobbed so violently I could barely breathe. Why wouldn't they let me go?

"La Toya, you belong here at home, don't you know that?" Mother continued, as if speaking to a child. "Don't you know you can't leave home?"

I felt like I'd died inside. Just a few feet away from freedom—*All I have to do is walk out that door*—yet I couldn't do it. Joseph's physical threats, Mother's planting fears in my mind, and Janet's pleas all held me back like some supernatural force. They'd let

Jackie and Randy go, and before them Rebbie. Why this irrational hold on me? I knew that no matter where I went or why, if my father wanted me home, he'd find me and drag me back against my will. And it wouldn't be a pretty sight.

Typical of our family, the following morning everyone acted as if nothing had happened, and the episode was never discussed again. Over the next few years variations on this scene were played out whenever I got up the nerve or felt desperate enough, but always with the same result. With each failed attempt I grew sadder and sadder, beginning to feel I might indeed remain at Hayvenhurst for the rest of my life.

Today I look back and reproach myself, *La Toya, you idiot. Why didn't you just leave? You had everything you needed.* But love and fear tore at me until I was paralyzed. It wasn't for several years that I realized I had a right to live my own life and finally saw a way out.

One of the strange things about my family was that nothing our parents did—no matter how much it hurt any of us kids—ever seemed to cast a ripple on the smooth facade of the happy Jacksons. We kept up this front not only for the public but for ourselves. Perhaps it seems contradictory that amid the brutality and humiliation I still treasure many beautiful memories of my family. The fun we shared, the practical joking, the intense closeness, while all genuine and heartfelt, were defenses that enabled us to deny what really went on at home.

Family life continued. Every few weeks one of the guys held a Jackson ritual called Family Day at his house. Usually these get-togethers had a theme, like Jermaine staging a carnival in his backyard, complete with amusements, animals, and games. We all looked forward to Family Day because it meant not only being with our siblings but with our nieces and nephews, too.

You can see my brothers' reaction to our father's cruelty in the love and kindness they shower on their own kids. When one of them became a dad for the first time, I remember him saying to me tearfully, "La Toya, I'm so scared that I'll do to my son what Joseph did to me." I'm happy to say that each treats his children nothing like our father treated us. All my nieces and nephews are well-mannered and just plain good kids, because of love, not beatings; encouragement, not insults.

Now and then I had to repress a tense smile upon overhearing one of my brothers tell his youngsters, "You know, when I was your age, if I did that my father would *kill* me." Because Jackie, Tito, Jermaine, and Marlon are such gentle, patient parents, their sons and daughters can't believe a father would actually strike his child. "Auntie La Toya," they sometimes asked me, "is it true Grandpa hit the guys when they were little?"

I only nodded and quickly changed the subject. Not that hearing the truth would have disillusioned them about Grandpa Joseph. I've learned from other families that the arrival of grandkids sometimes inspires grandfathers to mend severed relationships with their own children. Sadly, that didn't happen in the Jackson family. Until quite recently I don't think my father could even tell you the names of his sixteen grandkids. He'd wanted nothing to do with us as babies and was the same way with them. By contrast, whenever my brothers see an infant—any infant—they practically bowl over one another rushing to cradle it in their arms.

"Let me hold him!"

"No, you've had him long enough."

"Look how cute he is!"

"Yeah, look at the way he laughs!"

Some of my most cherished memories of home center on my mother and the many good times we shared. One day I teasingly told my brothers, "You guys go to Europe all the time, but I'm going to be the first person to take Mother there." It was going to be a special trip, just the two of us together. Before we left, Michael handed me an envelope. "Here," he said, smiling. "Give this to Mother when the plane is up in the air, okay?"

What is it? I wondered. Once airborne, I took the envelope from my bag and handed it to her. "Mother, this is for you from Mike."

"For me?" she asked, surprised. No matter how many gifts her children lavish on her, for Mother each is like the first one. Inside were $10,000 in cash and a piece of paper on which Michael had written the lyrics to one of her favorite songs, "Moon River." As we read the words—"Two drifters off to

see the world, there's such a lot of world to see"—
tears welled in our eyes. By the time we got to Michael's inscription, "Please enjoy yourself. Don't
hesitate to do anything. Just go for it. It's your life,
enjoy it. Love, Michael," we were crying like a
couple of idiots. All the passengers stared at us, and
the flight attendants kept asking if there was something they could do.

"I want the best for Mother," Michael always said,
bestowing upon her gift after extravagant gift. He'd
instruct jewelers coming over to the house, "Bring
the best you have." The two of us would hover over
trays of gold, diamonds, and precious stones, my
brother asking my opinion, then buying what he
wanted for her anyway: usually a big, bright, showy
piece that glittered like a tiny chandelier. "She's going to really love *this!*" he'd exclaim, holding up a
gaudy ring set with an enormous diamond.

"Mike, she's not going to like that ring! That's
something an old lady with no taste would wear."

"I don't care, La Toya, it's the most expensive and
the best, and I want it for Mother. Besides," he'd
sniff, "I know she wants this."

"No she doesn't." My woman's intuition was
usually correct. Mother has never worn any of those
things, though naturally she treasures them. I think
she felt guilty that she wasn't comfortable wearing
them, confiding to me, "It's so big, it's just not me."

The biggest celebration at our house was what we
called Mother's Day, held on a day other than the
traditional second-Sunday-in-May holiday, usually

just after her birthday. We didn't do it every year, preferring to surprise Mother, but each party outdid the previous one.

Our last big Mother's Day was in spring 1984. We spent months getting everything ready, and my job was to drive Mother to the Bistro Garden, an exclusive Beverly Hills restaurant, on time. The tiniest details were planned, down to which streets each of us would take to avoid accidentally passing one another on the way. Jermaine, as usual, assumed command, warning me, "Don't you blow this, La Toya. If she finds out ahead of time, or if something goes wrong, I'll kick your behind."

Joseph, in his inimitable way, nearly spoiled everything. I'd convinced Mother that she and I were going out for an impromptu lunch, just the two of us. But as I urged her to get dressed and get going, my father (who should have been at the Bistro Garden already) kept dropping hints like, "Yep, let me get ready and go to this *restaurant*."

A little while later he said, "Well, I have to go, Kate. Why don't you get ready to go to this restaurant?"

"What restaurant?" she asked.

"Aren't you going to this restaurant?" He was obviously doing his best to ruin her surprise. Anxiously glancing at the clock, I could see we were going to be late. Then Jermaine called.

"Where are you?" he hissed. "We're all here!"

"Jermaine, she's not even dressed," I whispered.

"Why don't you get her dressed? What's wrong?"

"Jermaine, just calm down. I can't force her, can I? Besides, Joseph keeps dropping hints. I think he might have even told her, out of jealousy."

"That Joseph!" Jermaine exclaimed. "I'm gonna kill him."

"Let me go. I'll see you soon."

My father finally left, and I drove my mother to the Bistro Garden. When we walked in, the huge room exploded with dozens of voices shouting, "Surprise!"

"Oh, my God!" Mother said, choking back tears, "I can't believe this!" She cried and dabbed her eyes with a hankie practically the entire day, during which we gave her one surprise after another. Each of us and the grandchildren did something special: wrote a poem, sang a song, made a speech; anything to let Mother know how much we loved her.

Michael sang. Then Jermaine—always having to compete with his brother—announced, "I've got the *best* song for her," and crooned "Dear Mother," bringing her to tears all over again. Whenever she hears Jermaine sing that song, she just breaks down.

Randy made a speech, which he began by saying, "I don't have very much to say—"

"So why didn't you prepare something?" Jermaine shouted from his table, laughing.

"Jermaine, you're so stupid," Randy retorted. "Shut up."

"Anyway, Mother, you know you're the greatest. And I have a very small gift for you." He handed her a box containing a gorgeous three-inch-wide antique pavé diamond bracelet. *Then* we brought out her favorite singer, country star Floyd Cramer, who was so gracious to fly out to L.A. and perform for her. The whole time he sang, she shook her head and repeated, "I don't believe this!"

Before the ice cream and cake, we led Mother outside, where we'd parked her present: a stunning burgundy and beige Rolls-Royce, "gift wrapped" with a giant ribbon that ran up the sides and from front to back, culminating in a colossal white bow on the roof. More tears. Last time we'd given her a Mercedes, so a Rolls seemed the logical progression. "Next time," Jermaine declared, "we'll buy Mother a *ship!*" I have no idea what our mother would do with a ship, but, knowing my brothers, I'll probably find out one day.

Back inside the restaurant, I distracted her for several minutes with a short speech. "Mother, this is the special moment we've all been waiting for. And we just want to say that we all love you, and we appreciate everything you've done for us all our lives . . ." While I spoke, her elderly father, Daddy, slowly made his way across the room to her table. When she turned around and saw him, she cried, "Daddy!" and leapt up to embrace him. They're both extremely sentimental, so the two of them were teary-eyed for the rest of the day, crying with happiness.

The whole time Joseph sat sullenly, smoothing his mustache and remarking snidely, "Well, Kate, they sure love *you.*" I could see in his face that he felt slighted, perhaps hurt. Mother told us that he sometimes said to her, "On Mother's Day this house is packed with so many flowers, it looks like a funeral home. These kids love you, but they don't love me."

None of us ever acknowledges our father's birthday or gives him gifts, a pretty sad commentary on our feelings toward him. It's hard not to feel sorry for him, though. Sometimes when we went out as a family, Joseph arrived by himself, stayed five or ten minutes, then disappeared without saying a word.

One year Jermaine assembled his brothers and said, "Look, you guys, Joseph feels so left out. We've got to do something for him."

"But he doesn't deserve it," someone inevitably replied. "He just doesn't."

"Aw, let's do it," Jackie put in. Despite receiving the worst abuse of anyone, my oldest brother always takes up for Joseph, no matter what. Since then the guys have occasionally taken their father out to dinner, but as opposed to the joyousness of Mother's Day, the atmosphere is tense, the conversation strained. It would be comforting to think that maybe these evenings out made Joseph regret having missed out on the joys of fatherhood, but sorry to say, they didn't.

In the summer of 1984, the Jacksons mounted the largest concert tour in history, named the *Victory* tour after the album that Jackie, Tito, Jermaine, Marlon, Michael, and Randy were recording together.

Since their last tour in 1981, Michael had soared

past his brothers in popularity, leading to wide speculation as to why the world's preeminent entertainer would bother to perform again as part of a group. It almost seemed like an act of charity. The truth of the matter was that Joseph, Mother, and the guys pressured him into it.

My father always made it a point to state publicly that while Michael was indeed a brilliant star on his own, he was better surrounded by his family. The more my brother distanced himself from Joseph professionally and personally, the more obsessed Joseph became with getting Michael back. His motives for staging this "reunion" tour weren't purely sentimental; it truly rankled him that he no longer controlled the guys' careers. Suddenly all the past disputes and dissatisfaction with his management were forgotten, and my father was back in charge as copromoter, with Mother, for which they would receive 15 percent of the net. Just as suddenly, my mother emerged as a force, perhaps the dominant force, in the family business.

From the moment it was announced the previous fall, the *Victory* tour was a headache for everyone. Things could never be like in the old days, when Joseph issued his edicts and everyone obeyed slavishly. Since firing their father and Weisner/DeMann, each of the guys had retained his own managers and advisers, which now complicated things. Michael had Frank Dileo and John Branca; the other brothers and my parents had their own representatives. Plus, springing up like weeds came a cast of would-be promoters, coordinators, advisers, and hangers-on, all jockeying for position with the family. Most were frustrated by the way we do business, discussing matters in meetings and then deciding through a vote, majority rule.

Mistake Number One was Mother and Joseph's decision to bring in flamboyant boxing impresario Don King to run things. We'd interviewed several big-name experienced concert promoters, but somehow my father convinced most of the guys King was right for the job. The self-proclaimed World's Greatest Promoter often came to the house to deliver long-winded monologues extolling his virtues. "I am the best," he'd boast, "the greatest . . ." And on and on. The whole time, Michael and I sat together in the last row of the family theater, staring incredulously at his electroshock hairdo and glittering rings, and muttering under our breaths, "Oh God . . ."

"Now, you should have a *black* person promote you!" King, an imposing presence, bellowed at us like we were little idiots. "Why make all these millions and millions of dollars and give it to the white man?" The dollar signs in his eyes blinded King to the bigger issue, which was the mind-boggling logistics of a tour this size. It wasn't about race or money, it was primarily about crowd control and the guys' security—especially Michael's.

Since *Thriller,* my brother had received untold death threats, one reason he'd opposed the tour from the beginning. "La Toya," he confessed, "I'm so afraid. I know we've gotten threats like this before, but it's different now.'' Little Sean Ono Lennon frequently visited Hayvenhurst, and I don't think there's a celebrity alive who wasn't profoundly affected by John Lennon's 1980 assassination by an obsessed fan. I know the specter of a similar fate preyed on Michael's mind constantly.

We were also concerned about fan safety. While the brothers' audiences are generally orderly, any crowd is potentially dangerous. In 1979 an oversight in basic safety procedures resulted in eleven fans being trampled and smothered to death outside a Who concert in Cincinnati. Knowing that this tour would attract an unusually high percentage of small children made us all extra safety conscious. Another problem we foresaw was overpacked venues. In Kansas City, for example, the official capacity was 45,000, but by the time you included all the friends and relatives of stadium employees and those even peripherally involved with the tour, attendance jumped closer to 60,000. With overcrowding on that scale, it's a miracle there were no disasters.

''We should have a promoter who is competent to handle the job,'' Michael argued, but his cautionary words seemed to fall on deaf ears.

''That's not the point, Mike,'' Joseph said. ''King has the money, and he wants to do the tour. I'm sure it will be fine. And if we're going to give away the money, we *should* give it to a black promoter.''

Jermaine added sourly, ''Besides, you and La Toya team up all the time,'' an increasingly common refrain of his.

"But you don't understand," I interjected. "A lot of things could go wrong, and we need to have the very best person available. There are other good black concert promoters."

"Don King is not even a concert promoter," Michael pointed out. Indeed, since 1974 he had presented some of boxing's most memorable fights, but no concerts. "He doesn't know the music, he doesn't know about the crowds; he knows boxing, and the two are completely different."

"What difference does it make?" Joseph asked irritably, glaring at Michael and me. "A promoter is a promoter. He can fill venues. And that's it!"

Of course, all the managers and lawyers were trying to put bugs in everybody's ears. Dileo and Branca raised the point that King had once been a numbers runner, had served time on a manslaughter conviction, and as a promoter constantly seemed to be fending off charges of financial improprieties. Michael was shocked by what he heard.

"This is why I don't want him involved," he argued one last time, in vain. When the others outvoted us, Michael declared, "Okay, Don King can be the promoter, but I don't want a penny from this tour. I'm going to give it all away to charity."

Don King's involvement wasn't the only thing my brother wanted to avoid. There was also Joseph, whose business acumen hadn't sharpened over time. Michael and I predicted the tour would be plagued by lawsuits, and even before it started, the legal papers started flying. Things were so chaotic that at one point Jermaine had to ask his accountant to find out if the tour was still on! Tito and Jackie complained that there were too many outsiders involved, all vying for power.

When the guys held a press conference at New York City's Tavern on the Green restaurant to formally announce the tour, King did most of the talking, pausing only to show a fifteen-minute documentary—about Don King. Afterward, Michael laid down the law to him, instructing the promoter in no uncertain terms that he was not to speak for him or represent him in any way. King was clearly chagrined.

Though Michael acceded to the tour, there was no way King, Joseph, or anyone could get him to do something he disagreed with artistically. Initially the *Victory* tour was to have included Rebbie, Janet, and me. We each had records scheduled for release either just before, during, or right after the tour, and my father, then managing Janet and me, thought this would be great exposure for us. He asked Michael to allow us to appear as openers and sing one or two songs apiece.

At first our brother said yes, then he changed his mind. "I don't want this to turn into an Osmonds thing," he explained, and I agreed. As much as we loved working together, most of us understood that the nine-member act was intended for family audiences, like the ones we'd drawn in Las Vegas. When Donny Osmond used to visit us, Michael always cautioned him, "You've got to get away from that goody-goody business,'' with the ultra-wholesome Osmond Brothers. ''One day you're going to regret it, because you'll want to be treated as a serious artist, and all the public will remember is, 'Oh, he was one of the goody-goodies.' '' I'm happy that Donny overcame that image in 1989 with his comeback hit ''Soldier of Love,'' but it took him a long time. Michael had been right: artists must seriously consider the images they project at all times.

When Michael delivered his ''no'' verdict, Joseph asked him to compromise and at least allow some of our records to be played during intermission. Again my brother refused, the others going along with him. It didn't matter that much to me one way or the other, but Janet took it personally. One thing about my sister, she can hold a grudge. Over five years later, after one of her albums became a hit, Jermaine asked her to open for him on the solo tour he was planning. Seeing as how his and the brothers' 1989 album *2300 Jackson Street* sold only moderately, Janet couldn't believe Jermaine's nerve.

''He hasn't had a hit in years, and he wants me to open for him!'' she complained to me.

''What did you tell him?''

My sister laughed wickedly. ''What do you think I told him? Remember the *Victory* tour, La Toya? Remember 'No, the girls can't perform one or two songs'? Remember 'No, we won't play the girls' records during intermission'? Well, I don't forget so easily, and I told Jermaine I wasn't going to do it.''

The *Victory* tour prompted some bitterness among

my brothers as well. While they were plotting out the show, Jermaine accused Michael of trying to dictate to him, when all he'd done was to suggest material for his older brother's solo segment. No one knows how to please an audience better than Michael, and he told Jermaine he felt certain songs would go over better than others, sincerely wanting him to do well. But Jermaine didn't believe that, confiding to me, "He wants me to look bad."

"No, he doesn't. You know that's not true."

"Yes, it is," Jermaine insisted in his thick voice. "You don't know Michael. He's a snake."

"Jermaine, he's only looking out for you and the entire group. He's not doing anything underhanded. He wants everyone to look good."

Predictably, the tune Michael suggested reaped the loudest applause every show, but Jermaine always had to compete, right down to his clothes. "When I go out there, I'm dressed better than all of them," he boasted. "And when this tour is over, I'm going to do a solo tour, and I'll draw more people."

What makes him think these things? I wondered. Based on his recent track record, there was no basis for such optimism. But that's Jermaine, who could certainly learn a lesson in humility from Michael. Whenever Michael was about to release a new album, he'd play me a track and ask anxiously, "What do you think? Do you like it?" Jermaine, by contrast, used to hand me his new record with a smug "Here's your prize!" then strut around the room, crowing, "It's a smash! It's going straight to the top! Just you watch!"

As the tour's projected summer kickoff date approached, the press teemed with stories about behind-thescenes friction and intrigue. After years of grumbling privately about the media's portrayal of her family, Mother decided to do something about it. She called her first press conference right outside our gates and spoke her mind, reconfirming that Don King and Joseph, both standing by her side, were still in charge. Funny, at that moment, *she* appeared to be the one in control.

In an interview with *Jet* magazine, she additionally pledged that black promoters would be used, appeasing the Reverend Al Sharpton, then a little-known black activist (some would say agitator) from New York, who'd threatened a boycott of the Jacksons' shows. Michael later called his own press conference to announce a change in the highly criticized ticket-sales policy that originally made the thirty-dollar seats available only in blocks of four. Clearly, with time running out, everyone was under a great deal of stress.

Amid the storm swirling around them, my brothers worked furiously to make everything perfect. Tito ran the band rehearsals; Michael, Jackie, and Marlon took care of the choreography; Randy was in charge of sound; Marlon oversaw the pyrotechnics; Michael designed the stage sets and overall concept; and Jermaine, Tito, and Jackie hired armies of personnel. At the same time, they were wrapping up the *Victory* album and preparing for about five months on the road.

Even before the tour's start, there were omens that the problems had only begun. First, Epic Records forbade Jermaine's new label, Arista, from releasing "Tell Me I'm Not Dreamin' (Too Good to Be True)," a duet he'd recorded with Michael. Jermaine was extremely upset, believing the single would have gone to Number One. Given the immense media coverage the *Victory* tour received throughout 1984, for a change he may have been right.

Then Jackie injured his leg. A "sporting accident" is how it was reported. Not quite. What really happened is that Enid accidentally ran him over with their car, pinning my brother against a fence and fracturing a leg! Jackie had to be hospitalized and used crutches for the next five months. Though he couldn't perform, he accompanied the group on the tour's final dates, hobbling on stage and waving to the crowd. Otherwise he stood with me in the wings, the proudest older brother in the world. "God, they're *ba-aaad*, aren't they, La Toya?" he'd exclaim. "They're really great!"

When the *Victory* tour opened on July 6 at Kansas City's Arrowhead Stadium, all problems were forgotten. Michael had really outdone himself with the staging. From the moment the lights dimmed and a firestorm of lasers, smoke, and thunder enveloped the stage, until the final note of "Shake Your Body (Down to the Ground)" faded into the night air, the audience was mesmerized.

The show opened with Randy portraying an Arthurian hero, freeing a sword from a mighty stone as a sonorous voice intoned, "Arise, all the world and behold the kingdom!" Seconds later the five materialized at the top of a gigantic staircase, backlit in brilliant white light. Looking invincible, godlike, they marched down the steps in unison, their thunderous footsteps reverberating throughout the stadium. The crowd howled deliriously as they made their way to the front of the stage, then broke into a frenetic "Wanna Be Startin' Something."

Every time I see the guys perform I'm always amazed, and the *Victory* tour was no exception. You have to remember that to me they're just my brothers. But when I watch them from the side of the stage, I realize how truly magnificent and uniquely talented they are. Sometimes I wish everyone could stand mere feet from them during a show. From that fantastic vantage point you can see the force behind every gesture, every glance, every note. Each time they spin, you actually hear and feel the *whoosh* of air and see showers of sweat swirl around them. Onstage my brothers are more than entertainers; they're a force of nature, full of a power and beauty that's hard to describe.

Throughout the show, the fans responded as a single entity, screaming every time Michael moonwalked, gasping at a laser's flash or a smoke bomb's resounding *ka-boom!,* and shrieking whenever one of the guys spoke. It was so wild! But the music is always what matters most, and they kept the crowd roaring throughout an hour-and-a-half set that included "I Want You Back," "Billie Jean," "Beat It," "Lovely One," "Heartbreak Hotel," "Thriller," "Working Day and Night," an a cappella "I'll Be There," "Human Nature," and "She's Out of My Life." Several writers pointed out that the only lull fell during Jermaine's solo numbers, but fans loved those, too.

It was so exciting to watch, and yet so sad, because I knew this would probably be their last tour together. Despite Michael's best efforts to be just one of the guys, he couldn't help but be the star. The public made sure of that. As far as Michael was concerned, though, Randy was the true star, and he said so all the time. My youngest brother's feet still gave him trouble from his car accident four years earlier, but he insisted on taking Jackie's place. Randy felt it was important that the fans see the brothers in the classic Jackson 5 formation, with Tito and Jermaine flanking the other three.

Each night Randy threw himself into playing percussion and keyboards, singing, and dancing, limping offstage following the final encore and moaning, "God, my feet are killing me." But after soaking them and resting, he was always ready for the next evening's show.

When the *Victory* tour ended that December at Los Angeles's Dodger Stadium, it was the highest-grossing concert tour in history. Michael stated afterward that he will never tour with the brothers again; whether that's true or not, no one can say.

Unfortunately, while the *Victory* tour was fantastic for bringing the Jacksons back together, it had its drawbacks too. Michael's fears about death threats proved well-founded; in one city police found a man armed with a live bomb and two front-row tickets. And his concerns about Joseph's involvement also turned out to be justified.

While it was fairly well known that the *Victory* tour would be Michael's swan song onstage with his brothers, neither fans nor the family suspected that Marlon planned to quit the group at its conclusion. So close in age to Michael, he'd never fully eluded the obvious comparisons. Like all the brothers, Marlon is a talented singer and songwriter, and it was only natural that he wanted to prove himself on his own.

Still, when he made his announcement at a family meeting, Michael was stunned. "Why are you breaking away?" he asked.

Marlon was candid. "I don't want to be part of it anymore. I want to have my own success, be my own entertainer."

Everyone understood, but we all felt the loss. For the first time there were fewer than five Jacksons to go onstage: just Jackie, Tito, Jermaine, and Randy.

Although we wouldn't find out until after the fact, another family member had already made a break: In September, midway through the *Victory* tour, Janet eloped with her longtime beau, James De-Barge, of the popular Motown family act bearing his last name. Before James, Marty, El, Randy, and sister Bunny formed DeBarge, their brothers Bobby and Tommy had been in a funk group called Switch, which Jermaine managed and produced. My older brother, in fact, helped DeBarge get a contract with Motown in 1981.

The DeBarge family had much in common with the Jacksons. They too hailed from the Midwest—Grand Rapids, Michigan—and the ten children were raised strictly. Janet and James had known each other for several years, but their elopement shocked my entire family. No wonder: they found out about it through the media!

In those years Janet and I were quite close. I was the only family member she contacted beforehand. I was traveling with the guys when she called me from back home to say she was flying to Grand Rapids that night. Then she told me why.

"Jan, don't do it," I said.

"La Toya, I have to. But please don't tell anybody."

"Let's talk about it first," I implored. "Are you really sure this is something you want to do?"

"It's something I *have* to do." There was no dissuading her.

"Okay, then, I won't tell," I promised, and I didn't. Upon learning of the secret marriage, the brothers were quite upset. One of them muttered protectively, "One wrong move from James, and he's had it!"

Janet was only eighteen and James twenty-one, so in many ways it was a typical Jackson marriage, except that soon the newlyweds were living at Hayven-hurst. James was kind and generous, but insecure. He and his siblings were not as sheltered as we'd been from the destructive influences that permeate the music business.

From the beginning, I suspected, correctly, that he had a drug problem. Although Janet pretended everything was okay between them, we all noticed that James acted peculiarly. Janet sometimes had to cruise dangerous areas of Los Angeles looking for him. One night after she returned from rescuing her husband, Michael pressed her for details.

"What was it like? Aren't you scared going out at four A.M. looking for him?" We were genuinely fascinated, because James's coming to live with us made my brother and me truly realize how removed we were from many of life's harsh realities.

"You see all kinds of people doing all kinds of things," was all Janet would say.

Our sister was learning about "real life" the hard way, which she didn't deserve. Like any wife, she tried to protect James by denying his problem, no longer confiding in me because she knew I knew the truth. Still my heart went out to her. At night I'd be awakened by James's screams from across the suite: "I can't help it! I can't help it! I have to have it!"

"No!" Janet shouted back. "No!" Then I'd hear the muffled *crash* of James tripping over furniture and struggling to get up. Sometimes I heard slaps. It was heartbreaking.

Many times I said to her, "Jan, you know we'll

pay for James to go into treatment. He needs our help.''

''He's *not* on drugs!'' she snapped. ''Don't you ever say that again!''

''Not on drugs, Jan? He's stumbling all over the house, he sleeps all day.''

''If you held a match to his feet,'' Jermaine once said, ''he wouldn't even feel it.''

Janet, stubborn by nature, still refused to admit James had a problem. Yet she was sufficiently embarrassed that she stopped traveling with security guards, not wanting them to see what was happening. The staff kept tabs on James anyway and reported to us about the unsavory characters he entertained whenever we were all out of town.

My parents dealt with an extremely sensitive situation the best way they knew how. Joseph hated James and threatened all the time to throw him out of the house, but Mother always intervened. ''No, Joe, leave him alone. If you say anything to James, I'm afraid Jan will run away with him. Then we won't know where she is or what she's doing. At least this way we know what's happening. If she's out there, and drug dealers come after him . . .'' She sounded so worried. ''It's better for her to be here.''

This was one of the rare times my father backed down, realizing his wife was right. The rest of us offered James support and love, but he refused to enter a treatment program. Janet became not only his wife, but his mother, father, and babysitter. The stress quickly took its toll on the marriage, and after less than a year, the two filed for divorce.

It was very sad, because my sister truly loved James. The press speculated that our family had a hand in separating them, which wasn't true. While Joseph was less than happy with Janet's choice of a husband, he didn't interfere, surprisingly. However, he and some people at Janet's record company did believe her career would benefit if she were single. In the end, professional concerns had nothing to do with the breakup. Things simply didn't work out.

Around the same time, Jackie and Enid were in the throes of a bitter divorce, during which she accused him of all kinds of terrible things. It broke all our hearts to witness his pain, but to tell the truth, we weren't surprised things ended up like they did.

After all the hoopla of the *Victory* tour, come 1985 everyone was relieved to get back to normal life and, for the guys, to take some desperately needed time off. But not Michael. He immediately got involved in what became U.S.A. (United Support of Artists) for Africa, set in motion by Harry Belafonte. Harry, whose lifelong commitment to philanthropic causes is well known, had been deeply moved by the starvation in Africa and wanted to raise money to alleviate it.

Initially he planned to hold a star-studded concert, but Ken Kragen, manager of such artists as Lionel Richie and Kenny Rogers, convinced him to record a special single. Bob Geldof of the Boomtown Rats had recently convened a group of British rock-and-roll idols for this same cause. "Do They Know It's Christmas," released under the moniker Band Aid, raised over $10 million for food and medical supplies.

Ken first approached Lionel, who in turn called Michael. We'd known Lionel since the early seventies when his former group, the Commodores, opened for the Jackson 5. They were a great bunch of guys to be on the road with, always laughing and joking.

Michael excitedly explained the U.S.A. for Africa project to me: "Quincy Jones is gathering a bunch of artists to record this song!" The only problem was that there wasn't yet a song to record.

Lionel came to our house, and after dinner he and Michael retired to my brother's room to write. Five hours later, after midnight, I peeked in on them.

"You guys still up writing? It must be going great!" I said.

"We wrote nothing," Lionel answered sheepishly.

"Nothing?"

"Nope," Michael answered. "Nothing."

The next day it was the same thing.

"You know, you guys, you have to have this song ready," I reminded them.

"Don't worry, La Toya, we're hot, we're cookin' tonight," Lionel said with mock enthusiasm. Michael cracked up. It was the laugh he employs when things aren't going well. Lionel has written so many wonderful songs over the years, but for some reason he was suddenly afflicted with writer's block. After he went home, Michael practically wrote the song himself, knowing it had to be finished the next day. When the two of them presented the demo to Quincy, he exulted, "This is great, Smelly! This is it! This is the song!"

It was the producer's job to "cast" the record. Like Band Aid, this was to be an all-star event. I was surprised, flattered, and honored when Michael told me that Quincy wanted me to be part of "We Are the World," along with Randy, Tito, Marlon, Jackie, and Michael. (Janet and Jermaine were not invited.) Quincy often included me in various projects, like appearing in the video for Frank Sinatra's song "L.A. Is My Lady," where I share a poolside toast with Dean Martin.

When word of the recording session got out, everyone wanted to contribute, but Quincy chose people for very specific parts. On January 28, 1985, right after the American Music Awards ceremony, we all proceeded to the A&M Recording Studio on North LaBrea Avenue, where Quincy and Michael were waiting. It was hard to imagine, but here were all these superstars together with *their* idols: Ray Charles, Bob Dylan, Harry Belafonte, Bob Geldof, Stevie Wonder, Willie Nelson, Billy Joel, Cyndi Lauper, Diana Ross, Tina Turner, the Pointer Sisters, Smokey Robinson, Bruce Springsteen, Dionne Warwick, Hall and Oates, and over two dozen others.

The music had already been recorded, so all that

was left was to teach each of the forty-six partici- pants his or her parts, rehearse, and record. Quincy instructed everyone to check their egos at their door, which we all did—with one glaring exception. But the spirit in the studio was so powerful, not even that person's misbehavior could dampen it. Before we rehearsed, Quincy eloquently reminded us why we were there and informed us of the seriousness of the crisis in Africa. Later that evening two Ethiopian friends of Stevie Wonder's gave personal testimoni- als. One woman spoke in her native tongue of Am- haric, the other in English. Standing in the ''choir's'' front row, with Randy on my right and Marlon, Tito, and Jackie behind me, I was deeply moved.

Before we got down to business, at Michael's be- hest Quincy acknowledged, ''There are going to be a lot of people who are offended because they're not a part of this project. But we can use only so many people. We can't have every entertainer in the world on this album. We have no space. I want you to know that I'm not neglecting anybody, and don't feel neglected if you're not one of those who are singing solos. I think you sing just as well, but we selected only a few people for these parts because we felt that their style fit.''

It was a wonderful, if long, evening. I got to re- ally talk to people I'd spoken to only in passing be- fore, such as Bob Dylan and the Pointer Sisters. I happened to be placed next to Bette Midler. At first she was very quiet, and I wasn't sure what to make of her, but soon she started spouting hilarious wise-

Home in New York. A great city, with tremendous creativity around every corner. (ALBERT FERREIRA/DMI)

The mid-1980s were a time of increasing tension at home, but no outsider would ever have guessed. **ABOVE:** *With Janet and Mother at the American Music Awards in 1986.* (BARRY KING/SYGMA) **BELOW:** *With Joseph at a concert in 1984.* (MARK REINSTEIN/PHOTOREPORTERS)

Recording "We Are the World" in January 1985 was an inspiring experience. I'm standing in the first row, second from the right. Michael is third from the left. (SYGMA)

By the time Michael embarked on the Bad *tour in early 1988, neither of us thought of Hayvenhurst as our home and we soon went our separate ways. (GLOBE PHOTOS)*

It wasn't too long before New York City felt like my real home.
(DANA FINEMAN/SYGMA)

Finally on my own, I believed I was safe and free. Little did I know how desperately my family wanted me back home, nor could I imagine the extremes they would go to. (JOHN CHIASSON/GAMMA-LIAISON)

With my manager, friend, and husband, Jack Gordon. (*JUDY BURSTEIN/PHOTOREPORTERS*)

The furor begins: me with a friendly boa constrictor during a press conference to promote the March 1989 issue of Playboy. (AP/WIDE WORLD PHOTOS)

LEFT: *For an appearance on Bob Hope's Easter special in the Bahamas, I wore the studded top some in my family found shocking. Bob and I turned out to be good friends. I love him very much.* (AP/ WIDE WORLD PHOTOS)

BELOW: *On virtually every program I appeared, "What does your family think?" was the most-asked question. Before long, I—and the world— found out.* (BARRY TALESNICK / RETNA LTD.)

Today's children need all the support and love we can give them. For two and a half years I was a national spokesperson for First Lady Nancy Reagan's Just Say No antidrug program. ABOVE: Left to right: Mrs. Reagan, me, Jack, and Just Say No founder Tom Adams. *(WHITE HOUSE PHOTO)* BELOW: Visiting children in the pediatric AIDS ward at Bronx Lebanon Hospital, New York City. *(JOHN BARRETT/GLOBE PHOTOS)*

Mother, Janet, Rebbie, Donald Trump, and me backstage after my American live debut at Trump's Castle, Atlantic City, March 1988. (JACK GORDON, LA TOYA JACKSON)

ABOVE: *With future New York City Mayor David Dinkins, 1989. (ANTHONY SAVIGNANO/GALELLA LTD.)* LEFT: *Outside the Plaza Athénée Hotel in Paris where in late 1990 I announced plans to visit the troops in Saudi Arabia. During my ten days with our armed forces they impressed me with their courage and dedication. (La Toya was the first entertainer to go to the Gulf. She left Paris on December 18 for Cairo, and entertained troops from December 20 through December 26, bringing Christmas to the troops who could not be home for the holidays.) (AP/WIDE WORLD PHOTOS)*

With Bob Hope during a show in Germany to celebrate the U.S.O.'s fiftieth anniversary, 1990. (JACK GORDON, LA TOYA JACKSON)

ABOVE: *Gay Paris... exciting... wild... fun. I love Paris every moment of every day. Here I am with Grace Jones at Maxim's in 1990.* (ERIC ROBERT/ SYGMA) LEFT: *With Whitney Houston, in New York City after one of her concerts.* (MONROE S. FRED- ERICK II)

ABOVE, LEFT: *Mother, the best friend I now wonder if I ever truly knew.* (SERGE ARNAL/STILLS/RETNA LTD.) ABOVE, RIGHT: *My oldest brothers (left to right): Tito, Jermaine, and Jackie, 1989.* (J. M. SIAUD/STILLS/RETNA LTD.) BELOW: *Jackie with our parents at the BMI Michael Jackson Award ceremony in Beverly Hills, 1990. No one is prouder of Michael and his brothers than Jackie.* (SMEAD, GALELLA LTD.)

For now, only telephone lines and love bridge the miles between my siblings and me. I'll never stop dreaming that one day we can be a real family, together, all of us laughing and talking, loving and understanding, not looking at the past but only to the future. I believe he who dwells on the past has no future. What a wonderful thing it would be if all of us could sit down together in one room and just cry, cry, cry. . . . (ALBERT FERREIRA/DMI)

cracks, and we ended up having a great time together. I was wearing a plain (for me, at least) bright mustard-color blazer with black pants. Several times Bette turned to me and cracked, ''Why are you so dressed? You make me feel like I'm *un*dressed.'' She was wearing a simple jumper, hardly any makeup, and seemed very comfortable just being herself.

Unlike most situations where you get a group of big stars together, there was no drinking or drugs, just people trying to help one another, massaging each other's shoulders (after all, it was late), and inquiring thoughtfully, ''You okay? Can I get you something?'' It was quite remarkable, really.

Although we were there for a serious purpose, between takes everyone had a lot of fun. Stevie Wonder started singing a soulful riff and had us all clapping and shouting, ''Go, Stevie! Get it!'' At one point we all sang Harry Belafonte's hit ''The Banana Boat Song (Day-O).'' No one planned it, we just started singing and clapping, and everyone fell into the groove.

Most of us finished recording by around three A.M., but Michael and the soloists were still at work come sunrise. My brother was very particular about how he wanted each person to sing his or her part, and that took some time. The record was released in early March of 1985 and since then has raised tens of millions to fight world hunger. It was a great honor to be among the artists who helped make a difference for so many. I know that ''We Are the World'' will always have a special place in Michael's heart, vividly demonstrating music's power to help benefit the world.

8

THE OUTSIDER

I begged my mother to come downstairs with me. We were in my hotel suite in Acapulco, Mexico, where I was performing at a music festival along with several top rock and Latin groups. Mother traveled everywhere with me, and I was leaving for the show at a nearby open-air coliseum.

"No, I don't want to go," she said, upset. "I didn't know *he* was coming."

No one knew that Joseph was coming. Though he managed me, my father never attended any of my concerts. Now he'd appeared unannounced in Acapulco, not to see me, I was sure, but to watch another act he managed, the Joe Jackson Dancers.

Mother was devastated. "It's bad enough I'm up here in your suite, and then here he comes, staying in his own suite. We're married, La Toya. That looks so bad. But I can't go down there," she insisted. "People will laugh at me again." She was referring to her husband's very public infidelities. That Joseph! At times like this, my heart went out to Mother. Trying to persuade her further was futile, so I kissed her good-bye and asked her to wish me luck.

The moment I boarded the private bus taking all performers to the show, I was thankful my mother had stayed upstairs.

"Okay, you sit here, and you sit there!" The familiar reedy voice belonged to Joseph's girlfriend Judy, one of several he'd continued keeping since Mother called off the divorce. I took a seat and watched her prance up and down the aisles, ordering dancers, musicians, and technicians around, all the while pretending not to notice me. Once my father climbed on board, though, his mistress made sure to flaunt their affair in my face. It was so sickening that just before the bus pulled away I bolted out the door and started walking briskly back to the hotel, burning with anger.

"What's wrong? What's wrong?" Joseph cried, running after me. As if he didn't know.

"Nothing," I said sharply and continued walking, refusing to look at him.

The minute I got back to the hotel that night, I told Mother, "We're taking the first flight out."

"But why?"

"We just are." Earlier, backstage, I'd confronted one of my father's chief assistants, telling him, "Don't you ever put me in a position like this again! I don't like it. It's disrespectful to me and to Mother. You *know* Mother doesn't like Judy, and yet she's here. We want a flight out tonight."

"But La Toya, there are no flights going out tonight. Besides,'' he appealed, ''what about the Joe Jackson Dancers?''

''I don't care about the Joe Jackson Dancers, and I don't care about Joe Jackson, or anybody except Mother,'' I snapped. ''Mother and I want out of here.''

''All right,'' he said wearily. ''I'll call you first thing tomorrow morning with the flight number.''

''And one other thing: Mother had better not find out Judy's here,'' I said. ''Because if she does, Judy might not live.''

Everyone knew what was going on, yet they all pretended as if nothing were wrong with this picture. It was just like at home. Joseph's subordinates reacted toward him like my siblings and I did, afraid to acknowledge his shameful conduct. At that moment, in Mexico, I hated my father more than ever and pitied my mother. His mistreatment of her compelled me to protect her in a way she'd never protected me.

I wanted to break away from Joseph so badly. But I saw no way out. Not only was he my father, he was legally my manager. Michael's repeated warnings—''La Toya, if you stick with him, you will never get anywhere; you'll be paying off lawsuits the rest of your career''—turned out to be prophetic.

No one can take away from Joseph his early accomplishments with the Jackson 5, but in the mid-1980s, without them or Michael to manage, he was not as successful. The music-business community is surprisingly small, and by now most producers and record-label executives had either clashed with him or had heard Joe Jackson horror stories through the grapevine. Minus a multimillion-selling act, doing business with him just wasn't worth the trouble. This frustrated the careers of his few clients, me included.

In 1984, after I cohosted two segments of the TV music program *Solid Gold,* a businessman named Jack Gordon saw me and contacted Joseph about my taping a pilot for another television music show. Though the series never panned out, Jack began working with my father, overseeing his personal finances and sundry show-business projects. Contrary to my family's recent claims, they liked him right away. He was a frequent guest at our house, sticking around after meetings with Joseph to chat, watch TV, or play games like Tonk or Scrabble with Mother, Michael, Janet, Jackie, and me.

Jack and my father became fast friends, making it all the more surprising that I liked him. He was good-natured and caring. Many people you meet in the entertainment field are self-absorbed, but Jack was different. At Christmastime he handed out toys to needy kids in the poor section of Los Angeles. Until meeting Jack I'd assumed that, with the shining exceptions of my brothers, all men were inherently evil like my father. I began to realize how wrong I was.

Now, I know you may be thinking, Sure sounds like she's ''liking him'' (an expression of mine). Though the media has speculated repeatedly about a romance between us, forget about it. He and I were only friends and are now also manager and artist, nothing more. My family's later claims that he courted me are totally false.

When the *Victory* tour came to New York that summer, I flew in to see my brothers play Madison Square Garden. Jack happened to be in town too and joined my family and me for dinner at the Helmsley Palace. We were having a nice evening, but I kept noticing our security chief Bill Bray staring at Jack suspiciously. With so much money at stake, it was routine procedure to investigate the background of any newcomer involved in the family business. Bill discovered that in 1981 Jack served four and a half months for a bribery conviction in Nevada.

When Bill told us, none of us could believe it. Jack seemed like such a nice, honest guy. No one was more surprised than Joseph, but once he heard the whole story, he decided to stick with Jack. My father reasoned that, for one thing, he hadn't been convicted of committing a violent crime; he'd paid his debt to society; plus there were extenuating circumstances in his arrest and conviction. I'll tell you about that in a moment.

You have to keep in mind that run-ins with the law weren't all that unusual in our industry, famous for its unsavory element. The manager of a multiplatinum rock group is a convicted former drug dealer, and many key executives have been found guilty of tax evasion and all manner of white-collar crimes. It's a hustler's business, with a great deal of money to be made. No matter how neat and clean the business suit, there's occasionally something dirty going on behind the scenes or under the table. In my family's many years in entertainment, we've encountered—and have been ripped off by—several of these swindlers, some whose names you might know. I'm not trying to downplay the seriousness of Jack's situation, I just want to place it in context. My family is in the music business, not the clergy.

In 1978 Jack owned a company seeking to introduce two new slot-machine-type games to Las Vegas casinos. When they failed to win the approval of the three-member Nevada State Gaming Board a day after the trio had assured Jack of a favorable outcome, the matter was brought before the State Gaming Commission. Because the Board didn't sanction the devices, Jack's company could obtain gaming licenses only if all five commissioners voted yes. One dissented, meaning that the machines could not be resubmitted for approval until the following year.

One of Jack's closest friends was a local businessman named Sol Sayegh. Having heard about Jack's striking out with the Gaming Commission, he offered to talk to its chairman, Harry Reid, on Jack's behalf simply as a friend. Sayegh had no interest in the machines. Now a U.S. Senator, Democrat Reid has long been an influential figure in Vegas politics. Both Jack and Sayegh had known the commissioner socially for years. Reid had even been Jack's personal attorney at one point. Jack left a meeting with Reid under the impression that a bribe had been solicited. Panicked and confused, Sayegh and Jack prepared for a meeting with Reid—to which they brought twelve thousand dollars.

Jack, planning to report Reid to the authorities if he actually accepted the bribe, had one of Sayegh's assistants copy down the serial numbers of the 120 hundred-dollar bills. After the two men met the commissioner in his office late one July afternoon, Jack went to another room and returned with the cash-filled envelope.

Within seconds he and Sayegh were under arrest and handcuffed. Reid, in what he later said was his anger at anyone believing he could be bribed, lunged at Jack and choked him until an FBI agent pulled him off. It appeared Jack had been caught in an FBI sting operation. During the next year's trial, the prosecution played tapes of ambiguous telephone conversations. The case ultimately rested on who the jury believed. Was Reid demanding a bribe as part of a sting? Or were Jack and Sayegh, two men who'd never run afoul of the law before, entrapped?

After studying the court documents and knowing Jack as I do, I believe there was more to this case than initially met the eye. For example, within three months of Sayegh's arraignment, his youngest child, a six-year-old boy named Cary, was abducted, never to be seen again. Over thirteen years after the boy's disappearance, it remains an open case. Because of this tragedy, charges against Sayegh were dismissed.

Jack, however, was convicted on one of three counts of bribery and in 1979 was sentenced to six months in a minimum-security facility. By 1981 he had exhausted his appeals and in January started serving his term. Despite the judge's recommendation that he do time in a local halfway house where inmates are allowed family visits, report to their jobs each day, and are "incarcerated" only at night, Jack was bounced from one federal maximumsecurity facility to another. Over the four and a half months he served, he was imprisoned under conditions usually reserved for mass murderers and hardened violent criminals: solitary confinement and unexplained withdrawal of basic privileges, even including food and medical care.

There were enough other irregularities and mysteries surrounding the trial and all that followed to fill a book. Suffice to say that Jack maintains his innocence.

Coincidentally, while Jack was appealing his case, another Las Vegas man, named *John* Gordon, alleged to have ties to major organized-crime figures, was shot in what authorities deemed an attempted mob rubout. Years later both my family and the media would shamelessly, "conveniently" confuse the two Gordons and suggest a link between Jack and Cary Sayegh's disappearance in their attempts to slander my manager. There is no link. For the record, Vegas authorities never so much as mentioned Jack's name in connection with this crime. That journalists requesting press files on Jack from a major Las Vegas daily also receive clippings on John Gordon only exacerbates the confusion.

Again, my whole family knew about Jack's prison record. It didn't matter to anyone at the time because once we were informed of the details, we believed he'd been framed. More important, he was our friend.

Working for Joseph, Jack couldn't help but notice how we kids had little to do with him. He was mildly appalled. "Why do you treat your father the way you do?" he often asked me. "He's only trying to help you." Joseph's abusiveness was a shameful family secret that I couldn't bear revealing to anyone then, so I always changed the subject. Besides, not knowing much about dysfunctional family dynamics at the time, I still wasn't sure if my siblings and I weren't somehow responsible for his behavior.

Before long my father gave Jack more responsibility in handling my career. In 1985 Jack independently arranged for me to discuss some possible film roles with Sam Weisbord, president of the powerful William Morris Agency. Though the meeting proceeded smoothly, I was nervous about being there. I knew Joseph would explode if he found out, accusing Jack of sneaking behind his back.

Mr. Weisbord, who'd shepherded the careers of stars such as Loretta Young, seemed to like me. "We groomed all those women," he said, pointing to several portraits on the wall, "but you already have what it takes." Then he turned to Jack. "I worked with her father many years ago in connection with the Jackson 5, so I have to warn you, we can work with La Toya only if he is not involved." I'd suspected many people in the industry felt that way about Joseph, but this was the first time I'd actually heard someone say it.

The two men asked that I leave the room so they could confer alone. When Jack emerged from the office, he appeared upset. "What did you talk about?" I wanted to know during the drive back to Encino. According to Jack, Mr. Weisbord said to him, "She's obviously a battered child. I know."

"La Toya," Jack asked intently, "be honest with me. Have you ever been battered or abused?"

"No," I replied.

"Does your father ever beat you?"

"Of course not, Jack. Why would you ask such a thing?"

"He does, La Toya. You're lying to me. Don't lie."

I thought my act was convincing, but Jack didn't buy it.

My fears of what would happen if Joseph learned of our clandestine meeting proved well founded. He got Sam Weisbord on the phone and spewed a series of racial and ethnic slurs before slamming down the receiver. The agent promptly called Jack to say, "I cannot and will not handle La Toya if this is how it's going to be." Once again my father's temper had sabotaged a golden opportunity. Jack, having yet to witness one of Joseph's raging fits, was shocked. "I can't believe your father did that," he said to me, incredulous.

"Forget it, Jack. That's how he is. You have to

listen to me; I don't want to go through this again.''
I tried to make him understand. ''My parents won't
let me live away from home. If you try advancing
my career, it will only blow up in your face. Mother
and Joseph pretend they want me to succeed, but
they really don't. Especially Mother.''

The older I got, the more she treated me like a
little girl, tightening her grip. She'd spent her entire
adult life being a mother; nothing was more important to her. Now that only Michael and I lived at
Hayvenhurst, the prospect of an empty nest must
have gnawed at her. Mother didn't even like for me
to leave the house to go shopping or out to dinner.
''If you go, who'll be here with me?'' she'd ask
plaintively.

Whenever reassured that I wouldn't abandon her
side, my mother used to say, ''You see, La Toya,
some of the others are like Joseph, running around.
But you know that staying with your mother is more
important than going out on dates. You're just like
me.'' How I'd loved to hear her compare us years
before. But not anymore. For the first time I found
myself resenting the way she made me feel that her
happiness, indeed her very life, depended on me.

It reached a point where in Mother's mind we
shared the same identity. Though I was in my late
twenties, she immersed herself in whatever I did. If
I took a college course in French, my mother enrolled in the same class. She still loved nothing better than to pick out my clothes. I truly believe that
she lived vicariously through me. No matter how

much Mother loved us all, she had to have felt some resentment over being a wife at nineteen and the mother of four at twenty-five. Perhaps in her eyes I was the Katherine she might have been were it not for Joseph. I now see that Mother equates love with control. Thus she especially loved me, the faithful daughter who willingly sacrificed my own needs to her happiness.

My mother's involvement in the *Victory* tour and her bitterness over Joseph's ongoing affairs had changed her. The woman I'd known all my life, so sweet and meek, had metamorphosed into a suspicious, petty individual. I understood her mistrust of strangers to a point, but not her sporadic flashes of mean-spiritedness at home.

She now talked about people, including her own children, viciously behind their backs. When Marlon completed his first solo album, *Baby Tonight,* he brought us a bunch of advance copies. My brother had fought hard for his artistic independence and was deservedly proud of the record. I was so excited for him, and as soon as Marlon left the house we put on a tape of the album. "This is very good," I commented, tapping my foot. But my mother snorted, "Marlon can't sing. Why doesn't he just hang it up? He has no talent." With that, she walked over to the cassette deck and shut it off in midsong. But the next time she saw Marlon, she pretended to have loved it. Observing her two-facedness a number of times, I remarked dryly, "Mother, you're really a great actress."

My confusion over her recent behavior only added to the stress of dealing with Joseph. Though still scared to death of him, I started standing up to him more. Something in me was beginning to change, and although I didn't fully realize it then, at last I was taking my first tentative steps toward independence. One afternoon he and I were discussing business over the phone and disagreed about something. The conversation quickly turned heated, and Joseph angrily swore.

"Could you please not use that language when you speak to me?" I never indulge in profanity and am put off by anyone who does.

"What did you say?" he bellowed in astonishment.

"I said, Would you please not curse?"

Click! Within minutes a frantic staffer at his office phoned me to warn, "Your father's very upset with you, and he's on his way home!" I estimated the driving time from Sunset Boulevard to Encino. But over an hour passed, and there was still no sign of him. We began worrying he might have been involved in an accident. When he finally walked in, my father said to me in a surprisingly calm tone, "You know, you're lucky traffic was so bad that I couldn't get to you quick enough."

I knew.

I'd never had a manager other than Joseph, automatically re-signing with him annually for a subsequent one-year term. Once, entertaining fantasies of finding myself someone else, I'd resisted signing my new contract. In my father's mind, however, there was never any question that he would continue handling my career. I stalled as long as I could, but he finally thrust a new contract into my hands and barked, "Sign it!"

"But—"

"Just sign the contract!"

"I haven't even had time to read it!"

"You don't need to read it," he said irritably. "It's a contract."

Here it comes again, I thought, and, predictably, it did: "You just perform," he said, "and leave the business to me." Lately this line had become my father's mantra. I *had* left the business to him, which was why I wanted a new manager!

That contract ran its course, and for over a year after its expiration, Joseph continued managing me. I secretly discussed with Michael how to get out of signing yet another "agreement." "La Toya," he said, "the day you break away from Joseph, everyone will know who you are."

"I don't know if I can, though," I whispered. Michael's downcast expression told me he knew exactly how I felt. Look how long it took him to shake free of Joseph's grip.

Even Mother seemed to realize I had to break away, advising, "Get away from him, he's no good. Get a lawyer." Which I did. Joseph knew I was unhappy, a fact underlined by the flurry of registered-mail letters my attorney sent him stating my refusal to renew the agreement. Yet all during those months, my father came home every evening and acted as if nothing had happened, leaving me to wonder, *Did he get the letters? Did he read them? Should I say something?*

I needn't have worried; he'd received the letters, given them a cursory glance, and ignored them. Whenever he did bring up at home the subject of my re-signing, Mother changed her position. Rather than speak up on my behalf, she simply said, "This is none of my business. I have nothing to do with it." I felt so betrayed.

I was scheduled to jet to Japan for some business negotiations, and Joseph opted not to accompany me, instead appointing Jack to take care of matters. Before we left, I begged Jack to speak to my father for me, which he did. "Let La Toya go, Joe," he said, trying to appeal to his sense of reason. "She's unhappy with you managing her, and you're not doing anything for her career. Let's work something out."

"Oh, she's not happy?" Joseph replied sarcastically. "Okay, I'll tell you what. You can manage her, and we'll split it fifty-fifty. I'll stay out of it completely. You'll have complete control."

I never would have predicted such an outcome. Even though my father wasn't fully out of the picture, I was thrilled. And even though Jack might not have been my first choice for a manager, he was a friend and an ally. It was a decision I could live with.

Jack recounted most of the conversation to me

later when breaking the good news. He did, however, deliberately omit mentioning Joseph's derisive tone when he said, "Oh, I'll let her have her freedom, all right. I'll let you manage her and see how she likes that." My father sincerely believed that with Jack, a relative novice in the music industry, managing me, my career would grind to a halt. This would be my punishment for wanting to leave him.

Departing for the airport the next day, I kissed everyone good-bye. Now, for as long as I could remember, whenever I leaned forward to kiss Joseph, he waved his hand at me and said disdainfully, "Don't kiss me. I don't kiss." On this day, though, he startled me by asking, "Aren't you going to kiss your father good-bye?" I did, stunned, and Jack and I left.

I boarded the plane feeling unshackled for the first time in my life. Although Mother's Jekyll-and-Hyde behavior continued to puzzle me, I couldn't resist thinking that things with my father, even at this late stage, just might change for the better. But I was wrong.

I was in Jack's suite at our Japanese hotel as he was making his daily call to Joseph, to keep him posted on developments. Flipping through a magazine, I overheard Jack say, "But Joe, you promised me I had control and that you were going to stay out of things . . ."

I started crying. I felt like such a fool. I should have known it was too good to be true.

"I own her!" my father shouted into the phone.

"I call all the shots! She's mine, and that's how it's always going to be! I will never let her go!"

All the years of humiliation and pain crested like a wave, sweeping me away. He'd done it again, lying to me and making me feel like a helpless child. Overwhelmed with frustration, anger, depression—you name it—I began punching myself in the arm and wailing, "I don't want to live if I have to be with him! I don't want to live!" I opened Jack's briefcase and took out a bottle of sleeping pills. Just as I got the cap off, Jack came running into the room and slapped the bottle from my hands.

"I can't live like this anymore!" I cried. "I just can't! I just can't! I can't stand this!"

Looking back, I know now that I didn't really want to die. What I wanted was for the constant pain and hurt to stop. I wasn't the only Jackson child to one day decide it was all too much to bear. In fact, at one time or another several of us have considered taking our lives rather than continue living under our father.

Jack eventually calmed me down and immediately called back Joseph. "Joe, you've got to let her go," he pleaded. "Let her have her freedom. If things keep going like this, you're not going to have anyone to manage—because La Toya won't be here. She's so unhappy, she wants to die. Don't you understand what you're doing?"

Apparently the latter remark shook up my father a bit. He thought a moment, then told Jack, "Well, all right. It's still a split, but I'll stay out of it."

* * *

In 1986 I signed a deal with Private Eye Records, a CBS affiliate, and set about finding a producer for my third album. This was the first time I and not my father got to determine who I'd work with. One of the people at my new label, Danny Davis, suggested I meet with Phil Spector, whom he knew quite well.

Of course I was aware of Phil's many million-selling records in the early 1960s for such acts as the Ronettes, the Righteous Brothers, Ike and Tina Turner, and the Crystals, and his unique, symphonic "Wall of Sound" style. He'd also produced the Beatles' *Let It Be* and albums by George Harrison and John Lennon in the 1970s. Since his heyday, though, Phil had recorded only John's widow Yoko Ono, the punk group the Ramones, and one or two others. His taste certainly seemed eclectic, and he was a legend with a capital *L,* so I looked forward to meeting with him.

As Danny and I drove to Phil's house off the Sunset Strip in the Hollywood Hills, he told me how some people found the producer a little bit . . . well, strange. "But you and Phil should get along fine," he assured me. I had no reason to feel apprehensive until Danny pulled onto the circular drive. Bouncing over a couple of speed bumps, we saw several signs warning that the fence was electrified and the premises patrolled by attack dogs and armed guards. One sign that caught my eye read: YOU ARE HERE AT YOUR OWN RISK.

Phil's mansion was an imposing Italian-style

structure that would have made a great horror-movie set. We were greeted by his servant, a tall, expressionless man I'll call Lurch, because it seems to fit. Walking through its portals was like entering a different era. Though it was just early evening, the sun not even about to set, the house's interior was eerily dark, lit, it seemed, only by candles. The decor was antiquated and very European, with lots of garish candelabras, marble tabletops, dusty-looking satin and velvet couches, gilt wood, ancient books, and heavy velvet drapes that hung from the twenty-foot ceiling down to the plush carpet. Everything smelled musty, as if no human had set foot there in years. Piped-in chamber music and Lurch's menacing presence added the finishing creepy touches.

Danny and I sat in the living room for about half an hour. I wondered if Phil was ever coming down to see us, while Danny snacked from a plate of cheese and fruit Lurch had served. When Phil finally arrived, he looked as much an anachronism as his house, dressed in black Cuban-heel Beatle boots, bell-bottom pants, and an overgrown Prince Valiant haircut. It was like he thought it was 1966, not 1986, and that he was still a teenager and not a man in his mid-forties.

Throughout this visit, Phil never took his eyes off me. He boasted that he was working on material for me to record.

"Well, I'd love to hear what you have in mind," I said and gestured toward a black concert grand piano. "Maybe you can play something for me."

"No!" he replied nervously, then just as quickly composed himself. "No, let's get together again. I have a lot of ideas."

"Well, okay." Maybe he was just shy.

As Danny and I drove home, I expressed some reservations. "To be honest, Danny, I found Phil a little bit strange." Again he told me not to worry, that the producer was admittedly eccentric but in no way dangerous. "Okay, Danny, if you say so . . ."

The next day Phil called me at home. "Listen, La Toya," he said intensely, "I want to work with you alone. I don't want anybody from the record company to come. Just you and me, the two of us. We'll get a lot accomplished."

That evening around dusk I drove to his house myself. Lurch greeted me at the door and showed me into the living room. As I sat on a satin couch, I noticed the cheese and fruit from the day before languishing on the same table, untouched and obviously unrefrigerated. Ugh. Lurch left the room and closed the door behind him, which is when I heard the lock go *click!* In the next hour and a half, he returned a dozen or so times to ask politely, "Would you like to use the bathroom?"

What an odd question, I thought. "No thank you, I'm fine." Later I learned that Phil's bathroom had peepholes, through which he spied on guests.

"Would you like something to eat or drink?"

"No. No, thank you." I wandered about the huge room, admiring the furnishings and thumbing through some old books. The one paperback was

about Phil. I paged through it, digesting uneasily
how he regularly kept visitors trapped in his house,
threatened them with guns, and so on. While reading, I had the distinct sensation of someone spying
on me. But how could that be? I was all alone. Then
I happened to glance up at one of the portraits and
noticed holes where the eyes should have been.

Lurch reappeared again. "Gee," I said, "it's getting awfully late. Are you sure Phil is coming down?
We should get started." Finally, a few minutes later,
Phil slipped in through the door. Wordlessly, he
crept toward the sofa, sat down uncomfortably close
next to me, and, staring intently, asked, "Would
you like to go to the Bates Motel?"

"The what? Of course not," I said, laughing. I'd
never seen Alfred Hitchcock's *Psycho*—thank God!—
and had no idea what the Bates Motel was. I thought
he was just trying to be funny. "We're here to work,
Phil," I said, anticipating a punch line. "Why would
I want to go to the Bates Motel?"

Phil wasn't laughing. He wasn't even smiling. And
he seemed to be barely breathing. "I want to take
you to the Bates Motel. I have the key, the key to
room number one. I own the key to the Bates Motel." He held up a motel-room key, and although I
smiled a tight-lipped smile, I realized this was no
joke. He was clearly trying to scare me, and he was
doing a fair job of it.

"What's the matter?" he asked impatiently.
"Haven't you ever seen *Psycho*?"

"No, I haven't."

I got up and walked toward the piano. Phil followed. In a flash he changed personalities, thrusting sheet music into my hands and commanding, *"Sing!"* while he banged out a discordant "melody" I'd never heard before.

"But, Phil, I don't know the melody—"

"Sing!" So I sang, any notes that came into my head, while Phil stamped his foot to keep time and raved at the top of his voice, "We're gonna make good work together! We're gonna be the best team ever! Your fucking brother Michael is nothing! He has no talent! I'll show him! Everything he's done is shit!"

I stopped singing and stared in disbelief as Phil continued his mad tirade. "Your brother, that punk, he's nothing! Nothing! And you: sit down!"

He pulled me down beside him on the piano bench. Phil would start to play an indecipherable tune, *Plonk! Plonk! Plonk!,* then jump up and scream, "I'm sick of you! I'm so sick of you! I'm sick of Michael!" before running out the door and locking it behind him.

How am I going to get out of here? A few minutes later Phil reappeared, now stumbling about and laughing, suddenly an amiable drunk. "How're ya doin'?" he asked, slurring his words and unsteadily negotiating some steps. Then he ran out again, only to return and act like someone else. He did this seven or eight times, assuming a different "personality" with each entrance.

Finally, I'd had enough. "Phil," I said firmly,

"listen to me." He stopped his hysterical laughter and fixed his gaze on me.

"I have to go. I have a meeting," I lied. "I'm expected at nine o'clock, and the people will be worried if I don't show up."

"Oh, didn't I tell you?" he said slyly. "Your meeting's been canceled."

"What?" Of course he was lying.

"They called."

"Who?"

"You don't know?" he asked suspiciously.

"They couldn't have called here. I—I didn't give anyone the number. But it's a very important meeting," I added, my heart pounding in my ears. No luck.

"You're staying here for two weeks straight, and I'm not letting you out of this house!" he said. "You will not leave until we get this album completed. Do you understand me?"

I changed tack. "Yes, Phil. Of course. I'm willing to work just as hard as you. And . . . and I truly believe that you and I will do wonderful things together. But I do have to go."

Now he went from tyrannical to imploring, crying, "You can't leave me! You can't leave, La Toya!"

"But Phil, you know I'm coming back," I said as sweetly as I could.

"No you won't! Once you leave here, you'll never come back. I know you won't . . . That's why I'm not letting you out of here."

"Please, Phil, let me go. Those people I'm to

meet, they know I'm here, and if they have to come get me, they'll never let me come back. They'll interrupt our music. But if you let me go, I can come back. Just let me go for five minutes. I want a hit record more than anything, and I know you're the man who can do it for me."

"You promise?" Now he sounded like a little boy. "You promise you'll come back?"

"Of course I promise."

Finally Phil relented and reluctantly instructed Lurch to let me out. I casually strolled out the door, but once I was clear, I started running as fast as I could. *Please, God,* I thought, *let my keys be in the car,* and luckily they were. I jumped in, locked the doors, and gunned the engine. As I turned to look behind me I saw Phil standing in the doorway, gesturing for me to come back, then shouting to Lurch, "Catch her! Catch her! Close the gate! Don't let her out!"

I floored the gas pedal, speeding through the iron gate just before it closed, then carefully wended down the narrow street. Shaking, I drove to Randy's ex-girlfriend's house, but Julie wasn't home. Now what? I drove to Jack's, but he was out too. Feeling too distraught to drive back to Encino, I circled the block for a while. Passing Jack's place again, this time I saw the lights on. When he answered his door, I collapsed into the foyer.

"What's wrong with you?" he asked, bewildered.

"Just please help me," I gasped, out of breath. "You've got to help me."

"What? What is it, La Toya?"

"Phil Spector." Jack gave me a look that said, "Say no more."

"Okay, call your parents and let them know you're okay. Everything will be all right."

He dialed their number and handed me the receiver. All I could say was, "Don't worry about me; I'm all right," before hanging up.

I had no idea that the minute I escaped from Phil's house, he'd called my parents and started threatening them, screaming at my father, "I know you have her there, and you're not letting her come back to me! She promised she would come back! I'm coming over there to blow your brains out!"

One thing about Joseph: nobody but nobody intimidates him. "You just do that," he huffed. "Because I'm coming up there to blow *your* brains out!"

"Oh yeah? I'll be waiting for you with my Magnum! You just dare come over here!"

As I learned later that night, my call home had come in the middle of this, so naturally my parents assumed that Phil was holding me captive and had forced me to say I was safe. They were immediately alarmed, because Phil pretended to be talking to me, as if I were still there. My father yelled that he'd call the police. What a mess.

After pulling myself together, I drove home. I walked in the door and trudged up the stairs to my room, where I found Mother, Joseph, Michael, and Janet all congregated, worried. When I recounted my bizarre evening, Michael the film buff pointed out, "La Toya, don't you know what the Bates Motel from *Psycho* is? It's where people get murdered!"

"And the cut-out eyes in the painting," Janet noted observantly. "There's a peephole in the movie too!"

Who needed to see *Psycho*? I'd just endured a couple hours with one. The nightmare may have been over, but it remained with me for a long time afterward. For the next month or so I couldn't stay in the house alone or sleep in my room without Janet there and the lights on. I just remember thinking how grateful I was for a change to be safe at home.

9

BREAKING AWAY

As a public figure, you grudgingly accept reading many things about yourself in the press that are far from flattering and some that are downright libelous. But Michael was victimized by the media, particularly the tabloids, more than most celebrities. It seemed like every week there was a new "exposé" about my brother filled with allegations ranging from ridiculous (Michael building a shrine to Elizabeth Taylor) to hurtful (Michael being gay). These rumors—which just by virtue of being published become "the truth" in many readers' minds—upset Michael and our whole family terribly.

For example, where his plastic surgery is concerned, the fact is that my brother was a very handsome young man who simply wanted to improve his looks. I don't understand why any fair-thinking, reasonable person would object to that. Not to mention that while Michael may be a public figure, it's really nobody's business but his own.

But the media developed this fascination with his face. Although we never bought them ourselves, we often found copies of the tabloids lying around the house, left there by workers, I suppose. Mother has always taken anything said or written about her children very personally. I wish I could say that more than twenty years in the spotlight has given us all thick skins against damning press, but there are some things that go too far. When my mother saw alleged pre- and postsurgery photos of Michael, tiny arrows indicating all the rumored procedures, it was too much for her.

She spread out on a table pictures of Michael and with him at her side angrily pointed to each photograph, explaining, "This is when you were going through adolescence and your face was so full and round. Now, this one is from when you first became a vegetarian. See how slim you are and how your cheekbones stand out? Here your skin is darker, because it was summer, but it's lighter in this photo because even I can tell that the flash was too close." She harrumphed bitterly, pounding her fist on the table for emphasis. "Why can't *they* understand that?"

"Mother, the public doesn't know all this," Michael said.

"But it's so unfair. Why are they treating you like this? It's not true, and I'm going to do something about it."

"But what?" Michael asked. "Mother, you know what the lawyers say. These magazines, all they have to do is cover themselves with one little word or phrase. They can print whatever they want, but if they add, 'It's rumored,' or 'It appears,' they're off the hook legally.''

''I know, I know, but . . .''

''Just forget it, Mother,'' I put in, trying to comfort her. ''It's best if we just act like it doesn't exist. We know the truth.''

Yes, but the truth is so elusive sometimes. We began wondering, What *won't* the papers say about Michael or any of us? It was crazy. One of the more bizarre incidents involved the so-called hyperbaric chamber. According to the tabloid wags, Michael slept in one at home, supposedly so that he would live forever. European reporters have their own version: according to them, my brother sleeps in it in order to stay lighter-skinned. That a photograph exists showing Michael lying on a table under a glass dome is sufficient evidence, apparently, to convince the masses it's all true.

In truth, the ''hyperbaric chamber'' was actually a museum display case. Michael was touring a museum, and someone thought it would be funny if he posed in the case. He obliged reluctantly. Who knew it would snowball into this? When the hoopla about the mystery chamber was splashed in all the papers, Michael resignedly said, ''Leave it alone, let them think what they want; they're going to make up rumors anyway.''

Sometimes my family and I suggested that he speak out more publicly and not be so reclusive. My brother's answer to us was always the same: anything he had to say was contained in his songs, and there was nothing he felt compelled to add. He used to give interviews freely, until one national news weekly distorted a comment of his. Michael said he wanted to visit starving children overseas and help them. But the reporter misquoted him in such a way that he seemed to be saying he would *enjoy* watching them starve to death. My brother, angry as I'd ever seen him, vowed, "That's it! No more interviews." And with precious few exceptions, he's kept his word. Since 1983 he's given no more than a handful, so much of what you read purporting to contain direct quotes from Michael Jackson is pure fiction.

Not surprisingly, considering everything that had happened to him in the whirlwind past few years, Michael became more protective of himself and suspicious of people and their motives. He believed, with some justification, that he could never know enough about whom he was dealing with in business and checked them out at every opportunity, even going so far as to snoop through their desks.

I've witnessed firsthand Michael's practice of "rambling," as my maternal grandmother called it, a number of times. Arriving early for an appointment, we're seated in some executive's office. As soon as the secretary closes the door behind her, my brother tiptoes around the desk and deftly opens and shuts the drawers, perusing their contents in mere seconds. "Will you please sit down and stop it?" I hiss at him, but Michael keeps opening, looking and closing, opening, looking and closing. The second he senses a hand on the doorknob—*Zippppp!*—he's back in his seat, pretending to study a painting on the wall.

Once an executive hurried in and joked, "I hope you kept yourselves occupied while you were waiting."

"Yes," I replied deadpan. "Michael went through all the drawers in your office." The man laughed and laughed; he'd never heard anything so funny.

"Oh sure!" he said, lowering himself into his chair, still chuckling. "Like Michael Jackson would be interested in my office! Very funny!" Oh, it was, all right.

My brother once explained to me why he did this: "People always put on a facade when they meet you, La Toya. Looking at the books they read, or seeing what's in their medicine cabinet or in their drawers, are the only ways you can get to know their true personalities. If you want to really know somebody," he theorized, "look in the very bottom of their bedroom drawers, and you'll know everything!"

Michael could never break his rambling habit. In 1986 my maternal stepgrandfather passed away. His wife, my mother's mother, Mama, was living in an Encino nursing home, having suffered a series of debilitating strokes. Except for Joseph, our family flew to Hurtsboro, Alabama, to be with Mother, with the understanding that Michael and I wouldn't go to the funeral. Not that we didn't love Papa dearly, but once when we were very young, the two of us attended a service and for some reason found the experience terrifying.

The morning of the funeral, as everyone filed out of my grandparents' house on their way to the church, Michael solemnly bid each good-bye. "See you later . . . So long, Marlon . . . Bye, Tito . . ." As soon as the last brother was out the door, he slammed it shut, spun around, and exclaimed, "Come on, La Toya, let's go! You take this room, I'll take that room, and we'll work our way back here." Time to ramble.

"What? Michael, I can't believe you!"

"Come on, we don't have much time," he said, glancing at a wall clock. "Funerals don't last long." My brother eagerly eyed all the chests, drawers, and closets in that wonderful old house, full of antiques, knickknacks, and Mama's precious figurines.

"Michael," I repeated, "Papa just *died*."

"That's right, La Toya, and if we don't find his and Mama's things, people are going to help themselves." I wasn't fully comfortable with this logic, but as usual my brother was right. In fact, Mother herself was quite concerned because Papa owned a lot of land and had squirreled away large sums of cash somewhere in the house.

"You've got to dig deep, real deep . . ." Michael buried his hands under the contents of a drawer. "That's where all the good stuff is."

Bill Bray, who stayed behind with us, wanted to search for the money, but Michael cared only about our grandparents' mementoes. What a scene: Michael ripping through drawers, while Bill wandered about, musing aloud where someone would hide their money.

"Forget the money!" Michael yelled impatiently. "We can always get money. There's great, beautiful stuff here. Like this. La Toya, you've got to keep this. It's Mama's." He held up a flowing strand of lustrous pearls. "I'll bet Mama had these when she was really young, and I know she'd want you to have them."

"No." I shook my head. "I can't take things like that, and neither should you, Michael."

"If we don't save these things now, La Toya, we'll never see them again, and you know it," he argued, stuffing his pockets with trinkets, jewelry, and items of sentimental value. I didn't take anything, and now I'm sorry, because other relatives later cleaned out the house. When everyone returned from the funeral, Michael was again his subdued, soft-spoken self. No one would ever have imagined what went on while they were gone.

With the media busy unearthing every tidbit about my brother, it was inevitable they would discover his devotion to the Jehovah's Witness faith. On the *Victory* tour, despite daunting logistics, he'd hired someone whose sole task was to locate a Kingdom Hall in each town so that Michael wouldn't miss a single meeting.

At one stop on the itinerary, he and Mother were late to a meeting. They quietly found seats at the rear of the Hall and settled back to listen to a Witness at the podium exhorting, ". . . I don't want any of you here today to be hypocrites like Michael Jackson, who professes to be a Jehovah's Witness yet performs on a stage for people all over the world!"

As Michael listened tearfully, the man went on, unaware that the object of his disapproval was right there in the Hall. ". . . Do not look up to him! Do not idolize him!" This wasn't just one person's opinion, but was in accordance with the religion's beliefs. An article in the organization's official publication, *Watchtower,* encouraged Witnesses to dispose of any record albums and videotapes they might own that contained "verbal or visual references to witches, demons, or devils," and never to wear "T-shirts or jackets that advertise such performers." This elder wasn't singling out Michael per se, but it still wounded my brother to hear it. After the service, though, he approached the man, shook his hand, and said, "Your speech was very good."

Michael realized by now that his popularity, music, videos, and dancing onstage deeply troubled some members of the faith. That he was drenched in wealth was another mark against him, for Jehovah's Witnesses don't believe in striving for success, as this is a fleeting world. I know I once worried that my fellow Witnesses would judge me materialistic because I preferred wearing natural fabrics to less expensive polyester.

Whatever long-standing reservations these Witnesses held about Michael being a pop idol crystallized the night he won those record-breaking eight honors at the 1984 Grammy Awards. The very next morning one elder issued him an ultimatum that my brother must choose between music and the religion. "What you're doing is wrong," the man declared.

Because Michael diligently studied the Bible, he could usually cite chapter and verse supporting his contention that entertaining people was not wrong. "I'm still living according to the teachings," he pointed out, as he'd done so many times before. "I still go door to door wherever I am, even if I'm on tour. I can't help it if people hang up my poster on their wall or tear my picture out of a magazine. I don't *ask* them to idolize me. I only want them to enjoy my music."

"Then you shouldn't make the posters, Brother Jackson," one of the elders countered.

"Other people make the posters," Michael replied. "I am being idolized, true, but that isn't my fault." Unless he disappeared completely from public view, there was no way to prevent people from adoring him. Truth be told, many Jehovah's Witnesses used to congregate outside the Kingdom Hall hoping to catch a glimpse of Michael Jackson, knowing full well this kind of adulation was forbidden. But then there were those parents who warned their children to stay away from him. This hurt my brother more than anything—though the admonitions usually went unheeded.

Michael did everything humanly possible to demonstrate his dedication to Jehovah. Once when an elder criticized, "Your movements on stage suggest sex; don't do them anymore,'' my brother complied without protest and promptly changed the routine. He also invited an elder on tour to see for himself that he lived in harmony with all the faith's rules, canvassed door to door, and attended all the meetings.

Sometimes it seemed these efforts were in vain. A lover of horror movies since he was little, Michael was extremely proud of the eleven-minute "Thriller" video, a special-effects extravaganza in which he turns into a werewolf and a dancing corpse. To squelch criticism from other Witnesses, it opened with a disclaimer reading, "Due to my strong personal convictions, I wish to stress that this film in no way endorses a belief in the occult." But that did not satisfy critics, who felt it sinful merely to portray demons and other occult figures.

While Michael and Mother always urged me to attend the Kingdom Hall with them, I usually declined. Though I continued to conduct my life within the teachings, as far back as my brother's and my stay in New York while he filmed *The Wiz* in 1977, my attendance had tapered off—grounds for expulsion. Why I stopped going, I couldn't say for sure. I only knew that from the day I was ordered never to speak to my disfellowshipped friend Darles, certain aspects of the faith had troubled me.

For example, the teachings forbid voting in elections because we follow God's law, not man's. Discussing this with me, Michael used to say, "That's fine, except we live on this earth, and man rules it now. So shouldn't we try picking the better man?'' I agreed. This was only one of countless points in which my thinking veered from the faith. I knew that if I raised my doubts at a meeting, the answer I received wouldn't likely be the one I was looking for. So I pretty much stopped going.

The religion had meant so much to me, I didn't know what to do. Eventually Rebbie called and lectured me that I'd better make up my mind and ''stop straddling the fence.'' Straddling the fence? Inside I was the same person, living the same way, respecting the rules, reading the Bible, and believing in God. When you grow up with such deep religious convictions, they become an integral part of you. I certainly didn't feel any less religious just because I didn't attend the Kingdom Hall as often as some people felt I should have.

One day I walked into Janet's room to find Michael crying his eyes out. When I asked him what was wrong, he jumped up, ran into the bathroom, and closed the door. Hearing his muffled sobs, I turned to my sister. ''Jan, what's wrong with him? Why is he crying like that?'' My first thought was that someone was seriously ill or had died.

''I can't tell you, La Toya,'' she answered, then retrieved Michael from the bathroom. After several attempts to get him to explain, he finally broke down and said, ''Okay, I'll tell you what's the matter.'' He drew a deep breath and looked at me sadly.

''La Toya, I . . .'' The words came out in a torrent. ''I can't talk to you ever again.''

"What do you mean?"

"The elders had a big meeting, and they told me never to speak to you because you haven't been coming to the Kingdom Hall. They asked me what I planned to do about it. I said, 'That's La Toya. That's her life.' But they said that if I don't stop talking to you, they'll kick me out of the religion. They said I have to make this decision now."

I was furious. *"I'm* the one who isn't going to the meetings. Why didn't they come to me? It's wrong of them to put this on you. I'm so sorry you have to go through this."

My brother kept crying, then excused himself, saying he needed to go out for a ride and think. He drove to his friend Marlon Brando's house, and they talked. Marlon advised him, "For heaven's sake, Michael, that's your sister. She will always be your sister. If that's the way they're going to do things, you don't need to be part of that. You can always get another religion, but you can never get another sister."

Michael decided to disobey the elders' edict and after that never attended any more meetings. To this day we've never discussed exactly what happened, but I know he subsequently severed his ties to the organization through a formal letter. What made this painful episode even more agonizing was that for a long time I believed Michael might be one of the Remnant, the select 144,000 on the earth today who will be part of the next world.

This crisis was just one of many my brother faced

during this time. He may have been out of the public eye from 1985 to mid-1987, but he was busier than ever. Even when Michael isn't *working,* he's working. Believing time is a precious gift, he doesn't waste a moment.

Mostly he wrote: his autobiography, *Moonwalk,* which took nearly five years to complete, and the songs for *Thriller*'s follow-up, *Bad.* My brother composed and recorded something like three dozen tracks, from which he picked the nine (along with two by other writers) that made up the album.

As you've no doubt gathered, Michael is a perfectionist who demands a lot from himself. How many artists, having created the biggest-selling LP in history, would honestly expect to top it? Michael truly believed he could.

Michael wasn't the only Jackson looking to top *Thriller.* Janet had emerged from her divorce determined to have a hit no matter what it took. Now, my sister had a habit of conducting business calls over her speakerphone, talking so loudly I often had to go across the hall and ask her to keep it down. Right before the release of her third album, I overheard her telling someone she worked with that she knew she was going to be bigger than Michael and that her new record would surpass *Thriller* in sales. I shuddered at her cattiness and told Michael about it. "That's terrible," he said, hurt and confused. "How can she be that way?"

But that's how she was, tremendously competitive. Janet was so threatened by some of the other female artists on her label's roster, she'd often complain to powerful business associates that someone else's record was on the charts and on the radio, and that she didn't like it. Hearing that, all I could think was, *I hope she never turns against me.*

Upon its 1987 release, Michael's *Bad* sold a staggering 15 million copies and became the first album ever to launch five Number One singles: "Bad," "The Way You Make Me Feel," "Dirty Diana," "I Just Can't Stop Loving You," and "Man in the Mirror." Musically and lyrically the record was every bit as accomplished as its predecessor and a phenomenal success by anyone's standards. Anyone, that is, but Michael Jackson. He was deeply disappointed by the album's showing, especially when it won no Grammy Awards. My brother had set himself a near-impossible goal, and in his eyes he'd failed.

But Michael does not accept failure. Rest assured that for his next LP he is working himself to exhaustion trying to write even better songs and put them across with even more conviction—if that's possible. Someday somebody will surpass *Thriller*; I'm betting it will be Michael.

The 100-plus-show *Bad* world tour was scheduled to open in Japan that fall. Before leaving, Michael had to complete several videos, a difficult feat complicated by his reluctance to delegate the smallest detail to anyone else. It was a hectic period, with my brother shuttling between video sets, trying to get everything done perfectly and on time.

Ever since I played a dance-hall girl in "Say Say

Say,'' Michael's guest duet with Paul McCartney, my brother wanted me to appear in several of his videos, including "The Way You Make Me Feel." Michael described the scene for me: "Okay, La Toya, I'm the guy, and you're the girl. At first other guys are after you, fighting over you, and you don't really care. But I'll be the one who gets you."

"Great! It sounds like a lot of fun."

As far as we were concerned, the two of us would merely be playing parts. But Frank Dileo and several other advisers pointed out to Michael that because "The Way You Make Me Feel" has such overtly sexual overtones, and I am his sister, people might read something into it.

"Maybe I shouldn't think about what people are going to say," he said to me, annoyed. "The way I look at it is, you're just playing a character, like in a movie." We'd had a similar discussion three years earlier about the casting of "Thriller." Ultimately my brother couldn't ignore the fact that the media would have sensationalized it. I could just picture leering tabloid headlines like "Are Michael and La Toya Jackson Really *Lovers*?" just below the Elvis sightings and fudge-brownie diets.

As Michael prepared to go on the road, the massive problems of the *Victory* tour threatened to repeat themselves. Although Joseph was completely cut out of his son's business—my brother saw to that—Mother's involvement now increased. Everyone connected with the *Bad* tour feared that if she asked him not to go out of concern for his safety, he wouldn't.

Their worries were well founded. With Michael, anything Mother says, goes.

My brother and the rest of us were saddled with Joseph's financial entanglements. We had no idea he was in such dire straits until Jack Gordon told me, "Call a family meeting. Your father's in real trouble."

"What kind of trouble?" I asked.

"Your father is broke. He has no money."

"What? No money?! That can't be true."

But it was. Among the many people to bilk him was an unscrupulous tax adviser who'd persuaded our father not to pay his taxes directly to Uncle Sam but to make the checks out to *him*. And do you think he forwarded all that money to the government? Of course not. He deposited it in his personal bank accounts. This went on for years, putting Joseph hundreds of thousands of dollars in the hole to the IRS. And that was only the beginning. It was a disaster.

My siblings and I discussed how we could help Joseph. I figured out that the net proceeds from just one of Michael's Japanese concerts could go a long way toward settling that debt. I talked to Mother about approaching Michael, knowing that only she could convince him to help the father he despised. For some reason that I couldn't fathom then, she seemed reluctant to bring up the subject. Another time after she'd promised she would, I walked up to her and Michael.

"Mother, did you . . ." I nodded in Michael's direction.

"Did I what?" she said quickly.

"Did you tell him about Joseph?"

"What about Joseph?" As if she had no idea what I was talking about. And we'd discussed this for the better part of a week!

"*Mother,* you were supposed to ask him about giving Joseph money from a concert."

"For what?"

Michael, meanwhile, kept looking back and forth between us, totally confused.

"Because Joseph needs the money, Mother. You know he's in trouble."

"No, he isn't, La Toya," she reprimanded. "You know he doesn't have money problems." Denial, sad to say, was a hallmark of our family.

"Joseph's in trouble?" my brother asked.

"Yes, Michael. Bad trouble."

"No, he's not," Mother snapped. "Don't listen to her." I then realized my mother had no interest in helping her husband. Why? Because, as she often said, "If Joseph is penniless he'll stay home. As long as he has money, he'll run the streets."

Our attempts to solve his financial problems stretched over many months. At one family meeting Michael not only generously agreed to bail out his father, he proposed a plan that would generate even more money. "I'll give Mother all the merchandising, except the posters," he explained. "This way I won't have to do the date specifically for Joseph, but he'll still be out of trouble." What Michael did, in essence, was to cleverly ensure that our father never received a penny. Instead he gave the considerable proceeds solely to Mother. She now controlled the Jacksons' finances—and by extension, Joseph.

I told Michael that I wanted to give our father ten thousand dollars, just so he'd have some spending money of his own. "Don't, La Toya," he said, "I'll do it," and gifted Joseph the ten thousand dollars, accompanied by a touching note that read, "I want you to know that I love you very much. Michael." Aide Miko Brando delivered it to Joseph's office. After perusing the envelope's contents, my father showed it to Jack, who remarked, "That's a very nice gesture, isn't it, Joe? That's a lot of money."

"Hnh," was the indifferent reply, "he's got plenty of money."

Throughout this crisis, Jack assisted my father, firing his old tax adviser and bringing in a more qualified team that got Joseph's liability reduced substantially. Instead of gratitude, my manager received only Mother's resentment. She disagreed with every one of the new firm's legal suggestions, just to be contrary, and muttered anti-Semetic insults behind Jack's back. As a white man and a Jew, he would never be fully trusted or accepted.

With the end in sight, we held another family meeting. Jack explained that Joseph still needed some additional help in erasing his enormous debt once and for all. Michael spoke up, asking, "Why should I help him again?" Jack, who'd never dealt with my brother in business, was taken aback by his cold tone. "If I help him this time, I'm going to be helping him for the rest of my life. And all he's done is cost me money and misery.''

''But, Michael, he's broke.''

After a moment's silence, my brother said, ''Okay, I'll help him one last time.'' Everyone else also agreed to contribute money to bail out our father, with the understanding that he close his office and get out of the music business forever.

''I'll put him up in a beautiful home, and he can fish and hunt and do whatever he wants,'' Michael offered. ''But he's to close down the office. He can't keep getting into trouble like this. It's got to stop.''

Jack presented the plan to my father, who initially agreed to the conditions. But the day before the final settlement, the two of them were driving to the office when suddenly Joseph bellowed, ''I'm too young to retire! I ain't gonna retire, and they don't tell me how to run my business.'' So my father continued going to work every day. Sometimes he just sat moodily in his private office all day, shades drawn, lights off.

None of us ever challenged him about reneging on the deal. You'd think that after all the trouble he'd caused, one of his nine grown children would have said to him, ''Wait. You agreed to get out of the business.'' But we didn't. We were still afraid.

One time Jackie and I were sitting around the house chatting when security announced over the intercom, ''Mr. Jackson has arrived.''

''Oh my God, Joseph's here!'' my brother exclaimed, jumping to his feet. ''I've gotta go.''

"Where are you going?"

"Home." Each of us thought the same thing: how sad that a grown man should fear his father. "La Toya," he lamented, "I have children of my own, and I'm still afraid of him. I never come over here unless I'm sure he won't be home. I stop out front and ask security if he's here. If they say he's not, I drive in; if they say he is, I turn around and go home."

"Oh, Jackie . . ." I said softly.

"Do you know how I feel?" Jackie's eyes were watery, and his voice broke. "I hate him," he said. "I hate him."

During the late 1980s my career kept me traveling constantly. On one flight I met an attorney who knew First Lady Nancy Reagan. We started talking, and I mentioned how interested I was in child-related issues, especially drug abuse. He told me that he'd inform the First Lady, then launching her "Just Say No" campaign, that I wanted to help in some way.

He was true to his word. A short time later I was invited to the White House, where Mrs. Reagan and I talked for quite some time. It was in October 1987, only days following her mastectomy, so I was surprised that she would see anyone. I found her genuinely concerned about the escalating adolescent drug problem and committed to making a difference. She was very kind as she said, "I can tell that you really care about these children. A lot of people don't. We'll be working together. It will take a lot of your time and a lot of hard work, but it's something we believe in.''

I agreed at once to become a national spokesperson for Just Say No, the national organization of youth clubs that provides educational, recreational, and service activities to encourage a drug-free lifestyle. In that capacity I crisscrossed the country for the next two years, talking to kids about drugs, and recorded the song ''Just Say No.''

My busy schedule kept me away for months at a time. Michael, too, was rarely home. Yet my siblings and I remained close, now speaking on the phone instead of holding family meetings. I don't think a day passed where I didn't talk to at least one of my brothers and sisters.

The nest at Hayvenhurst wasn't empty for long. Michael phoned me from Japan to say Jermaine and Hazel were divorcing after a fourteen-year marriage that had produced three children. We'd seen this coming for a while. Ironically, as much as Jermaine resented Joseph's cheating on Mother and having a ''second family,'' he repeated the same pattern in his own life, having a child out of wedlock with a woman he met one night in a restaurant.

Hazel loved Jermaine so much that she overlooked his infidelity, even offering magnanimously to adopt the baby. This enraged Berry Gordy, who saw his daughter being made a fool. It was, I must admit, a pretty bizarre situation. On our regular Family Days, Jermaine brought along his out-of-wedlock child.

Hazel obviously loved Jermaine enough to try

making the marriage work. As always, my heart went out to the children. And to the child's mother, who, I later found out, had no idea her baby was being cradled in Hazel's arms. Once Jermaine and Hazel's breakup seemed imminent, my parents begged him to come home again. He did, bringing his girlfriend and their new baby, later joined by a second child.

Mother wanted me at Hayvenhurst as well. Every time I called her from the road, which was often, she implored, "La Toya, when are you coming home?" The longer I was away, the more desperate the pleas. It was increasingly apparent to me that she secretly hoped to see my career fail so that I would return to Encino. Then things could go back to the way they'd always been, and we could be together all the time.

Whether or not my father was in cahoots with her, I don't know, but Joseph seemed to be doing his best to hamper me professionally. He'd broken his promise to stay out of my business and still had me under his thumb. Nothing had changed. When I objected to his managing me yet another time, he issued this threat: "Before I let go of you, I will sit on you for five years, and you'll go nowhere! I'll call every radio station in the country and tell them not to play your records! You fool with me, you're messin' with your career. If you don't want me to manage you, *nobody* will know about you, you're history.

"You're the last Jackson," he said, "and I'm not letting you go!"

This was no bluff. My father may not have managed any more mega-selling acts, but his last name still gave him enough industry clout to do everything he claimed. I couldn't believe anyone would do this to their client, much less to their own flesh and blood.

Mother was in the room with us, silent as usual. "Can you believe what he just told me?" I asked her. "Can you believe he would do this?" I appealed to her to take my side against Joseph, just this once. But she stared at me blankly, turned, and walked up the stairs.

Despite the fact that I was a grown woman, my mother grew obsessed with my being away from home so much. In early 1988 my itinerary returned me to Los Angeles for a few days. It was good to be back at Hayvenhurst and especially to see Mother. She'd been acting increasingly odd, but I'd missed her terribly.

Two days before I was to leave, she came into my room and remarked, "La Toya, you look very thin. Why don't you eat?"

It sounded like the kind of thing all mothers say. "No, I'm really not that thin, Mother," I replied. "In fact, if you ask me, I think I'm a little bit fat."

"Well," she offered, "I have some Lasix. Why don't you take some?"

I couldn't believe my ears. Having just claimed I was too thin, why was she offering me this prescription diuretic, or water pill? Lasix is far from harmless, sometimes causing a fatal imbalance of electrolytes and crucial minerals even in healthy people. I know, because as a teenager overly concerned about my weight I'd taken it and on three occasions suffered severe reactions. Mother knew this. She also knew that after the third emergency, doctors had warned me never to ingest it again, or it could kill me.

The side effects were awful: my jaw locked, I couldn't breathe, and paralyzing cramps inched up my body until I felt my heart would stop. One night I was so certain I was going to die that I lay down in Janet's room and begged her, "Please, just watch me." My sister had a recurrent weight problem, and having learned my lesson about Lasix, I remember telling her repeatedly, "Jan, don't worry about how much you weigh. It's not worth this. You're fine the way you are."

My mother returned to my bedroom with a bottle in hand. "You know I can't take those," I said to her. "You know what will happen."

"No, really," she replied, as if she hadn't heard me. "I have a whole bottle of them. I'm only going to throw them away. Here."

She placed several of the small white tablets in my hand. "Here," she repeated.

"But Mother!" Her behavior frightened me. The minute she left the room, closing my door behind her, I phoned Jack. Knowing my medical history, he told my father right away. When Joseph got home, he stormed into my bedroom and demanded, "La Toya, give me those Lasix!" Then he marched down the hallway to Mother's room and threw the pills on her bed.

"Kate, did you give her these?" he demanded.

"No," she said innocently. "I don't know what you're talking about."

"Kate, you know damned well what I'm talking about! Did you give her these?" he asked again.

"No."

"Then where did she get them?"

"I don't have the slightest idea," Mother answered. "I don't know."

"Kate, what are you trying to do? You know what will happen if she takes them. Are you trying to kill your own daughter? Is that what you're trying to do?"

My father called me into the room. In front of Mother, he asked me, "Did she give you these Lasix?"

"Yes," I replied softly.

"La Toya," Mother lied. "*I* gave you those?"

"Mother, you know you did!"

"But La Toya," she said sweetly, "I'm just trying to help you." My mother, the actress.

With that, I left the room, knowing there was no way to reason with her. How could she do this to me? What was she thinking? Was this how she planned to keep me at home? I was so upset, but I was leaving the day after tomorrow. What could possibly happen in one day?

The next afternoon I was home when I heard Joseph snarl, "Where is that Jack Gordon?"

"Wasn't he at the office working with you today?" I asked.

"No, he's not at the office."

"Well, maybe he's at home," I suggested. "Why don't you call his house?"

"He's not home!" My father stepped toward me and, shaking his finger in my face, shouted, "From now on, I want to know every move you make before you make it. Do you understand?" I had no idea what he was referring to but knew better than to ask. After glaring at me a few seconds, he stormed off. As was so often the case with Joseph, his rage seemed to materialize out of the blue. But whereas it was usually directed at his children, I could see that an unsuspecting "outsider" was about to walk into Joseph's trap.

Knowing that Jack was probably on his way over to discuss some business with my father, I notified security at the front gate to warn him to go home. Too late. Jack stepped into the foyer, all smiles. My father was waiting for him in the hallway near his study. Standing behind Joseph, I urgently mouthed, *Go back! Go back!,* but Jack either didn't see me or didn't understand. Then, as Jack approached him, my father pushed him into the room, threw him into a chair, and locked the door.

"What's going on, Joe?" Jack asked, puzzled.

From the hallway, I could hear them tussling, and I feared the worst. My father was so large and strong, especially when enraged. Jack, on the other hand, is of average size and not the physical type. He rose from his chair, but Joseph grabbed him.

"No!" he commanded. "You sit down. I want to talk to you. I want to know every move La Toya makes! I want a daily report! You hear me?"

"But, Joe, Joe," Jack replied, flustered, "I can't do a daily report on her—"

"I want a daily report! And I want *him* to know what goes on too." My father pointed to another man present, an aide I'll call Robert.

"I don't know you," Jack said to Robert, then turned to my father. "I have nothing to say to that man, but I will report to you and tell you everything that I do—like I've always done, Joe."

Listening from the hall, I thought of all the times my father refused to talk to Jack or even see him. Then he couldn't be bothered with the daily reports. And now it was an issue? Something else had to be going on. This was about me and about my parents' refusal to accept that they would not always control me.

Suddenly I heard muffled shouts, Jack screaming, and Mother, in a monotone, saying, "Put him down, Joe. Just put him down. Don't do that." What he'd done was to grab Jack by his collarbone, lift him straight up out of his seat, and then throw him to the floor.

"W-Why did you do that?" Jack asked, gasping for breath.

"What'd you just say to me?" Joseph's furious tone reminded me of the countless nights I listened

to him torment my brothers back in Indiana. Again he picked up my manager by the clavicle and hurled him to the floor. My father was trying to do to Jack what he'd always done to us: provoke you until you got so mad and hurt that you had no choice but to fight back. Then he had an excuse for beating you up but good. As always, his victim was someone smaller.

Jermaine's girlfriend had wandered into the hall. "Oh my God!" she cried. "What are they doing to Jack? This is terrible!"

The door finally opened, and I ran in to find him on his knees, doubled over in pain, crying. He pleaded with my parents, "Please! Don't you understand? I'm just trying to help her. That's all I want to do. She wants to succeed. I'm not trying to hurt or harm her."

Mother looked at him contemptuously. "You're nothing but a big act!" she hissed, then turned to her husband. "Can't you see he's just putting on a big show for us?"

"Leave him alone!" I shouted. "This man has bleeding ulcers; he's not a kid. What are you doing to him?"

Joseph stepped toward me menacingly. "Get out of here."

Ignoring him, I slipped my arms under Jack's elbows, raised him to his feet, and helped him to the door. But before we made it out of the study, my father grabbed me from behind, tearing my hands away from Jack, punched him in the back, and pushed him down into the same chair. As for me, I was picked up by the waist and tossed through the portal like a rag doll. *Wham!* I smacked into the wall, back first, and fell to the floor sobbing. This was a nightmare.

From the hall I heard Mother's voice. "Joseph, don't. You're gonna kill him. You shouldn't do things like that, Joseph." It was like an animal tamer calming a ferocious beast. And just like that, my father stopped. For years he'd dominated her; now it was the other way around. Meanwhile, I sat shaking in the hallway, ashamed of my parents. At that moment, I knew I would never come home again.

Amazingly, just minutes later Joseph acted as if nothing had happened. I'd taken Jack down to the kitchen to give him some water. My father casually joined us at the table, politely inquiring, "Would you like some coffee, Jack? Maybe some cake? Some Seven-Up?"

What he needs, thanks to you, I thought, *is a doctor.* Jack couldn't believe it, but I'd seen this bizarre behavior many times before. Joseph excused himself and strolled out of the kitchen, and I could see in Jack's eyes that he believed my father clinically insane.

When Jermaine got home late that evening, his girlfriend told him everything. "I'm gonna go in there and talk to Mother and Joseph," he said angrily. "I'm getting so tired of this. They treat everyone like children. It's got to stop. What's wrong with them?"

"Jermaine, just forget it. It's over now," Jack said, trying to calm my older brother.

"Didn't you hit him back?" Jermaine asked, still agitated. "You should have hit him back!"

"He's your father, and it's his house. Let's just forget about it."

The next day Jack and I left for a Just Say No function. As Jermaine drove us to the airport, he couldn't stop talking about Joseph's unprovoked attack. "I can't believe he did this," my brother kept saying. "He was totally out of line."

Today Jermaine will deny this, and he and the other guys will claim to have hated Jack from the start. But in fact, at one time or another each remarked to me on what a great job my manager was doing and how they respected his commitment to me. Beginning the morning Jack and I left Los Angeles, however, everything began to change.

10

PLAYBOY

For a sheltered person wanting a crash course in "the real world," there's no better classroom than New York City. I'd spent over a year there recording my fourth album, 1988's *You're Gonna Get Rocked,* and often performed in Europe, so Manhattan was the ideal location. After moving into the Helmsley Palace and then the Waldorf-Astoria Hotel, I eventually settled in a spacious apartment at the Trump Parc, overlooking Central Park.

What a radical change from what I was used to! In Encino, we never saw drug deals, street fights, homeless people curled up on the sidewalk under grimy blankets. Of course, some of these sights are more common now in Los Angeles, too. Living in Manhattan, where these things are as much a part of daily life as blaring car horns and foul-mouthed taxi drivers, really opened my eyes about many things. An unrelenting series of dramas seemed to unfold on every street corner. I found the city frightening yet fascinating.

It took me a long time to fall into New York's fast-paced rhythm. On the sidewalk I felt like a revolving door, getting spun this way and that by the rush of pedestrians. Waiting to order lunch at a delicatessen counter was a lesson in assertiveness training. I quickly learned that if you didn't speak up, you didn't eat.

I was preparing for my American concert debut at Trump's Castle Hotel and Casino in Atlantic City, New Jersey, when Michael came to Manhattan to play Madison Square Garden and to attend the 1988 Grammy Awards ceremony at Radio City Music Hall.

My brother too had moved out of Hayvenhurst— not coincidentally, just days after I left home. The only thing that had held us there, I now see, was each other. Like me, he never formally announced that he was leaving; he just left one day.

Michael bought a sprawling seventeen-hundred-acre ranch in Santa Ynez, just north of Santa Barbara, California. Five years earlier, when we'd shot the video for his and Paul McCartney's "Say Say Say" there, my brother and I stayed in the guest house. I remember him looking around and saying, "I'm going to buy this place and live here someday."

Michael called me from his hotel. I particularly remember this conversation, because he blurted out some things that left me speechless. We got on to talking about our parents, who'd flown in, along with Rebbie, to see him perform.

"I hate Joseph so much," Michael said.

"But why, Mike? You've never felt this way before. I know you dislike Joseph, but I never heard you say, 'I hate him,' or 'I can't stand him.' "

"I *do* hate him, La Toya," he replied with uncharacteristic venom. "Let me ask you a question: If Joseph died tomorrow, would you cry?"

I didn't want to answer, though I knew my honest response would be, No, not at all.

"Mike, it doesn't matter. We should love him, and I do, if only because he's my father. And he's your father too."

"He's not my father!" Michael exclaimed bitterly. It was so strange to hear him talk like that. I thought back to an evening we'd spent at Jane Fonda's house just after she and her famous father had costarred in the film *On Golden Pond*. Her relationship with Henry was strained, to say the least, and it was apparent that it bothered her greatly.

"*On Golden Pond* is really our story," she admitted sadly. "My father and I have no communication. We don't talk to each other, we don't even say hello. I don't know how to say to him, 'Daddy, I love you.' It's very awkward when I'm around him." Michael and I felt so sorry for her, understanding how she felt. Shortly before Henry Fonda died, Michael urged Jane, "Go see your father. Tell him how you feel before it's too late." For obvious reasons, it pained my brother that anyone should go through life distanced from their father.

But on this day in 1988, he wanted none of his own advice, railing against Joseph. "I'll never forget the times he hit Mother,'' he added, ''and I hate him for it!''

The words echoed in my mind: *hit Mother.* Most of my childhood memories were so vivid; why didn't I remember that? ''You're lying,'' I said. ''Joseph may have done a lot of things, but he never hit Mother.''

''But he did!'' Michael insisted. ''I saw it so many times!''

As soon as we hung up, I dialed Rebbie's hotel to ask her if what my brother said was true. I wasn't prepared for her answer. ''Joseph used to hit her *all the time,*'' she said. ''I used to jump on his back and hit him over the head with my shoes to make him stop. Then he'd beat me, too. Don't you remember this? Back in Gary?''

''No . . . I never saw it.'' Or had I?

''Sure you did! They had big fights all the time.''

The next day Jackie called, as he almost always did. I couldn't refrain from mentioning what Michael and Rebbie had told me, and my oldest brother confirmed everything. ''You were too young to remember what Joseph did. But *I* remember.'' Now he came forth with a torrent of anger, the likes of which I'd never heard from him.

''That man is no good,'' Jackie said. ''He's never been a father. I look at him now and know he never cared for any of us. And we're all still afraid of him! Do you know how badly I would feel if I knew my own son was afraid of me? I hate him.''

While I understood Jackie's bitterness, I could

never bring myself to say those words. In my own way, I still loved Joseph, out of respect and wanting things to be the way they should be. Intellectually I knew he didn't love me, but I needed to believe he could. As I'd begun to see, even as an adult, part of you deep inside is always a child, always searching for the love you need.

I remember the first time my father said, "La Toya, I love you." It was over the phone; in *1988,* about thirty years too late. Stunned, I could muster only a hurried "Okay. Good-bye," and hung up the phone.

When I told Janet, she replied, "Oh, he's so full of it. He makes me sick." She went on and on. Michael was as astounded as I was, but skeptical, sneering, "I can't believe it. It's a fine time to tell you now; who does he think he's fooling? Though he says that he's 'changing.' He's around the house now all the time."

Maybe he was changing. But it really didn't matter anymore. Still, Joseph's saying those three words was headline news in the Jackson family. Michael and Janet wanted to know all about it. Michael especially pressed me for details: how he said it, the inflection in his voice, his tone. I must have imitated our father saying, "La Toya, I love you," a dozen times that week.

"How did you feel when he said it?" Michael asked.

"Like . . . it was a lie," I admitted.

If you ask my parents or most of my siblings today, the Jackson family unity began crumbling either the day I left home or when I appeared in *Playboy* magazine. Now I see that our undoing as the perfect family began decades before, its seeds planted and nurtured in Joseph's abuse, Mother's denial, and the lies we all told ourselves and one another so that we could continue being a loving family. Since, in our eyes, Joseph was beyond anyone's control, and Mother was a victim like us, we couldn't confront him or blame her.

What really changed us was this deluge of revelations and my parents' attempts to dismiss them as unimportant. It was another manifestation of the insidious denial my mother and father lived by and passed on to us.

After this rash of outrage, most of my siblings went back to doing what my parents always wanted us to do: excuse and rationalize. There were no confrontations or discussions, no accusations or demands. Because I was the only one who brought it up, the only one to suggest that my parents were accountable for their actions, I would be branded the troublemaker and made an outcast.

While Michael was in New York for his three Madison Square Garden shows, my manager met with his manager. Frank Dileo had assigned Jack the task of keeping Joseph away from the arena, taking seriously my brother's threats not to perform if he spotted his father in the audience. Dileo was extremely concerned that Joe Jackson would worm his way back into Michael's business.

My family had by now turned against Jack, believing he'd taken me away from them. In keeping with our lengthy history of denial, no one wanted to face the truth: that I'd left of my own free will, and gladly.

Dileo assumed Michael's managership in 1984 fully believing his new client was the same mild-mannered, childlike character my brother presented to the world. ''All I have to do,'' he'd boast privately, puffing on his ever-present cigar, ''is wind Michael up, point him in the direction I want him to go, and he does it.'' He soon found out that when it comes to business, no one gives my brother marching orders; it's the other way around. Only Mother can convince Michael to do something against his will.

Dileo didn't understand that not even Joe Jackson controlled my brother anymore. Yet his agenda was to try isolating Michael from the rest of the family (a common manager ploy; in fact, the very one my family accuses Jack of), convinced this would somehow empower him. Suddenly it became increasingly difficult to get calls through to Michael. Security chief Bill Bray, who answered the phone in my brother's hotel rooms, insisted this was for the best.

I still spoke to Mother almost daily; at least once during each conversation, she pleaded, ''La Toya, please come back home.'' Even so, she, Rebbie, and Janet came to see me at Trump's Castle in late March. It was an extravagant production, with an eight-piece band, three backup singers, and four dancers. The days before the opening were a blur of interviews, rehearsals, costume fittings, and so on. I was a little nervous but really looking forward to it. Out from under my father's management, I loved entertaining more than ever and was determined to succeed. I knew this would take time, but that didn't dampen my enthusiasm one bit.

The casino had scheduled a press conference the afternoon of the first show. Mother and Janet, sitting with me in my dressing room, discouraged me from showing up. "Don't go downstairs," my sister said.

"Why not, Jan?"

"Nobody's there," she snapped. I was disappointed and not a little embarrassed.

Then my manager burst into the room. *"Where have you been?"* He was frantic. "You can't keep the press waiting forever. Let's go!"

"You don't have to go down there, La Toya," Mother interjected.

"There are *five hundred people* down there!" Jack replied. "Of course she has to go!"

"Don't do this to my sister!" It was Janet, yelling at Jack. What on earth was she talking about? Don't do *what* to me? Before I could ask, Jack pulled me out of the room by my arm and led me to the large room downstairs where a mob of reporters, photographers, and cameramen were waiting. And there, in front of my microphone, sat my sister Rebbie! As if this were all in her honor! What was going on here?

A thinly veiled attempt on my family's part—no doubt originating with Mother—to sabotage my career, that's what. They knew that missing my own press conference would guarantee no coverage of my show. And no coverage of my show would make it harder to gain exposure and get future bookings. Etcetera. The anticipated outcome: La Toya returns home for good.

The shows went over terrifically, receiving some great reviews, and two more dates were added to accommodate ticket demand. I suppose because I'd been repeatedly described in the press as "quiet," my new image came as a shock. Entering the stage on a black motorcycle amid smoke and lasers, decked out in skin-tight black leather and a rhinestone-studded top, I was certainly the "new" La Toya. Donald and Ivana Trump warmly congratulated me backstage. That made me feel very good, somewhat offsetting my uneasiness over my family's behavior.

I was becoming more outgoing and comfortable in new situations, but I didn't revel in my newfound independence by trying to make up for lost time and rebelling against my moral upbringing. For one thing, I was still extremely withdrawn around the opposite sex, which some men misinterpreted as snobbishness, Eddie Murphy, for one.

We had all known Eddie for years, and several times he invited me out to dinner. I politely refused.

Eddie's incredibly talented, but I was put off by his reputation as a notorious womanizer and confirmed bachelor. In short, he's just not my type. I still believe dating is a very serious thing.

This apparently irritated him to no end, because I heard through the grapevine that he'd told friends he was furious with me. "One day she'll want to work with me," Eddie supposedly said, "and then she'll be sorry." Perhaps I'd inadvertently wounded his king-size ego, but it wasn't as if I'd broken his heart.

A short time later, my manager and I were ringside at the Mike Tyson–Tony Tucker International Boxing Federation heavyweight-title fight in Las Vegas. Jack, a gregarious type, was shmoozing with people from all over, including Eddie, there to cheer on his friend Mike Tyson. From my seat, I saw Jack slip the comic a note. (It's impossible to discuss business at these star-studded events; people pretend to listen while scanning the room for other celebrities they can then rush off to, feigning interest all over again.) Jack, having no idea that America's most bankable box-office attraction harbored a grudge against his client, had scribbled on a slip of paper that I wanted to be in an Eddie Murphy movie.

Following the fight a special presentation was made to Mike Tyson, and Eddie was there on the raised dais with him, standing alongside the champion. During a lull in the ceremony, Eddie unfolded Jack's note and read it, his face suddenly breaking into a lopsided grin. Eddie punched Mike's shoulder to get his attention, pointed at me from the stage and in front of thousands of spectators howled that goofy laugh of his: "Ah-hahahahaha!" He'd look down at the note, up at me, point and rock with laughter. Of course, I had no idea why. I asked Jack, "What did you write in that note?"

"Oh, just that you wanted to be in his next film—"

Mortified, I bolted from my seat and ran back to my room at the hotel.

Later that night I was walking through the lobby when Mike and his entourage passed by. I heard them whisper, "There she is! There she is!" But he pretended not to see me, so I was surprised to pick up the phone several weeks later and hear his soft, boyish voice.

"I've been trying to call you ever since that day I saw you in Las Vegas," he said. It turned out that Mike hadn't ignored me, he was just too shy to introduce himself. "I walked those hotel floors for hours waiting for you to come down. Finally, when I saw you, I got so nervous, I pretended like I didn't know you. I couldn't even say a word, so I walked the opposite way. It's been so hard to get in touch with you. Now I'm glad I did.

"You know," Mike added, "I fell in love with you the first time I saw you . . ."

The two of us struck up a phone friendship, talking for hours at a time. I know there's been a lot written about Mike's alleged violence against women, but I found him sweet and sensitive. Because he was under constant pressure and public scrutiny, he needed someone to confide in. He was casually dating actress Robin Givens then, but never indicated to me it was serious. That's why I was stunned to read about their marriage in early 1988.

A few days later he phoned me long distance from Japan, where he was fighting, and over the next three hours opened his heart to me. The union was already in trouble. "I married Robin because you wouldn't say anything to me, La Toya," he said. "If you had shown just the least bit of interest in me romantically, things would be different."

This kind of talk made me uncomfortable. "Mike, you shouldn't be saying that. You're married."

"But I have to tell you how I truly feel."

"No, Mike. You have to work on your marriage." I thought to myself, *I sound just like Mother advising my brothers.* Robin did not appreciate his calling me, which created a lot of friction, even though we were just friends. It was a bad situation all the way around, and I'd be lying if I said I was surprised that she and Mike divorced less than a year later.

Around this time, I learned that Donald Trump wanted to present Michael at the Atlantic City Convention Center that fall, offering him the biggest payday in entertainment history. For my brother, who loves breaking records, it seemed irresistible. One of the billionaire developer's chief entertainment executives, Tom Cantone, asked Jack and me to act as liaisons between Trump's people and Michael's. When my manager presented the deal's specifics to Frank Dileo, he was interested, dispatching men to the venue to determine if it could support the *Bad* tour's massive lighting and sound equipment.

Yet at the same time, Dileo was playing as hard-to-get as a prom queen on a first date. "I'm going to have to work on Michael, because I've really poisoned him against you," he told Jack cryptically. Why he'd done that, he didn't say. "But he'll come around," Dileo added confidently.

Donald Trump must have wondered what was happening, appealing to me to talk to my brother personally about playing the Convention Center. In one of the rare times I was able to get through to Michael without weaving through a maze of handlers, he sounded surprised by all the confusion. "Of course I'm going to do the date," he said, perplexed. "I thought Frank had taken care of it. I'd love to do this for Trump."

"Well, it's not taken care of at all," I answered.

"Are you sure?"

"Yes, I'm sure."

I could imagine him frowning on the other end. "Okay," he said, "I'll take care of it." Calling back Mr. Trump, I assured him that everything would go as planned.

Not coincidentally, it soon became next to impossible for me to get in touch with my own brother again. Each time I phoned, Bill Bray promised to relay my message, but my brother never returned my call. That wasn't like him at all. Certain that something was wrong, I called Mother, traveling with him, and got her to put him on.

"Mike, I've been trying to reach you for days!" I said, exasperated. "Are you going to do the Trump date or not? Come on! You're really hanging everyone up."

"La Toya, I want to do it," he insisted. "I don't know what the problem is—"

The line went dead, and just minutes later Dileo was on the phone to Jack. "Jack Gordon," he said, "you *know* we were never going to do those Trump dates. You *know* I told you no in the beginning. You *know* Atlantic City is not good for Michael Jackson."

It looked as if the deal was off for good, but I decided to give it one last shot. I soon found that in the process of turning Michael against Jack, Dileo had also helped to poison my already deteriorating relationship with my family.

That summer, my brother was touring Europe. At the same time he was in Hannover, Germany, I was in another German city, just two hours away, to sing on a television show. I called Mother, accompanying Michael as usual, and asked, "Would you please come visit me? I really miss you." When we first talked, she sounded mildly enthusiastic, but as I spoke to her over the course of the day, something changed. Suddenly she was complaining about the distance and the inconvenience.

"But I really want to see you," I said.

"I'll think about it." She sounded so indifferent.

"It's really not very far. I'd just like to spend some time alone with you." Despite her icy manner ever since I'd moved away from home, I missed her so much that I sometimes cried.

"Well, I don't know . . ." She called back later to say she wouldn't be able to see me because "I don't want to miss any of Michael's shows." Having been on the tour since New York City, she'd seen him perform dozens of times already but hadn't seen me in months. "I understand," I said, though I didn't and still don't to this day. As I hung up the receiver, my heart broke.

When Jack couldn't take any more of my moping around, he said, "That's it; we're going to Hannover so you can see your mother and Michael. We'll get this whole Trump business straightened out, and you'll feel better."

We watched Michael's show from the wings. As always he was brilliant, whipping the audience into a frenzy. Afterward, he, Mother, Jack, and I climbed into a car, to return to Michael's hotel. But when Bill Bray saw my manager in the backseat, he pointed at him and shouted, "You! Get out of this car!"

Michael intervened. "It's okay if Jack rides with us," he said. "It's all right."

At the hotel, Mother's behavior was stranger than

ever. She knew all about the apparently aborted Trump deal and kept running interference so that Michael wouldn't get to speak to me alone. Despite her efforts, my brother and I managed to slip away into a bedroom and talk. We didn't discuss business at all, just gossiped, reminisced, and laughed. But Mother came into the room time and again, asking suspiciously, "What are you guys talking about?"

"Oh, nothing," I said, giggling. The two of us were so happy to see each other. My mother, there to spy on her own children, planted herself in a chair.

"Mother," I said at last, "don't you have guests out there you should be with?"

"Yes," Michael agreed, "you should be in the living room."

Reluctantly, she walked out. Not a moment later, Bill burst in. "Well, we gotta go!"

"Oh, come on, Bill," Michael replied. "I haven't seen La Toya in a long time. Let me spend just a little more time."

"No, Joker. You gotta get up early."

"But it's my *sister*—"

"Let's go."

A look of sadness crossed Michael's face. We went into the living room, where I hugged and kissed everyone good-bye. When we got outside, Jack asked me, "So what did he say?"

"About what?"

"The Trump deal?"

I'd been so thrilled to see Michael and Mother that

it had completely slipped my mind. "I didn't even mention it," I replied.

"What? Get up there right now and find out!"

At this point, I could have cared less about the concert, but I knew Mr. Trump needed an answer. So I went back inside and took the elevator to Michael's floor. Wherever he stays, security people line each side of the hallway, so that going to his room is like walking down the aisle at a wedding. I felt so silly saying hello to everyone again when I'd just left five minutes earlier.

I knocked a secret knock, and Bill answered the door. "What do *you* want?" he demanded. I couldn't believe that years ago I'd used to wish this man were my father. How he'd changed.

"I need to see Mike."

"Hi!" My brother's smiling face popped up from behind Bill. "What are you doing back?"

"Mike, I want to ask you something."

We moved away from Bill, but I knew he could still hear us. "Are you going to do this Trump thing or not? Just give me a flat-out answer, because I'm fed up with this."

Michael was quiet for a minute. "La Toya, let me tell you something," he said. "Trump has an ego, and I have an ego, and when two egos get together, it doesn't always work out." It didn't sound like something Michael would say, and I left convinced that wasn't true. I was right. A few weeks later he called me in Atlanta and blurted out the real reason:

"I can't do the Trump dates," he began, "because . . ."

"Why, Mike?"

He lowered his voice. "Don't tell anybody this, but Frank says Jack is tied to a bunch of gangsters, and if just one of them doesn't get paid off, they'll kill *me*. I can't be involved with anything that has to do with that."

A few weeks later my brother phoned and said, "I love you too much to see this happen to you. You have to get away from Jack, La Toya."

"What are you talking about?"

Michael went on to tell me that he and some other members of the family had seen Jack's "criminal record." What they'd seen were the standard documents and court transcripts from his trial, which they'd known about in detail for nearly four years. Someone was obviously misleading Michael, but there was no talking to him. Or any of my other siblings, now all convinced that, as Joseph said, "Jack's got a record as thick as a Bible."

"Aren't you afraid of him?" my brother asked. "Frank said he would kill you." I immediately thought back to Dileo's remark to Jack: "I've really poisoned Michael against you."

I couldn't believe my brother's gullibility when it came to Dileo. In September, Michael played a relatively small (by his standards) Pittsburgh venue for Frank Dileo Day. It was later reported in Frederic Dannen's book *Hit Men* that Dileo had two misdemeanor convictions for bookmaking. Between the

Bad tour and early 1989, their relationship cooled until finally one day my brother phoned his manager and uttered two words into the receiver: "You're fired."

Why this conspiracy against Jack Gordon? Simple. The family line of reasoning went that if they eliminated him, once again, I'd come home. For their campaign to publicly discredit him (and thus embarrass me into firing him) they enlisted their friends in the press. In a *People* magazine feature story about me, a reporter I'd known for many years described my manager as a Svengali. In that article Jack was a "former carnival operator and Las Vegas businessman." In a second, he was something else.

Both pieces depicted my parents as bewildered by Michael's moving out and Janet's severing her management contract with Joseph. My father came across as a misunderstood victim of his heartless children. Not coincidentally, a writer who had contributed to both pieces was soon shopping a proposal for Joseph's autobiography, which he was to coauthor with my father.

Not content merely to slander Jack's reputation, my father began threatening him with bodily harm. "I'll come through these phone lines and strangle your ass, you Jewish bastard! Why don't you meet me at my house, behind closed doors?" The two of us would listen quietly as he ranted, "You're gonna get arrested! You're gonna get arrested! You don't know what's coming. You have no idea what I've got planned for you. It's hanging right over your head. You just wait and see."

My recently declared independence and outspokenness took everyone by surprise. After the release of *You're Gonna Get Rocked,* Janet called to alert me I'd been the subject of several family meetings.

"About what?"

"About your new album cover. Jermaine's called meetings about the way you're dressed." At one of these, I later found out, Marlon defended me, saying, "I'm not attending any more of these meetings. It's ridiculous. Let her live her own life. Why are you guys always trying to control her? Besides, the album's out. It's over and done with."

The controversial article of clothing was a rhinestone-encrusted leather brassiere-style top—provocative, but hardly revealing by today's standards. Still, Jermaine was outraged, as was Mother. You'd have thought they just came off the farm, with no idea of how pop music and a sexy image go hand in hand. "La Toya," Mother cautioned, "you have to be careful about the kind of pictures you take. Be really careful."

I listened, my heart pounding in my chest, as I thought, *Wait until she sees what's coming next.*

I've been asked a million times why I posed for *Playboy* magazine, and I have to confess that I approached the whole thing very naively. Originally I was to be photographed fully clothed, but even then my guilty conscience overwhelmed me, and I backed out of the deal. The funny thing is, I'd never really seen a copy of the magazine. One time I looked at a piece it ran on the Jacksons, but I didn't dare look at any of the pictorials, since reading a magazine like *Playboy* constituted grounds for immediate disfellowship from the Jehovah's Witnesses. Back then I sincerely believed there was something dirty about it, without really knowing why.

Before posing I looked through several issues of the magazine. I knew some of the women who'd posed nude over the years. This impressive list included Sophia Loren and Elizabeth Taylor, both guests at Hayvenhurst and women I admired immensely. Then it just struck me, *What is wrong with appearing in* Playboy? *Why shouldn't I?* I realized that my initial reaction wasn't based on my true feelings, but on what the faith thought, or on what my parents would think. What about what I thought?

This was one of the first times in my life when I made a decision based on what I felt was right for me. My parents' hold spanned thousands of miles, and they were wearing me down with their constant pleas and threats. I'd told them repeatedly that I was on my own at last, yet they persisted in asking when I was coming home to live. What could I do to show them unequivocally that I planned to live my own life? That I couldn't be forced home? That I couldn't be told what to do anymore?

It was one of those crazy things. Had *Playboy* not approached me, I certainly wouldn't have contacted it, and had I not been in that particular state of mind, I undoubtedly would have turned down the offer. The negotiations went on for months under utmost secrecy, with all *Playboy* personnel aware of the planned pictorial having to sign strict confidentiality agreements. You'd have thought the magazine was about to publish vital Pentagon secrets. The project even had its own code name: Toyota. The photo sessions took place in New York in November 1988. When I arrived back in New York, a contingent of people from the magazine met me. Until the moment they spotted me, they had no idea who they were photographing. "You're 'the person'!" one of them gasped.

Because of privacy considerations, *Playboy* rented the entire Neil Simon Theater on Broadway. As I prepared for the shoot, an assistant remarked casually, "We heard that you have your own ideas about how you want the nude poses done."

I gulped. "The what?"

"The nude poses."

"I'm not showing anything," I told him firmly.

For the first two days I held my ground. From the beginning I insisted that everything be done tastefully and artistically. In my mind, that still meant not showing "anything." Poor Stephen Wayda, the photographer, and make-up artist Clint Wheat! I didn't allow any other assistants present, so Steven had to arrange everything, move the lights, and change the scenery himself. Sweat poured off his body the entire time. Unbeknownst to me, *Playboy*'s editors were getting so exasperated with my prudishness that contingency plans were underway to substitute Hugh Hefner's wife-to-be, Kimberley Conrad, for me if necessary. Then a funny thing happened.

Stephen had me pose for the picture that opened the layout, in which I have a finger raised to my pursed lips, as if I'm saying, "Shhhh!" Well, my robe slipped down, exposing a nipple. When I realized it, I thought I would faint on the spot But when Stephen showed me the test Polaroid, I saw it wasn't so bad after all. The third and final day of shooting went very smoothly. I had the most fun posing with the snake, though I was disappointed there was only one. I'd envisioned six or seven.

People don't realize how much hard work goes into photo sessions. To make models look their best, there's a whole range of positions and poses that, um, *enhance* one's appearance. Once the pictures hit the newsstands, Arsenio Hall joked on TV that my breasts weren't real. Sorry, Arsenio. As a matter of fact, my layout was one of the few done without full body makeup or any kind of photo retouching. When I first heard his comments, I considered sending Arsenio X-rays to prove him wrong. But then I decided, Why give him any satisfaction? Besides, in the grand scheme of things, controversy over my breasts' "authenticity" seemed pretty silly. (One good thing to come out of the *Playboy* pictures: speculation that Michael and I were the same person was permanently laid to rest.)

Between the time of the photo session and publication, several months later, I was contractually forbidden to disclose anything about the pictures to anyone, including my own family. I *had* to tell somebody, though, and decided to confide in Janet when she visited me in New York around Christmastime.

"Jan, I'd really like to talk to you," I said. "It's important."

"Well, then start talking," she snapped without looking up from her coloring book. We used to be so close, talking on the phone several times a week, but lately she'd grown as distant as Mother.

"It's personal. Can't we go into another room and talk privately? I hardly ever see you."

"No, we can talk here." There were other people around, so I let it drop, somewhat hurt by her abruptness. Maybe I'd tell her some other time.

Several weeks later I saw the proof sheets from which I was to select the pictures for the layout. When I first laid eyes on them, I thought to myself, *That's not me; that's somebody else,* and felt like I'd just taken a punch to the midsection. Then reality set in: I'd done it. It was over. My family and millions of readers were going to see it and think what they wanted. In my own mind I was satisfied that there was nothing at all wrong with my posing. It was no different from the bare-chested fashion models in *Vogue* magazine, or the nude women I saw on beaches throughout Europe.

Several weeks before the issue hit the stands in late February, I phoned home. As usual, while I talked to Mother, Joseph listened in on the extension. We were having a pleasant conversation for a change, when suddenly he interjected, "Kate, tell her!"

"Tell her what?" Mother asked innocently.

"Tell her, tell her what you heard," he urged.

"I didn't hear anything . . ."

"You know what you heard, Kate!" Joseph said in annoyance. "All right, *I'll* tell her. La Toya, I heard that you posed for the centerfold of *Playboy*. Did you?"

"Of course not," I answered nervously. "I would never do anything like that."

"Okay. You'd better be telling the truth," he said, "because somebody said that they saw some pictures."

"No, I didn't pose for the *centerfold*," I said, which, if you want to get technical, was true.

Janet called later to ask the same question. Again I denied it. Then Michael phoned a few days after that. This was the one I'd been bracing for, because Hugh Hefner had called to let me know that Michael showed up unexpectedly at the Playboy mansion, ostensibly to visit its exotic animals. I'm sure it's no coincidence that a staff meeting about the issue was in progress there at the time.

"Did my sister pose for your magazine?" Michael asked. Hef told me he said he didn't know, perhaps not the most convincing answer from *Playboy*'s publisher. Somehow Michael pirated photocopies of the layout; I know it wasn't from Hef.

When my brother called, I guessed he might know something, but I had no idea he'd actually seen the photos.

We spoke for three whole hours without one mention of the pictures. I couldn't stand it any longer. "I heard you were at Hef's house the other day," I said.

After a moment's silence, Michael replied, "Yeah. How did you know?"

"They told me. What were you doing there?"

"Just visiting."

"Do you want to ask me something, Mike?"

"Uh, no."

"Are you sure?"

"Uh-uh." We were quiet for what seemed like a very long minute, then he said, "I saw your pictures."

"What pictures?"

"*Your* pictures, La Toya."

"You couldn't have!"

"Well, I have them right here. And I'll prove it to you: okay, here you are with the snake . . . and here's one where you have a white terrycloth bathrobe, and you have your finger up to your mouth, like you're saying, 'Shhhhhh' . . ."

"My God, you do have them!"

"Yes," he said, laughing, "and I think they're great! Diana Ross thinks they're great, Frank Dileo thinks they're great—"

"All these people have seen them?!"

"Yeah, Diana thinks they're fabulous. You know,

you're going to sell more copies than any other issue in *Playboy* history.'' That Michael, always concerned with sales records. As usual, he would be proved correct; the issue was the magazine's all-time best-seller. Then Michael got serious.

''La Toya, you have to tell me why you did it. When I used to walk into your bedroom at home, if you were in your bra and teddy, you screamed for Mother and threw things at me. And now you've posed. I think it's great, but I just can't believe you did it. Why?''

''Well . . .''

''Wait! I'm going to tell *you* why you did it.''

''Go ahead, Mike.'' I found this amusing. As perceptive as he is, how could he possibly know?

''Okay,'' he said excitedly, like a detective solving a crime, ''the first reason is, you did it to get back at Joseph, to let him know he can't tell you what to do; to tell him that you're grown now and can make your own decisions.''

My jaw dropped.

''The second reason is that you want to get back at the religion.''

''Oh my God!'' I gasped.

''Now the third reason—I don't know if it's true or not—is that you wanted to get back at Mother too. I hope that one isn't true, La Toya.'' *But it is,* I thought.

''I never told anyone any of this, Mike. How could you know what I was thinking?''

''I know,'' he said, ''because that's why I wrote

'Bad.' And that's why I wiggle the way I do and grab myself in that video and 'The Way You Make Me Feel.' It's to get back at Joseph and the religion, and tell them I can do what I want, and they can't control me. So when I heard you posed for *Playboy,* I knew why you did it. You hated doing it at first, but you knew you had to do it, to show them, to tell them that you're in control from now on. And it will tell them, too. It will set them straight.''

There was never any question in my mind that Michael was rebelling just as I was. From the first line of ''Bad'' or the video for ''Leave Me Alone,'' I'd seen a difference in the persona Michael chose to present to the world. He was more aggressive, no longer the victim. Months after our conversation, when I began thinking a lot about my family, I started interpreting my brother's work the same way he'd interpreted my appearing in *Playboy.* Equipped with words and images, he painted a far more explicit and—to me, at least—painful picture of growing up in the Jackson family.

One of the wonderful things about creativity and self-expression is the escape. I don't think any artist knows exactly where his ideas come from, or why. Sometimes your work transports you; other times it maps familiar terrain. In Michael's case, I can't separate the creation from the creator.

While I believe my brother's videos are some of the best ever made, I'm at a loss to reconcile someone who loves children as much as Michael producing entertainment that so graphically and relentlessly depicts violence. Take, for instance, the "Smooth Criminal" segment of his motion picture *Moonwalker*. I can't watch the scene where the little girl is repeatedly kicked, slapped, and stomped on without cringing. To me, that's not merely effective filmmaking, that's a memory.

In several of Michael's (and my other brothers') videos, intimacy is usually crushed by betrayal, anger, secrecy, or persecution. Pain is always eluded by Michael Jackson becoming invincible, invisible, uncatchable, or unbeatable—every battered child's fantasy. What I find so telling, though, is how in so many of his works Michael casts himself as a do-gooder. Yet no matter how admirable, his ends are inevitably accomplished through force or violence, as in "Smooth Criminal."

Of all Michael's videos, I find "Thriller" the most disturbing. The metamorphosing monster, its creeping forehead, its yellow eyes: Joseph. Sometimes I wonder what my brother meant, and if he imbues these images with the same meanings. Then I wonder if I even have to wonder.

In conjunction with the March 1989 *Playboy*'s publication, I embarked on a promotional tour, appearing on virtually every major television program, including *Donahue* and *The David Letterman Show*. Of course, the first question was always, "What does your family think?" to which I honestly replied, "Some agree with it, some don't." That proved to be the understatement of the year.

The issue hadn't been out more than a few days

before Jermaine went on TV's *Entertainment Tonight,* condemning what I'd done. I'd posed for *Playboy,* he charged, because I couldn't get a hit record and couldn't sing. It proved to me something I'd realized a long time ago: without a hit record, you don't count in my family. Tito, however, sitting silently beside Jermaine, looked into the camera and said simply, "We love you, La Toya." Tito has always been a quiet, steady voice of reason and logic. I'll never forget that.

I'd done the right thing for me, but as I found out, even before *Entertainment Tonight,* few in my family shared that view. Janet called me, furious not that I'd posed but that I hadn't told her about it. My explanation that I'd tried to when she visited me in New York did not sway her. As I hung up, I remember thinking, *This is only the beginning.* John Maclain, a family friend then working with my sister, called to tell me my brothers' positions, which were as varied as their personalities.

"Are you sure everyone saw it?" I asked him. "Because I talked to Jermaine and Jackie, and they didn't say anything about it."

"No, they saw it all right," he answered.

Later I found out that Jermaine had been dying to jump down my throat about it during that call, but Jackie had persuaded him not to. When Jermaine finally did call, I got an earful.

"I want you to know that you're a piece of shit! And I'm saying this because I know you're mad at me for cursing. But I want you to know that's what you are! You've degraded our family, and you've made us all look bad.'' I found that criticism interesting coming from the father of two out-of-wedlock children.

"And when I see your manager,'' he continued, "I'm gonna kill him, because I know it was his decision, not yours!''

"Jermaine,'' I said quietly, "when you calm down and can control your temper, then call me back, okay?''

He just shouted over me. "Another thing: I don't like you going on television and saying that we agree with what you've done! *None* of us agrees, so stop saying it!''

"Well, Jermaine, I think it was awfully low of you to go on television and say the things you said about me. If you really feel that way, you should have said it to me, not to the whole world.''

Thank goodness not all my siblings agreed with Jermaine. Michael urged me not to reply to him publicly, as several publications and television programs were dying for me to do. "Don't take Jermaine's bait,'' he warned, adding, "I want you to know that what you did is really great. But if they ask you what I think about it, please don't tell them.'' As much as I love Michael, recently he always seemed to play both sides of the field.

Jackie's call was the most touching. "What Jermaine's doing is very wrong,'' he said. "And I want you to know that I agree with whatever you do. I haven't seen the pictures, and I don't want to see them, because you're my sister. But I support you one hundred percent, and I love you.''

I felt so choked up. ''Thanks, Jackie.''

Of all the calls, the one that said what I really wanted to hear was Marlon's. Having broken away from the family to live on his own terms, perhaps he best understood how I felt. Somehow he too had gotten an advance copy. ''I saw the pictures, and I want you to know that they are beautiful,'' he said, ''though I think the business with the snake went a little too far, and I don't agree with what you've done.''

I felt a twinge of hurt, but said, ''Marlon, you're entitled to your own opinion. Thank you for telling me what you thought.'' Before hanging up, he added tenderly, ''Don't let the other members of the family get to you; your father, your mother. Just do what you have to do. If you don't want to go back home, you don't have to go back home.''

Mother, not surprisingly, was bitterly upset with me. ''Don't you ever, ever pose for *Playboy* again!'' she sputtered when we finally spoke. ''You've embarrassed me, La Toya!''

''I understand how you feel,'' I answered. ''But don't you think Jermaine's overreacting?''

''Don't you know that Jermaine got on television and said those things because he loves you so much, La Toya?'' she replied, as if that made sense.

''You call that love, Mother?! You know better than that.''

''Well, anyway, I know you didn't really want to

do it. It wasn't you, it was that damned Jack Gordon. He forced you to do that—''

''Mother, nobody forced me,'' I said firmly. ''I had the final say-so. I could have said no, but I didn't. That's what I wanted to do. But I'm still the same person inside. Can't you see that I am still your daughter?''

''Don't you ever do that again!'' was all she said before hanging up.

I certainly didn't expect Mother to be thrilled by the pictures, but I didn't think our relationship would dissolve over them. I was wrong. From then on, if I called home and said, ''Hello,'' she'd answer, ''Hi, Jan!'' Realizing her mistake, she'd then claim to be too busy to talk. It was as if I didn't exist. Upset, I told Michael about it, but he didn't believe me, saying, ''Doesn't sound like Mother to me'' or ''Maybe she really is busy.'' I realized I would never convince him that Mother was anything other than a saint. That hurt too. Michael and I had shared everything. All I wanted from him was a little moral support, a shoulder to cry on.

I couldn't stand the coldness any longer and finally confronted my mother over the phone. ''What is it?'' I asked her. ''We used to be best friends. What happened?''

''*You're* the one who decided to leave,'' she sniffed.

''But Randy left. Janet left. Michael left. You don't treat them like this.''

She had no answer. But I did. This wasn't about love, this was about control.

The biggest surprise of all was Joseph's response: none at all. As Michael observed so insightfully, one reason I posed nude was to show my father he couldn't dictate to me anymore. But I realized afterward that I'd wanted to accomplish something else. Subconsciously it was a test to see if he or Mother could love me as the woman I was now, not as the little girl they'd tried so hard to make me. I'd hoped to hear my parents say what they'd never said before: that they loved me, unconditionally. That whether or not they agreed with everything I did, I was still their daughter. Sadly, I had wished in vain.

II
HOME

If, in my family's eyes, my appearing in *Playboy* drove a wedge between me and them, my writing this book created an unbridgeable chasm. Through their attorneys, they bombarded me with letters full of veiled threats. Their outrage still mystifies me, since at that time there were at least *four* other Jacksons then pecking away at typewriters: Joseph and two of my brothers were each shopping his story, but in the end found no takers.

Mother, too, wrote a book. Initially unable to publish it in America, she blamed the stateside lack of interest on my manager. Her misguided conviction that an industry which valiantly defended Salman Rushdie's *The Satanic Verses* against Moslem terrorists' death threats would capitulate to Jack Gordon's "demands" was absurd. But it was typical of the bunker mentality that seemed to have overtaken Hayvenhurst. My parents always saw the world in terms of us against them. In their eyes, I was now one of "them"; an outsider. Mother's story eventually found a publisher overseas, then was later issued here in paperback.

According to the newspapers, Michael was so vehemently against my writing a book that he investigated the possibility of buying a controlling interest in my original publisher. He was also reputed to have offered me millions to scuttle the project. But at the same time my brother and I were allegedly in the thick of a "sibling feud" (so claimed *Newsweek),* we spoke on the phone constantly. Rarely did he raise the subject of the book, and when he did so, only indirectly, as is his way.

"By the way, La Toya, I hear you're writing a book . . ."

Right, I thought, *as if you didn't know.* I'd already received a flurry of sharply worded letters from his lawyer, filled with groundless threats against a book that didn't yet exist.

The most Michael ever said to me was, "You know, I said all good things about you in my book . . ." Another time he inquired slyly, "La Toya, do you know what's going to be in your book? . . ."

Not once did he say he was angry or upset that I was writing my autobiography, just as he'd written his. More important, he never asked me not to. Deep in my heart I believe that Michael knew I was going to print the truth about our family, and while he would never deny it privately, he preferred it be kept secret. Yet there seemed to be another side of him that wanted the truth out. He'd made this evident with his *Moonwalk,* which more than hinted at our father's abusive ways.

Over the next several months, conversations between me and my family dwindled. And speaking to either Mother or Jermaine only made me wish I'd never dialed their numbers. My mother remained distant yet continued to plead, ''When are you coming home?'' while my older brother repeated threats against my manager. ''I'm gonna kick Jack's behind, then step on him like a cockroach,'' he'd growl, sounding more and more like Joseph all the time. I didn't take him too seriously, but Jermaine repeating Joseph's cryptic warning that he would see to it Jack was arrested made me uneasy.

Distraught over my family situation, I was surprised and delighted when Jackie called to ask me to sing on *2300 Jackson Street,* the album he, Tito, Jermaine, and Randy were recording at Hayvenhurst and in Tito's home studio. I thought the plans were definite, but strangely, nothing ever came of them.

Jackie and Jermaine kept insisting I fly home to add my vocals to the title track. I explained that I was doing two days of television work before departing for Europe on business, so we then agreed that Jermaine would record me in a Manhattan studio the next time he was in town. When he did come to New York, however, he never called; I discovered my brother was in the city only through a friend. I phoned the hotel he usually stays in but was informed he'd checked out. I couldn't reach Jermaine, he never called me, and I never heard from him about it again.

Living away from home was drastically different in almost every way, except for one: I still had to travel with a few security guards. Reliable security people are rare, so those who are really good usually work for a relatively small number of public figures. You see the same guards everywhere, and they all know one another.

My manager hired one guard I'll call Tim, a menacing-looking three-hundred-pounder, nearly seven feet tall. Because he'd worked for me before and had been assigned to my father on the 1984 *Victory* tour, I felt he was trustworthy. But Tim had changed since then. He'd become belligerent and, basically, too difficult to be around. So after a brief time I had to let him go.

I was making quite a few personal appearances. In addition to my security, the promoters hired some of their own people from a pool of free-lancers; mostly moonlighting policemen and bodyguards. In the summer of 1989, Jack and I noticed that Tim seemed to turn up like a bad penny wherever I was. A hunch told me it was more than mere coincidence.

In early August I was scheduled to appear at the Music Summit Rock Festival in Moscow. Between that and an important concert in Reno, Nevada, I was very excited about my career and felt that despite all the recent intrafamily conflicts, I'd made some intelligent decisions. It was satisfying to know that after a lifetime of being denied autonomy, I could ably direct my own life.

There was a lot to do before the trip to Russia, and at one point Jack flew to Reno and Las Vegas for some meetings and then on to Los Angeles. I stayed behind in New York. When Jack stepped off the plane in Burbank, he was accosted by three Los Angeles Police Department detectives. The reason: Jack had $178 worth of outstanding traffic tickets. But it made no sense for three LAPD plainclothesmen—who have no involvement in traffic infractions and who certainly had far more pressing cases—to drive to Burbank for something so minor. They couldn't even arrest Jack, just detain him at the North Hollywood police station until he paid the fines. He did, and the matter was settled quickly.

The incident struck me as peculiar. How did the police know Jack was going to be in their jurisdiction? Joseph and Jermaine's dark threat—"I'm gonna have him arrested"—played back in my mind. And I'll never shake the feeling that my family assumed I would be on that plane too.

While in Los Angeles, Jack met with my father's former aide Robert, the witness to Joseph's attack on him. Robert had recently left Joseph's employ and now recast himself as our ally. I'd never really liked him before and did not particularly trust him. But he claimed to have some information he was sure Jack would find intriguing. He said that one reason for my brothers' insistence I return home to sing on *2300 Jackson Street* was that they planned to forcibly keep me there. He mentioned Tim by name and said of my ex-security guard, "Watch out for him. He's part of this. He'll have a van. Be very careful around him."

I knew Mother wanted me home desperately, but to go that far? It was simply, literally, unbelievable. And in view of the source, I felt it best to put it out of my mind.

There was a great deal of publicity before the trip to Russia. As is usually done, we took a suite for one day at the Waldorf-Astoria Hotel, and there I met with a day-long stream of reporters and photographers, including some from the Soviet news agency Tass. Jack, my press agents, Richard Rubenstein and Dan O'Connell, our friend Sidney Bernstein (an industry figure perhaps best known for bringing the Beatles to America), and several other people were on hand to escort the press people into a separate room where I conducted interviews and posed for photos.

I was in that back room when suddenly who walked into the foyer but Tim, his young son in tow. Since my suite number was supposed to have been kept secret, this made Jack uneasy, but he let the little boy take a picture with me and then led him back out. As father and son walked out the door, the burly bodyguard turned around and demanded abruptly, "I'd like to talk to La Toya."

"She's busy," Jack replied.

"I've got a message from Michael for her," Tim

replied. "They're having a Family Day, and he wants her to come. I want to tell her personally."

Jack knew this was a lie, for Janet had been calling me about the get-together for the past few days, begging me to go. And besides, if Michael wanted so badly to reach me, he could have called directly. Jack thought quickly and reasoned, How would Tim have known about the upcoming Family Day? Was he working for my family again? One thing was clear: he had more on his mind than just personally delivering a message.

"La Toya already knows about it," Jack said tersely as Sidney, Richard, and Dan looked on. "If you want, I'll tell her again. But right now she's working, and you are not going to tell her anything."

Tim had just stepped across the threshold and into the hall, and Jack started closing the door, when suddenly Tim turned and leaned his considerable weight against it, forcing it back open. My manager slipped out into the hallway and looked up at the much taller man. In his best Jimmy Cagney, he said, "Let's take a walk," then turned and whispered urgently to Sidney, who'd stuck his head out the door, *"Close the door and lock it!"*

Down the hall, Jack confronted Tim. "I don't know what you want or why you're always there every time I turn around, but I don't want you here or any place around me or La Toya. Stay away."

Tim glared down at Jack. "What have you got against me?"

"Nothing. I just don't want you around, that's all." With that, Jack turned to go back to the suite but heard the big man's heavy footsteps behind him. When Jack spun around to again warn Tim to leave immediately, he saw him whispering into a walkie-talkie, "Calling all units, calling all units!" Sidney let Jack into the room and slammed the door just before Tim got one of his meaty hands on the knob and shouted, "I'm coming in!"

"Come on!" replied Dan, a martial-arts expert. Someone inside had already called hotel security, and either the sight of the approaching guards or something in Dan's voice made the bodyguard back off.

The whole time this was happening, I was in the other room, oblivious. All I knew was that someone knocked on the door, said something to the photographers, and they quickly grabbed me and locked me in the bathroom. As I sat there alone wondering what was going on, five hotel guards escorted Tim and his bewildered little boy out of the building.

When we cautiously came downstairs later that afternoon, several bystanders told us that a man fitting Tim's description had been standing in front of the Waldorf on Park Avenue for hours, screaming my name and cursing, before finally climbing into *a van* and driving off. Just to be on the safe side, we snuck out a side exit on Fiftieth Street and hurried to our cars.

It was with a sigh of relief that I left for Russia the next morning. I've performed in nearly every country on the globe, but the reception I got from the over fifty thousand packing the Olympic Stadium was so gratifying. Though American records are rare behind the Iron Curtain, the entire audience knew and sang along to all my songs, so that after the first concert, the organizers made me the headliner. It was an experience I'll never forget, not only for the great shows (which benefited a Soviet children's charity) but for the Russian people. Despite living under deplorable conditions, they were so warm and generous, and I truly admire their spirit. Talking to them on the streets of Moscow, I gave them whatever I had on me—little items like lipsticks. From their reaction, you'd have thought I was passing out gold bullion.

The trip was a welcome distraction, but then it was back to New York, to rehearse for my upcoming show in Reno. The night before we were to leave for Nevada, my band and I ran down the set one last time at a Manhattan rehearsal studio. Perspiring and weary, I rode back to the Trump Parc around eleven with my trusted bodyguard, Johnny, and a new driver. Jack stayed behind at the studio with Richard Rubenstein and a private investigator to finalize some details.

Everything about this night is so sharply etched in my mind, it's as if it happened yesterday. It was cold and rainy, and driving along Central Park South the streetlights made the wet pavement gleam like onyx. My town car stopped in front of the Parc's gold canopy, and I stepped out, with Johnny at my side. For a second I thought I spied someone lurking around me. I can't say exactly why; I just recall being overcome by a feeling of being watched. But I kept walking straight ahead until we were inside the automatic glass doors. Safe in the vestibule, I stole a furtive glance behind me.

Johnny caught my eye and whispered, "What's wrong?"

"Nothing . . ." *Strange, I don't see anyone . . .*

I shrugged, and we proceeded two steps to the marble concierge's desk to check for any packages. Then from the corner of my eye I saw him again: a man in a blue or purple shirt, standing behind and left of me. He was speaking into a walkie-talkie, his eyes trained on me. The thought *This is so creepy* popped in my head, when I heard "Calling all units! She's just entered the building." I froze, and Johnny asked, "Is that Trump security?"

"No!"

Johnny quickly pushed me into a corner, ordered, "Stay right here!" and hustled outside.

"Who are you, buddy?" he demanded of the stranger. While I watched Johnny, I thought, *I don't believe it. My parents are trying to have me kidnapped!* Within seconds my bodyguard trotted back inside. One of the doormen approached him and said, "Her parents were just here looking for her. They're next door at the Jockey Club," a landmark New York restaurant no more than twenty paces from the Trump Parc entrance.

This is it. This is it, I kept thinking. They were

right there, and I was trapped. I began crying and knew I had to get out of there fast. "Don't panic," Johnny said calmly, holding me tightly. "I've got the car ready outside. All you have to do is jump in it and go."

"But I don't know the driver," I whispered in panic. "What if—"

"Just go!"

"Please, Johnny, just walk beside me until I get to the car."

"Don't worry," he assured me. "I've got you." The car sat idling only thirty feet away, but it seemed like a mile. Traversing the wet sidewalk that stretched between the glass doors and the car, I felt like I was going up a down escalator, walking, walking, but not getting anywhere. From the main entrance Johnny screamed to the driver, "Open the door! Open the door!"

The next few seconds are a blur: frenzied shouts of "Get her! Get her!" A hand grabbing at my shoulder as I slipped under it and into the backseat. *Slam! Click!* Three men running across Central Park South while someone else yelled, "Block the car! Don't let her go!"

It was a chase scene right out of a James Bond film. My driver pulled away from the curb, whipped the car into a U-turn, raced west on Central Park South and, tires squealing, turned sharply left onto Seventh Avenue, and raced back downtown to the studio. I knew to kneel on the floor and keep my head down, but I couldn't resist peering out the rain-splattered rear window. I strained to see what was happening and possibly catch a glimpse of my parents.

Suddenly it dawned on me that I may have escaped my would-be captors, but I wasn't necessarily safe.

"Who are you?" I screamed at the driver, terrified. "What's your name? How can I trust you? Where are you going? How do I know you're not with them?"

"Don't worry," he replied. "I'm not one of them. I'm taking you where you'll be safe."

"Oh no! Oh no!" I couldn't stop crying. "How do I know? How do I know you're not one of them?" I leaned back in the seat and rocked myself gently, just trying to hold on. Until we pulled up in front of the rehearsal studio a few minutes later, I was more frightened than I'd ever been in my life.

While I made my escape, Johnny found himself on the sidewalk surrounded by four ominous men, among them the ubiquitous Tim. "Joe Jackson wants to talk to you," he said, then walked Johnny next door to the Jockey Club. There my father and my mother were having dinner with a white man Johnny didn't recognize.

"Where is my daughter?" Joseph demanded.

"She's gone."

"What do you mean, 'she's gone'?"

Mother cut in, saying sweetly, "All we want to do is see our daughter."

My bodyguard retorted, "Mrs. Jackson, if you

want to see your daughter, why don't you pick up a telephone and call her? Did you have to do this?''

"We didn't do anything," she snapped. "We were just having dinner here at the Jockey Club." Mother made it sound as if they lived across the street, not across the country.

Johnny was so brave. Joseph rose from his seat, flashed one of the police badges he owns, and threatened, "I'm gonna bust you, and then I'm gonna break you."

"Well, there's no time like the present," Johnny countered coolly. My father backed down.

"I'll tell you what I'll do, Mrs. Jackson. I'm going to see La Toya now, and if she wants to see you, I'll bring her back with me. And if she doesn't want to see you, I'll come back and tell you."

"We'll wait right here for you," my mother said.

Jack was sitting in a coffee shop around the corner from the studio. My road manager came out to the car, and, seeing how distraught I was, ran to get his boss. "La Toya's in the car, hysterical!" he shouted. Jack, Richard Rubenstein, and the private investigator hurried out to the car, got in, and locked the doors.

"What's going on?" Jack asked.

I was so shaken, my teeth chattering, all I could say was, "They tried to hurt me! They tried to hurt me!" Between sobs, I eventually blurted out the whole story.

Johnny later arrived and described his encounter with my parents. "They had their security with them," he reported. "Also some pasty-faced white guy who said he was their lawyer."

Jack asked me, "Do you want to see your parents, La Toya? If you do, we'll take you back."

"No." If they'd really wanted to see me so badly, why had they come to New York without calling first? I couldn't understand it.

As promised, Johnny returned to the Jockey Club to deliver my message, but Mother and Joseph were gone! A waiter there told him they'd hurried from the restaurant as soon as he'd left.

Before I could return to my apartment, Jack called in some more private investigators and enlisted extra security. That night I slept fitfully. There was one guard stationed inside my apartment, another posted outside my front door, and two more patrolling the lobby, all armed. Everyone was so fearful of another kidnapping attempt, they accompanied us to the airport the next morning and even searched the plane before we boarded.

Upon landing in Nevada, a contingent of eight guards took over, never leaving my side the entire time I was there. Needless to say, work was the last thing on my mind. But I had shows to put on, so I concentrated all my thoughts and energies on my work, trying to forget.

Thinking about it now, there was no reason to think Nevada would be a haven from harassment and possible abduction. My parents had recently purchased a second home there, for the specific purpose of fleeing the Great California Earthquake. Mother believed the whole family would be able to seek refuge there and live together once again. How we would be alerted to the impending disaster and evacuate in time is beyond me.

It was quickly clear that trouble had followed us. Because of Jack's 1979 conviction, he must register with the Nevada police within forty-eight hours of entering the state. On the second day, he went to register, but the officer present told him not to bother; that he could come back the next day. How bizarre: an officer of the law encouraging Jack to break it. As my manager turned to go, another cop said, ''Be careful.''

Of what? We were to find out. Right before our arrival, the police had been tipped off that three men were in Reno to kill Jack Gordon. According to our sources, which I can't reveal for fear of reprisal against them, the cops warned the trio they would be closely monitored. Defeated, the men left town. The reason the Nevada police wouldn't register Jack was that in the event something happened to him, they wouldn't be responsible, they wanted to be able to claim that they didn't know he was in the state.

The same day, Jack heard from our friend Tom Cantone of Donald Trump's organization. ''I just got the strangest call from Mrs. Jackson,'' he said. ''She was very upset and pleaded with me to tell her where her daughter was. When I said I didn't know and suggested she try to call La Toya herself, she said, 'Oh. I never thought of that.' Isn't that odd?''

Perhaps to Tom, but not to me. Clearly Mother was trying to make people believe she had no idea where I was. I guess she didn't want to appear responsible for anything either.

I tried to relax as much as I could, but it was so hard. I soon discovered I couldn't even trust my new security staff. I couldn't put my finger on why, but one of them just bothered me. No matter where I moved or what I did, his eyes followed me constantly. He reminded me of a coiled cobra, ready to strike.

One day I walked into my dressing room without knocking and found the guard and a secretary huddled together whispering. From their startled expressions, I just knew they were spies hired by my parents. "He's one of them," I warned Jack.

My suspicions were soon confirmed. Jack and I were in my suite talking about the upcoming show when I heard the chain on the door rattle softly. "Shhh!" I whispered, cutting off Jack in midsentence. "Quick! Turn off the lights, so they can't see us if they get in!" At least I'd learned something from all those years of being surrounded by security.

Jack hit the switch, and in the darkness we saw the door being slowly but firmly pushed, as if someone were trying to break the chain quietly. Jack sprinted to the door, slammed it shut, then shouted, "What do you want?"

The guard I'd suspected spluttered, "I . . . I just wanted to say good night." He was let go the next

morning. But where was the guard who was supposed to be posted outside in the hallway? We found
out later that the would-be perpetrator had instructed him to take his break, promising to cover
for him.

What next? I was a nervous wreck from constantly
looking over my shoulder. And the knowledge that
my own family was behind it all . . . If it wasn't
happening to me, I wouldn't have believed it.

At least I could forget about it onstage. The night
of the show, everything went smoothly. At least it
was one place I knew I'd be safe. At one point I
glanced at the wings and saw Jack, his face pale as
a cadaver. Something was wrong. After the final encore and a few minutes of photographs, a phalanx
of security guards brought me back to my dressing
room. I was ready to collapse, but Jack grabbed my
arm and said, "Come on!"

"Where are we going?"

"Just come on. You have to go somewhere."

It was only after we'd pulled up in front of a nondescript little building that Jack announced, "Come
on. We're getting married."

I screamed, "What? What are you talking about?"

"La Toya, listen to me. We have to. This is the
only way I can protect you. If we're just manager
and client, your family can do whatever they want
to you. If you're my 'wife,' they can't, because I'm
then your legal guardian. You've got to do this for
yourself and for me. If you don't, you're going to
end up kidnapped, and I'm gonna get killed."

The last few days' events had really taken their toll on both of us. I buried my face in my hands and cried. "No! No way, Jack! I can't do this. You know what marriage means to me. I've never been in love; I don't even date. And you're asking me to marry you for reasons that have nothing to do with being in love. It's not right. I don't love you. I don't have feelings for you."

"La Toya, you're not doing it for those reasons. If you want a life and a career, you have to do this."

Being man and wife, in the legal sense only, wouldn't protect us fully from my parents, but if it at least served as a deterrent, then it was worth doing. Drying my eyes, I got out of the car, still moaning, "I can't do this. I'm sorry. I just can't," even though I knew I had no choice.

Next thing I knew, we were standing before a woman who took down all the relevant information, then handed us a marriage license and instructed us to go across the street. There in another plain little building two older women were waiting for us. They politely showed us into the room where the ceremony would take place. One woman began reciting the brief, no-frills ceremony as we stood stiffly, both staring straight ahead.

What am I doing here? The instant I heard Jack intone, "I do," I spun on my heel and stalked out. "I just can't do this," I said, bursting into tears again.

Once again Jack had to calm me down, and back we marched to the altar. After the official's "I now pronounce you man and wife!'' we thanked her and silently stepped out into the warm night air. She must have thought we were the strangest couple she'd ever wed! I know poor Jack was hurt because I refused to even kiss him, but I was frightened and angry. I couldn't help snapping, ''I just want you to know one thing: We are *not* married. Sometimes I don't even like you, but now I'm married to you *in name only.* One other thing: I want the original copy of the marriage certificate!''

How ironic, that my mother and father's detesting Jack had resulted in his becoming their son-in-law! I was furious that their interference forced me to do something I wouldn't have done under any other circumstances. All my life I'd hoped I'd marry once and forever. Now, of course, that's impossible.

We went to dinner with one of Jack's other clients and never mentioned the wedding. I didn't have a ring (and still don't). Though the women at the marriage office assured us everything would be kept confidential, within hours every major news organization was calling us to verify the rumors of our marriage. Everywhere we went, photographers and reporters dogged our steps, shouting, ''La Toya! Are you married?'' I kept shaking my head no. What a nightmare. When one writer suggested, ''Could it have been an imposter?'' I replied, annoyed, ''Maybe.'' Naturally it appeared in the press the next day as me saying, ''It must have been an imposter,'' sounding like an idiot.

But that should have been the least of my problems. The next morning (and, no, there has not been a honeymoon), Jack was on the phone with a Mr. Edwards, who was claiming to be my parents' attorney. He requested that the two of them meet privately later that day. Jack's lawyer, Oscar Goodman, suggested instead the three of them meet in his Las Vegas office. Edwards's insistence that Jack meet him alone smacked of another underhanded plot. Was there no end to this?

"This has got to stop," I told Jack. "I'm calling Mother."

The first few minutes of our conversation were just chat. When I couldn't stand it anymore, I said, "Mother, I want you to know right now that I know what you're doing. I know that you and Joseph threatened to have Jack killed. I also know that you tried to kidnap me. Twice. Now, you should know that if anything happens to Jack, I'll go straight to the police and tell them that you did it! Do you understand me? *You!* So you'd better pray that he doesn't get hit by a car tomorrow!

"Another thing: Don't ever forget, Mother, I know you better than anyone else in the world. I was your best friend. You can fool Joseph, you can fool Mike, you can fool everybody in the house, but you can't fool me. I know all about you. You throw the rock, then hide your hand."

Mother was screaming hysterically, "Don't you talk to me this way! I'm your mother! What gives you the right to talk to me like that?"

I waited for her to deny my accusations, but she never did.

"You had an attorney with you at the Jockey Club too, when you did what you did," I added.

"What do you mean, 'when you did what you did'? We wouldn't kidnap you."

Joseph, on the extension as always, added, "You're over twenty-one; we can't kidnap you. Besides, what would we do with you if we did?"

What would they do? They'd keep me at home.

"Mother, I'm tired of playing these games with you. Good-bye."

I hung up feeling like a huge weight had been lifted from my shoulders. "I can't believe I just did that," I said to Jack, amazed at myself. "I can't believe I did that. And it was long overdue."

Within minutes, Marlon called. He'd been visiting Hayvenhurst when I called, so I knew Mother put him up to it. My brother offered his congratulations on my "marriage," then abruptly asked that I relinquish my deeds for the share of Hayvenhurst I owned. I refused. Jack asked Marlon to tell my parents and all the guys to phone Oscar Goodman's office later that day for a mass conference call. "I really believe that if we all talk, we can resolve these problems," he said.

"Yeah, that's a good idea," Marlon agreed, promising to spread the word.

My bodyguard Johnny accompanied Jack to Vegas for the meeting at his attorney's office, running into Mr. Edwards at the coffee machine. The minute they came face to face, Edwards's eyes lit up with fear, and he took off for the front door. Hearing the commotion, Jack and Oscar came out of the inner office to see Johnny holding Edwards and saying breathlessly, "Jack, this is the guy who was with La Toya's parents at the Jockey Club!" The pasty-faced white man.

They all sat down to talk, but it was soon clear nothing would be accomplished. Despite Marlon's promise, not one member of my family ever called, and when Jack noticed Edwards was wired, recording the entire meeting, he exploded. "Apparently the family doesn't want to bring this to a peaceful end," he fumed. "And I ought to report you. A licensed attorney getting involved in an attempted kidnapping!"

"I wasn't there to do what *they* were doing," Edwards protested.

"Then why were you there? I'll tell you why you were there: so that if the police happened to intervene, you could introduce yourself, tell them this was a private family matter, and send them on their way."

"Who's writing the book?" Edwards abruptly asked, deflecting the question.

"La Toya's writing the book," Jack replied.

"Can you stop the book?"

"No. She wants to write the book."

"Are you sure it's not *you* who wants to write it?"

"No. It's her book."

"And what about the deeds to the property?"

"It's her property. You'll have to ask her."

"Will she give them back?"

"Why should she? You've got to stop this harassment."

"Well, I'd like to resolve this matter . . ." He had one more question: "Are you two married or not?"

"We're married," Jack answered.

With that, the meeting ended. Inexplicably, when Jack, his attorney, Oscar, Johnny, and another security person got downstairs, a reporter was waiting, apparently tipped off that something was about to happen. But what?

We left Nevada the following day.

A month later I again tried to assemble all the family attorneys together to smooth out the problems. I still didn't feel safe, having subsequently learned that several of my siblings attended family meetings where the kidnapping was discussed. This hurt me a thousand times more than anything Mother or Joseph did. If among them not a single one thought enough of me to call and warn me, who knew where it would end?

Edwards, Michael's attorney, John Branca, Oscar Goodman, and another attorney representing me met in Los Angeles. I let it be known to all that my book was on the table for discussion, that I was ready to do whatever it took to bring the family together again. All I wanted was for them to mind their own business, let me live my life, and stop this insanity before somebody got hurt.

Despite my peace offering, the meeting quickly

collapsed. The attorneys couldn't even agree on what to discuss. Before they departed, though, Oscar approached Branca and said, "I know there are a lot of problems, but they can be settled."

A few days later TV newscasters were reporting that Jack Gordon, manager of La Toya Jackson, had been accused of murder. The tabloids had a field day, calling for our comments. On the condition that we grant him an interview, one television muckraker offered to show us footage that would prove the allegation was a story my powerful family had planted in the media. I no longer trusted anyone and refused. For the record, Jack has never been formally accused, suspected, or even questioned regarding any such matter.

The whole business reached surrealistic proportions. In late 1989 I still had my apartment in New York City but was planning to go to Europe to work and, possibly, to live. One day I got an urgent message from Julie, Randy's ex-girlfriend and now Janet's secretary, to call home immediately. When I reached her, I said, "Hi, Julie, it's La Toya. I got your message. Is something wrong?"

"How are you, La Toya? How are you doing?" She must have asked me this five or six times. In the background, I distinctly heard Janet on another phone: "Shhh! Shut up. It's La Toya!" A few seconds later: "Hold it, Michael. La Toya's on the phone." *Another setup,* I thought. As I later learned, things I'd told Janet in confidence had been relayed to my parents.

"Julie, you've asked me how I am now about six times," I remarked calmly.

"Well, your grandmother's very sick, and you should be here. She's been sick for the longest time, and we haven't been able to reach you. Everybody's worried that you won't see her."

"Please give me the number of the hospital," I said. As Julie recited the number, I could still hear Janet in the background spreading the word, "It's La Toya!" I phoned the hospital where Mama had been living in a vegetative state for several years.

Michael came to the phone. "La Toya," he said, "it's really bad, it's really bad. It's the last days for Mama. You should come out on the next plane."

"I'm leaving town for Europe tomorrow. I just can't."

He handed the phone to Mother, and when I explained it to her, she replied emotionally, "Cancel wherever you have to go. Just cancel it. Come here."

I felt my resolve crack. I thought, *What if they're not lying, trying just to lure me home? What if Mama really is dying?* "Okay," I said, "I'll do it."

Mother's tone changed. "I'll pick you up at the airport," she offered happily.

"No, that's okay. Just give me the directions. She's in the same hospital, right? I'll find it. If things are so bad, you should really be with Mama."

"No, I insist." *But why?* Later in the conversation, I asked Mother how long Mama had been so desperately ill. She replied that she'd taken the bad turn "just this morning." That was interesting, since earlier Julie had told me that Mama had been near the end "for the longest time."

Once again suspicious, the second I hung up, I called the hospital again, only this time to speak with a family friend who works there. When I inquired about Mama's declining condition, she sounded surprised. "Why, she's fine, just the same as always." She added how unusual it was that the entire family was there to visit Mama.

Though racked by guilt, I decided not to go home. I just couldn't trust my own family. Not so strangely, I never heard any more mention of Mama's dire condition, not even the following year, when she did pass away.

Thinking back over all those years, I realized that Mother was the guiding force behind the cruelty and abuse. This lady who pretended to be so gentle on the surface had in fact caused all the turmoil in our lives. We'd always thought that it was Joseph, but it was her, telling him what to do and how to do it. Like I'd said to her before, she was always throwing the rock and hiding her hand, convincing everyone— outsiders and my own siblings—that she was sweet, kindhearted, and compassionate. Little did they know that the minute they were out of earshot she talked about them very, very viciously. After seeing it so many times, I finally had to face the fact that this was her true personality.

I was glad to spend most of 1990 in Europe, where, with an ocean between my family and me, I felt safer. Yet during a music festival in Cannes, France, one of my father's employees followed me around the resort city, photographing my every move. As much as I could, though, I tried to keep my mind off them.

So many times I longed to pick up the phone and tell Michael what I was going through, but no one in the family can call him directly anymore without going through his security. And if I did reach him, I'm afraid he loves Mother so dearly that he probably wouldn't believe me. I'll never know which of my siblings is aware of what really happened.

As I write this, I can honestly say that despite everything I'm happier than I've ever been. When I'm not working very hard at my career, recording and touring, I devote time to various children's causes, among them babies born with AIDS.

I can't say it's not painful being estranged from most of my family. I wish it could be otherwise, but my parents have made it clear that unless I acquiesce, forfeit my freedom and my career, and go home, nothing will change. Strangely, what hurts the most is when I read my family's comments to the effect that I'm not "the La Toya" they knew and loved at home. I stop and think, *But who was she?* An adult woman whom everyone treated as a child. Terrified of my father, suffocated by my mother, I was miserably unhappy, a prisoner of what they thought was love. My heart breaks to think that my family would rather have me back

like that than living a full, satisfying life anyplace
else.

I live alone, but for the first time it actually seems
possible that I could one day marry (for real) and
have children. If that doesn't come to pass, I'd love
nothing better than to adopt. I know I could give
them the love, support, and freedom all children deserve. I can't imagine anything more fulfilling than
knowing you've given a child a start to a good, happy
life.

I often find myself thinking back to the last time I
was home. It was summer 1989, before the kidnapping attempts and all that was to follow. I wanted so
badly to see Mother and my family that I became
homesick and despondent. I told Jack, "I want to
go home."

He looked at me and sighed. "Okay," he said
reluctantly. "After you go to your house, if you get
out, you call me. This is the end, though, because I
don't think you're ever going to come out again. But
that's your decision."

Jack took me to the airport. As I boarded a private jet, I reassured him I'd return. "I just have to
collect my things. What about my book? I need the
pictures from my files, my diaries. And my jewelry,
of course." I smiled, wanting him to laugh, but he
wouldn't. Frankly, I knew that one kind word from
Mother, and he was probably right: I'd stay at Hayvenhurst for the rest of my life.

A friend picked me up in Los Angeles at the airport and drove me to Encino. My mind raced. Who would be home? Would I see Mother? What would I say? What would I do?

Before I knew it, we were there. A security guard approached the car, and I smiled brightly. "Hi! I'm in town and just stopped by to say hi!"

"Well, La Toya, nobody's home. Jermaine and your father are in Europe. And you just missed your mother by about three minutes."

"Darn it! Well, I have an interview, but I'll come back afterward. In the meantime, though, I just want to pick up a few things."

"Sure," he replied, adding, "It's good to see you, La Toya."

We pulled up to the house. It was a bright California day, but I found myself envisioning the house at night, with the Tivoli lights outlining the structure so that it looked like a gingerbread house. Outsiders had always described it like that, but this was the first time I saw what they meant. I lingered outside for a moment. This was the home my brothers gave us, the house my parents wanted us to live in forever. It did look like something from a fairytale. And it was.

I opened the front door and stepped into the large foyer, the sharp click of my heels echoing on the marble floor. Jermaine's girlfriend greeted me curtly before running to the phone. I knew she was calling my brothers to tell them I was home, but apparently she wasn't able to reach anyone. Meanwhile, my cousin Tony, who worked for the family, watched every move I made.

Climbing the green-carpeted spiral staircase to the second floor, I was surprised by how secure I suddenly felt, like a baby in her mother's arms. I remembered all the things I came to collect: the photographs of me with my siblings, my nieces' and nephews' drawings, Michael's sketches of me, the trinkets and gifts I treasured. I walked down the hall and peeked into Michael's room; it was just the way he'd left it. Messy. I smiled to myself, thinking, *They're still waiting for him to come home, too*.

Then I went to my room. I opened the door and gasped, stunned at what I saw. My bedroom had been turned into a storeroom for Jermaine's clothes. Several freestanding shoe racks cluttered the middle of the room, and chrome garment racks lined the walls. I jerked open drawers, ran to the walk-in closet, and searched everywhere, but all my things were gone: photographs, diaries, scrapbooks, everything that held any meaning for me. I thought back to all the times over the last two years when I'd asked Janet to send me something I needed. She would always say, "But it's not there," and I couldn't figure out why she couldn't find it. Now I understood. My parents must have cleaned out my room shortly after I left, long before *Playboy*, long before I confronted Mother about Joseph's abuse, long before this book.

I felt as if they'd taken my whole life and just

thrown it away, as if it were trash. How much more could they possibly punish me?

This can never be my home again, I thought. *No matter how much I wish, it will never be home anymore.*

The time! Originally I'd hoped to see some of my family; now I wanted to leave before anyone got home. I ran down the steps, but just as I reached the door, I stopped, drawn to my mother's room. If I couldn't see her and have her hold me, I needed to feel her presence, because despite everything, she still meant the world to me. No matter what she did, she was my mother, and I was her child. Even today, part of me can never let her go.

I hurried back up the stairs and into her room. As long as I could remember, she kept dozens of portraits and snapshots of her children everywhere, organized in little groups. I looked in the familiar places, desperately scanning each framed image for my own. But they were all gone: the pictures of Michael and me clowning around, of me alone, and a very special one of Mother and me. They'd all been replaced by other photographs. Looking around the room, I felt as if I no longer existed.

The pain of my disappointment was so deep, deeper than anything I could have imagined. I fought hard to hold back my tears, but they cascaded down my cheeks. I wanted to ask, ''What have I done to deserve this? I love you, no matter what! Can't you ever love me again? I'm still your daughter. I'm still La Toya.''

But no one was there. Closing my eyes, I heard the voices of my brothers and sisters singing and laughing throughout the house. I thought about the happy times, the wonderful memories I'd always cherish. My parents could destroy all of my mementos, but those memories would always be safe in my heart.

Closing my mother's bedroom door, I took a deep breath, wiped my eyes, and started down the stairs. The heavy front door closed behind me. I got into the car and rode through the iron gates for the very last time. I was going *home*.

THE INSIDE STORIES

Buy them at your local

bookstore or use coupon

on next page for ordering.

Save up to **$400** on **_TWA®_** flights with
The Great Summer Getaway
⃠ from Signet and Onyx! ⊜
Look for these titles this summer!

JUNE

EVERLASTING
Nancy Thayer
EARLY GRAVES
Thomas H. Cook

JULY

INTENSIVE CARE
Francis Roe
SILK AND SECRETS
Mary Jo Putney

AUGUST

AGAINST THE WIND
J.F. Freedman
CEREMONY OF INNOCENCE
Daranna Gidel

SEPTEMBER

LA TOYA
La Toya Jackson
DOUBLE DOWN
Tom Kakonis

Save the coupons in the back of these books and redeem them
for TWA discount certificates
(Up to a maximum of four certicates per household).

- **Send in two 2 coupons** and receive: 1 discount certificate
  for **$50**, **$75**, or **$100** savings on TWA flights
  (amount of savings based on airfare used)
  - **4 coupons: 2 certificates**
  - **6 coupons: 3 certificates**
  - **8 coupons: 4 certificates**

TWA®/SIGNET/ONYX BOOKS
"GREAT SUMMER GETAWAY"

TERMS AND CONDITIONS

This certificate is valid for $50 to $100 off the price of a qualifying TWA® published fare to any TWA destination excluding Las Vegas, Cairo and Tel Aviv. Travel is valid one-way or roundtrip provided the minimum fare is met. Ticket issued in conjunction with this certificate is valid for travel through October 31, 1993. See the chart below for amount of discount.

Purchase a one-way or roundtrip ticket for at least:	Receive the following discount:
$200	$50
$300	$75
$500	$100

Discount cannot be applied to V or T class fares anytime. Discount applies to fares BEFORE application of any departure taxes, customs and security charges, other governmental fees or surcharges not part of the published fare. Travel is valid one-way or roundtrip provided applicable rules and fare minimums are met before discount. Applicable discount will be applied only once to the total fare of the ticket. Only one certificate may be used per ticket issued.

Additional blackouts:

Domestic:	1992:	Nov 24-25	Nov 28-Dec 1	Dec 18-31
	1993:	Jan 1-5	Apr 2-4/8-9/16-19	
Additional:	Florida/Caribbean	Southbound:	Feb 11-13	
		Northbound:	Feb 20-22	
	Super Bowl	To Los Angeles/Ontario/Santa Ana:	Jan 28-31	
		From Los Angeles/Ontario/Santa Ana:	Jan 31-Feb 2	
	Mardi Gras	To New Orleans:	Feb 18-19	Mar 26-27
		From New Orleans:	Feb 24-28	
	Kentucky Derby	To Louisville: Apr 28-May 1	From Louisville: May 2-4	
	Indy 500	To Indianapolis: May 26-28	From Indianapolis: May 31-Jun 1	
International:	1992:	Jul 1-Aug 31		Dec 18-31
	1993:	Jan 1-5	Apr 2-4/8-9/16-19	Jul 1-Aug 31

1. When making reservations advise the TWA agent that you're holding a TWA/Signet $50-$100 discount certificate and provide the source code located on the front of this certificate.

2. Open jaw itineraries and/or additional stopovers may be taken only when permitted by the fare type purchased.

3. This certificate is valid for tickets issued on TWA stock for travel on TWA and/or Trans World Express flights 7000-7999. Travel is not permitted on TWA-designated flights operated by another carrier. Any travel on another airline must be ticketed and paid for separately.

4. Consumer is responsible for transportation to nearest airport served by TWA and/or TWE.

5. Tickets may be issued by TWA or your travel agent. All certificate travel must originate and be paid for in the U.S. Certificates must be presented when ticket is purchased and will not be honored retroactively.

6. Once redeemed for tickets, certificates may not be reissued. Certificates will not be replaced if lost or stolen. No copies or facsimiles will be accepted.

7. Certificate cannot be redeemed for cash or applied against a credit card balance. Certificates are void if sold, bartered or purchased in bulk.

8. Ticket refunds/itinerary changes are permitted only in accordance with the fare type paid. Ticket refunds will be issued only for the dollar amount actually paid TWA for the ticket, less any applicable penalties. When the ticket is wholly or partially refunded, the certificate will not be replaced, and further discounts or upgrades will not apply.

9. Tickets issued against this certificate may not be combined with any other coupon, Certificate, Frequent Flight Bonus award ticket or other promotional offer or upgrade program. This certificate is not valid with travel industry employee discounts, or with special travel programs, such as the TWA Travel Club℠, Senior Travel Pak℠, or Business Flyer Award℠ Program.

10. Use of this certificate for international travel is subject at all times to the applicable laws and regulations of foreign governments and is invalid where prohibited by local law.

Agency Commission: Travel agents receive standard commission on funds actually collected.
The check or money order is to be made out to TWA/Signet Offer for $2.50 postage and handling fee for each certificate ordered (maximum four per household).

Certificate requests must be postmarked no later than December 31, 1992.

Mail to: TWA/Signet Offer
Box 4000, Dept. P
Plymouth Meeting, PA 19462